From the Shores of Silence

From the Shores of Silence

Conversations in Feminist Practical Theology

Edited by

Ashley Cocksworth
Rachel Starr
and
Stephen Burns

scm press

Published in 2023 by SCM Press
Editorial office
3rd Floor, Invicta House,
108–114 Golden Lane,
London EC1Y 0TG, UK
www.scmpress.co.uk

SCM Press is an imprint of Hymns Ancient & Modern Ltd
(a registered charity)

Hymns Ancient & Modern® is a registered trademark of
Hymns Ancient & Modern Ltd
13A Hellesdon Park Road, Norwich,
Norfolk NR6 5DR, UK

Cover art: *Of Water and Spirit* © Jan Richardson. janrichardson.com

British Library Cataloguing in Publication data

A catalogue record for this book is available
from the British Library

ISBN 978-334-06096-3

Typeset by Regent Typesetting
Printed and bound in Great Britain by
CPI Group (UK) Ltd

Contents

For Nicola

Contributors

Al Barrett is an Anglican priest and has been Rector of Hodge Hill Church since 2010. Following training at the Queen's Foundation for Ecumenical Theological Education in Birmingham, he has attempted to reflect and write from a feminist perspective as a straight cis man, including chapters in *The Edge of God: New Liturgical Texts and Contexts in Conversation*, eds Stephen Burns, Nicola Slee and Michael N. Jagessar (Epworth Press, 2008) and *Presiding Like a Woman: Feminist Gesture for Christian Assembly*, eds Nicola Slee and Stephen Burns (SPCK, 2010). He published his doctoral research as *Interrupting the Church's Flow: A Radically Receptive Political Theology in the Urban Margins* (SCM Press, 2021), and has recently co-written with Ruth Harley, *Being Interrupted: Re-imagining the Church's Mission from the Outside, In* (SCM Press, 2021).

Stephen Burns is Professor of Liturgical and Practical Theology at Pilgrim Theological College, University of Divinity, Melbourne, Australia. His publications include *The Edge of God: New Liturgical Texts and Contexts in Conversation*, ed. with Nicola Slee and Michael N. Jagessar (Epworth Press, 2008) and *Presiding Like a Woman: Feminist Gesture for Christian Assembly*, ed. with Nicola Slee (SPCK, 2010), ed. of Ann Loades's *Explorations in Twentieth Century Theology and Philosophy: People Preoccupied with God* (Anthem Press, 2022) and *Speaking of Christ, Christa and Christx*, ed. with Janice McRandall (SCM Press, forthcoming).

Ashley Cocksworth is Senior Lecturer in Theology and Practice at the University of Roehampton. His publications include *Karl Barth on Prayer* (T&T Clark, 2015), *Prayer: A Guide for the Perplexed* (Bloomsbury, 2018), *The T&T Clark Handbook of Christian Prayer*, ed. with John C. McDowell (Bloomsbury, 2021), *Karl Barth: Spiritual Writings*, ed. with W. Travis McMaken, Classics of Western Spirituality Series (Paulist Press, 2022) and *Glorification and the Life of Faith*, with David F. Ford (Baker Academic, 2023).

Gavin D'Costa is Emeritus Professor of Catholic Theology at the University of Bristol and Visiting Professor of Interreligious Dialogue, Pontifical University of St Thomas Aquinas, Rome. He is author of nine books and one co-authored book, and has edited twelve books. His two most recent publications are *Vatican II: Catholic Doctrines on Jews and Muslims* (Oxford University Press, 2014) and *Catholic Doctrines on the Jewish People after Vatican II* (Oxford University Press, 2019). Gavin has also published a book of poetry (with Eleanor Nesbitt, Mark Pryce, Ruth Shelton and Nicola Slee), *Making Nothing Happen: Five Poets Explore Faith and Spirituality* (Ashgate, 2014). Gavin is an advisor to the Roman Catholic Bishops in England and Wales on matters relating to other religions. He has taught in Rome at the Gregorian (2001) and the Angelicum (2022), as Visiting Professor.

Michael N. Jagessar is Mission Secretary for the Caribbean and Europe with the Council for World Mission (London Office). Prior to this role Michael worked with various ecclesial communities and theological institutions. Some of his publications include *Ethnicity: The Inclusive Church Resource* (Darton, Longman and Todd, 2015), *Christian Worship: Postcolonial Perspectives*, co-authored with Stephen Burns (Equinox, 2011), *The Edge of God: New Liturgical Texts and Contexts in Conversation*, ed. with Stephen Burns and Nicola Slee (Epworth Press, 2008), *Postcolonial Black British Theology*, ed. with Anthony G. Reddie (Epworth Press, 2007) and *Black Theology in Britain – A Reader*, ed. with Anthony G. Reddie (Equinox, 2007).

Sharon Jagger is Lecturer in Religion at York St John University, where she teaches on intersections between gender, sexuality and religion and the sociology of religion. She gained her doctorate at the Centre for Women's Studies (University of York), following a career in the third sector working with women vulnerable to homelessness, and as a domestic abuse practitioner. Her research interests continue to develop applications of feminist theory, particularly focusing on women in the priesthood, women's goddess spirituality, and performance and ritual. Sharon has collaborated on several projects, including research into university chaplaincy support of trans and non-binary students and women in music production.

Deborah Kahn-Harris is the Principal of Leo Baeck College in London, where she also lectures in Hebrew Bible. Her most recent publications include '"If Not with Others, How?": Creating Rabbinic Activists Through Study', with Rabbi Robyn Ashworth-Steen, *Journal for Inter-*

disciplinary Biblical Studies 2, no. 1 (2020) and 'Between the Song of Songs and Lamentations: Violence in the Divine-Human Relationship', in *The Bible on Violence: A Thick Description*, eds Helen Paynter and Michael Spalione (Sheffield Phoenix Press, 2020). She holds a PhD in biblical studies from the University of Sheffield and has previously served as a congregational rabbi in north London and as the Teaching Fellow in Judaism at the School for Oriental and African Studies, University of London.

Rachel Mann is a priest, poet, scholar and broadcaster. Author of 12 books, her latest *Spectres of God* (Darton, Longman and Todd, 2021) explores some of the key influences on her theological writing. She is Visiting Teaching Fellow at the Manchester Writing School and Visiting Scholar at Sarum College. She broadcasts on BBC Radio 2 and Radio 4.

Jenny Morgans is an Anglican priest and a university chaplain at King's College London, and an Associate Tutor at St Augustine's College of Theology and the Queen's Foundation for Ecumenical Theological Education in Birmingham. Her research interests include faith and feminism, faith at university, emerging adulthood, faith development theories and practical theology – especially involving qualitative research and chaplaincy. She is writing a book with SCM Press about the faith and gendered experiences of Christian women at university, based on her PhD research. Other publications include 'Reflexivity, Identity, and the Role of the Researcher', in *Researching Female Faith: Qualitative Research Methods*, eds Nicola Slee, Fran Porter and Anne Phillips (Routledge, 2018).

Eleanor Nesbitt is a poet and Emeritus Professor (Religions and Education), University of Warwick. She is a Quaker, born into an Anglican family and married into a Hindu one. Her ethnographic research focused on religious socialization in Sikh, Hindu, Christian and 'mixed-faith' families in the UK. Her poetry has appeared in publications including *Making Nothing Happen: Five Poets Explore Faith and Spirituality*, with Gavin D'Costa, Mark Pryce, Ruth Shelton and Nicola Slee (Ashgate, 2014). Other publications include *Guru Nanak*, with Gopinder Kaur (Bayeux Arts, 1999), *Interfaith Pilgrims* (Quaker Books, 2008), *Intercultural Education: Ethnographic and Religious Approaches* (Sussex Academic Press, 2010), *Pool of Life: The Autobiography of a Punjabi Agony Aunt*, with Kailash Puri (Sussex Academic Press, 2013), *Sikhism: A Very Short Introduction* (Oxford University Press, 2016) and *Sikh: Two Centuries of Western Women's Art and Writing* (Kashi House, 2022). She co-edits *Brill's Encyclopedia of Sikhism*.

Karen O'Donnell is the Director of Studies at Westcott House, University of Cambridge. She is a feminist, practical and constructive theologian whose research interests include trauma, Mariology, and the body. Her most recent publication is *The Dark Womb: Re-Conceiving Theology Through Reproductive Loss* (SCM Press, 2022), which explores the experience of reproductive loss as a site of theological discourse.

Anne Phillips is a theologian and educator and has tutored for many years as a Baptist minister at Northern Baptist College where she became Co-Principal. She taught Christian education and faith development, theological reflection, and pastoral studies with an emphasis on women and children, in addition to researching, writing and training on issues of justice for women and girls. Her doctoral research explored the faith lives of pre-adolescent girls, and was published as *The Faith of Girls: Children's Spirituality and the Transition to Adulthood* (Ashgate, 2011). An original member of the Research Symposium on the Faith Lives of Women and Girls, she contributed to, and with Nicola Slee and Fran Porter co-edited, *The Faith Lives of Women and Girls: Qualitative Research Perspectives* (Ashgate, 2013) and *Researching Female Faith: Qualitative Research Methods* (Routledge, 2018). In retirement she became a Church of England priest, and works as a spiritual accompanist while continuing research into the spiritual flourishing of women and girls.

Mark Pryce is an Anglican priest, practical theologian and poet. He grew up in the Welsh Marches, read English at Sussex University, and trained for ministry at Westcott House Cambridge. Mark has served in Black Country parishes, as chaplain and fellow of Corpus Christi College Cambridge, and is currently Director of Ministry for Church of England Birmingham. Mark's theological writing and research traces connections between poetry, spirituality and liturgy. His book *Finding a Voice: Men, Women and the Community of the Church* (SCM Press, 1996) is a pioneering contribution to the development of critical masculinities from a theological perspective. Mark's recent publication, *Poetry, Practical Theology and Reflective Practice* (Routledge, 2019), explores the value of poetry in ministerial formation, professional development and qualitative research. He is a Visiting Scholar of Sarum College, Salisbury, and Chaplain to the King.

Anthony G. Reddie is the Director of the Oxford Centre for Religion and Culture in Regent's Park College, in the University of Oxford. He is also an Extraordinary Professor of Theological Ethics and a Research Fellow with the University of South Africa. He is the first Black person to get an 'A' rating in Theology and Religious studies in the South African National Research Foundation. This designation means that he is a leading international researcher. He is a prolific author of books, articles and chapters in edited books. He is the Editor of *Black Theology: An International Journal*. He is a recipient of the Archbishop of Canterbury's 2020 Lambeth Lanfranc Award for Education and Scholarship, given for 'exceptional and sustained contribution to Black Theology in Britain and beyond'.

Ruth Shelton is a poet and theologian, now working as a Creative Writing Tutor. She has worked in a wide variety of settings, most recently at Emmanuel House, a support centre for homeless and marginalized citizens of Nottingham, including roles as Reader-in-Residence in three Leicestershire prisons, and Poet-in-Residence at the then Shepherd School in Nottingham (now Oak Field School) for students with profound and multiple disabilities. She taught pastoral theology for many years at Campion House, Osterley and for EMMTC at the University of Nottingham and as Director of Social Responsibility for the Southwell Diocese. She contributed to *Making Nothing Happen: Five Poets Explore Faith and Spirituality* (Ashgate, 2014) and her full-length poetry collection *Arthur Talks* was published by Palewell Press in 2019.

Rachel Starr is Director of Studies at the Queen's Foundation for Ecumenical Theological Education in Birmingham. She completed her doctorate at *Instituto Superior Evangélico de Estudios Teológicos* in Buenos Aires, Argentina where she was a member of *Teologanda*, a network of women theologians. Recent publications include *Reimagining Theologies of Marriage in Contexts of Domestic Violence: When Salvation is Survival* (Routledge, 2018) and *SCM Studyguide: Biblical Hermeneutics*, 2nd edn (SCM Press, 2019). Her work on theologies of marriage has been published in Latin America and used in the Methodist Conference report *God in Love Unites Us* (2019). With Robert Beckford, she is editing *Behold the Men: Introduction to Critical Theologies of Masculinities* (SCM Press, forthcoming).

Heather Walton is Professor of Theology and Creative Practice at the University of Glasgow. She is a life writer and theologian and shares in the leadership of Glasgow's doctoral programme in theology through creative practice. Her works include *Writing Methods in Theological Reflection* (SCM Press, 2014), *Not Eden: Spiritual Life Writing for This World* (SCM Press, 2015) and with Elaine Graham and Frances Ward, *Theological Reflection Methods*, 2nd edn (SCM Press, 2019).

Alison Woolley is Director of Seeds of Silence, which supports people in developing a spiritual discipline of silence through online and in-person workshops, training and retreats and through its website resources. This project emerged from her PhD research at the University of Birmingham, through the Queen's Foundation for Ecumenical Theological Education in Birmingham. Rooted in feminist practical theology and published as *Women Choosing Silence: Relationality and Transformation in Spiritual Practice* (Routledge, 2019), it investigates the role, value and construct of chosen practices of silence in the lives of contemporary Christian women. After 24 years working as a music therapist in Yorkshire and recent lecturing and supervision of theology doctoral students at Chester University, she now combines her professional and academic experience with ongoing work as a spiritual director, and researching and running a grant-funded project that offers women beginning doctoral research in theology a unique form of additional support which intentionally addresses the intersectionality of their personal narratives, their spiritual journeying and their area of research. She lives in the Scottish Borders.

The River

Nicola Slee*

You let the river carry you along on its slow, unhurrying passage to the sea.
The river is composed of sunlight and moonlight, earth's tears,
and your own; mud puddles; rain that has fallen on city roads

and on mountains thousands of miles from here.
And rose petals, the pink and the white,
flowers scattered on moving water at a death.

The river is composed of sorrow: the loss of a brother,
waste of a life given over to the bottle; millions
of tears he drank down with the vodka, never shed.

Now you are shedding them for him. Crying
when the music comes, when someone speaks to you kindly.
Crying when you come home from work at night, exhausted.

The river absorbs your grief, the never to be repeated days of a life,
winks back light from every slanting angle
in which you catch sudden glimpses of

a little boy blowing out candles at a birthday party,
a visit from your brothers when you were at university,
a time you talked of Tolkein's world more real than Devon fields.

The river will turn up more as it carries you along;
from its unseen bed of stones and roots and darkness
it will bring up to its surface leaves of last autumn,

berries and fruits that the birds missed,
feathers fallen from nests, fragments of paper
torn from hedgerows, debris of a life now passed.

Trail your fingers over the side of your small boat,
lying back with your face to an empty sky. Catch what the river offers,
pick up each morsel, sodden and shining, examine it carefully.

Lay a trail along the deck of the craft, piece leading to random piece.
Boat, woman, flotsam and jetsom, strung along a rope of river,
bearing what has to be borne, singing, weeping to the sea.

* Originally published as Nicola Slee, 'The River', in Gavin D'Costa, Eleanor Nesbitt, Mark Pryce, Ruth Shelton, and Nicola Slee, *Making Nothing Happen: Five Poets Explore Faith and Spirituality* (Farnham: Ashgate, 2014), 43.

I

Introduction:
Exploring the Boundaries of Speech

ASHLEY COCKSWORTH, RACHEL STARR
AND STEPHEN BURNS

It
isn't
far from
the shores
of silence
to the
boundaries
of speech.[1]

Feminist practical theology emerges from multiple conversations, requiring careful listening to the stories, pauses and passions of women; conversations that are in themselves life-giving but which seek further impact beyond their boundaries. The hope that the distance between women's silence and speech can be breached pervades feminist practical theology, exemplified by Nicola Slee, the friend and colleague whom this volume honours. Much of Slee's work is painstakingly attentive to 'hearing into speech' the voices of women and others for whom silence has long been imposed.[2] Over four decades, Slee has debunked presumptions about what women have to say (and how they might say it), exposing skewed male-centred norms inflected in theological disciplines.[3] She has sought to attend to the faith lives of women and girls:

whose voices have never been heard
whose words have been consigned to silence
whose wisdom has not been heeded.[4]

Through its focus on Slee's words and work, this book invites readers into conversations taking place within contemporary British feminist practical theology.

For many years, Slee has been a central figure within the discipline of practical theology. In 2017, she was installed in the named chair of 'Feminist Practical Theology' at the Vrije Universiteit, Amsterdam, the only such chair in Europe.[5] In 2019–21 she was Chair of the British and Irish Association for Practical Theology (BIAPT). And as series editor for the 'Explorations in Practical, Pastoral and Empirical Theology' series,[6] she has had a significant role in establishing the direction of practical theology, encouraging emerging scholars, not least from her own doctoral students, and helping shape the conversation.[7] She has supported the emergence of women's voices and leadership in the church as well as the academy, as seen, for example, in her erstwhile association with WATCH (Women and the Church), of which she is an Honorary Vice President.

Out of her conviction that 'the life makes sense of the work, but in a reciprocal way, the work makes sense of the life',[8] Slee has shared freely about her own faith life, offering her experience and insights in poetry, liturgy and reflections. As the title of this collection suggests, themes of water pervade Slee's work. She grew up close to the ocean in rural north Devon, and water imagery is present in her earliest writing, and ever since.[9] Slee's love of the sea perhaps comes most into focus across adjacent pages of her *Praying Like a Woman*. Her poem 'Coming to Water' is an appeal for great attentiveness to water, which Slee deems 'a poultice for sickness'. She encourages 'wait[ing] for a long while' at any waterside, walking its edges, gazing at its surfaces and, if it rains, upturning one's face to the weather. In the imagination of this poem, Slee trusts herself to water's 'tenderness', from which she says it is 'never time for leaving', and which even when one is not right there, is continually ringing in the ears.[10] In the next poem, 'Sea Song', Slee's gazing at the sea evokes not just sounds but also rich colours:

bladderwrack and wheatsheaf,
blown meadow and metal rust,
mudflat, oyster.

The addressee of this poem is 'ballast and balm' for her, with tenderness emphasized once again: 'you were gentleness'. Here is how Slee the poet concludes her re-imagining of the divine in this piece:

All words drown in you,
as flesh and forest do.
Only the fish live in you
and do not know it.[11]

Along with water, the table, feast and food is another cluster of themes
in her work,[12] again pointing to a profound sacramental sensibility and
one that is complemented by major attention to the word – always com-
prising liturgical celebration and integral to sacramental action. For her,
'Liturgy assumes a prior address from the one who, from before time,
has called us into being, made us in the divine image and looks for our
response of love.'[13] Hence her desire to:

Wait for the riven word.
It will be spoken, it will be heard.[14]

Her liturgical and research-related listening no doubt intertwine with
each other. Two striking examples of Slee's evoking of the transformative
power of listening are present in another set of adjacent poems in *Praying
Like a Woman*:

Until there is not one last woman remaining
who is a victim of violence
We will listen and we will remember.

These are words from her 'Texts of Terror', which sits next to 'Stations
of the Cross' with its critique of Christian doctrine:

I cannot venerate the glorification of unnecessary suffering,
but I can venerate all those who work to alleviate suffering
and bring its causes to judgement.[15]

Slee has been grounded in the church as pray-er and prophet and preacher,
not only by raising her voice in the likes of WATCH and the Lesbian and
Gay Christian Movement, but in keeping close to a local parish and special relationships with religious communities of both men and women.[16]
Her poem 'Letter to the Church', conspicuously addressed to a 'brother',
determinedly states,

I will work with you,
but I will not work for you.[17]

Slee's feminist convictions come forward, never to retreat, in an early book, and notably one with another liquid allusion: *Swallowing a Fishbone? Feminist Theologians Debate Christianity*. Published in 1996, it is clear from Daphne Hampson's Preface that 'Nicky' Slee was integral to – not least to the instigation of – the extraordinary conversation the book captures. This early British feminist text still stands out for its emphasis on dialogue and process. Involving Slee, Hampson and four others – Sarah Coakley, Julie Hopkins, Janet Martin Soskice and Jane Shaw – post-Christians (such as Hampson) and still Christians (Slee among others) dialogue about feminism and Christianity through a series of papers, responses and afterwords.[18] *Swallowing a Fishbone?* remains a landmark of collaborative process in feminist theology in Britain – in Slee's own words, an attempt at 'the ideal of feminist friendship',[19] even if 'not always ... easy'.[20] *Swallowing a Fishbone?* turned out to be the first-fruits of the work a number of the participants would go on to do.[21] For her own part, the process of ongoing listening and dialogue involved in *Swallowing a Fishbone?* resonates with the detail and care at the heart of Slee's own work.

Slee's early work (a feminist reading of the Gospel parables) became well known not only because of Hampson's discussion of it in *Swallowing a Fishbone?* but especially because of its inclusion in an anthology that galvanized the challenge of North Atlantic feminism to both the academy and churches: Ann Loades's *Feminist Theology: A Reader*.[22] Nevertheless, the lack of many British feminist voices in the reader gives some fuel to Slee's own later assertion that 'feminist practical and pastoral theology have been slow to emerge within the broader field of feminist theology', at least on one side of the Atlantic ocean.[23]

Over time it was in the space of practical theology in which Slee would firmly establish herself, particularly with the 2004 publication of *Women's Faith Development*, a text based on her doctorate supervised by John M. Hull at the University of Birmingham. Hull later becoming her colleague at the Queen's Foundation for Ecumenical Theological Education. While alert to 'interlocking systems of discrimination' it focuses on gender, and while making numerous constructive proposals in order to correct bias in practical theology, its force can be distilled in its statement of problems needing to be addressed.[24] Referring especially to James Fowler's work on models of faith development and Fowler's influence on subsequent work in the area, Slee notes:

> feminist analysis reveals serious limitations in his work at a number of different levels. The sources drawn upon, the images and metaphors of faith employed, the models of mature faith adumbrated, the theoretical understanding and operationalization of faith, and the account of stage

development proposed can all be critiqued for their inbuilt androcentric bias.[25]

Slee's work puts up strong contest to Fowler's and others' assumptions that despite manifestations of faith in different contexts, they had nonetheless been presumed to possess 'certain formal characteristics at the deep level of structure'.[26] Her own reorientation of thinking involves emphasis on 'faithing' – a 'verbal form' as opposed to the noun 'faith' – so, she says, 'to highlight the dynamic and active process of meaning-making' involved.[27] Slee identifies six particular 'strategies' by which women's faithing emerges: the conversational, metaphoric, narrative, personalized, conceptual and apophatic, and she reveals women's faithing preferences for metaphor, story and exemplar as vehicles of expression. This is an especially striking finding given that it seems to happen even when access to more conceptual and analytical discourses is available to women.[28] Slee highlights, therefore, women's choices not to employ some of what androcentric bias in the discipline had mistaken as norm and standard. Furthermore, she draws special attention to processes of faithing which are as significant for women as the presumed content of faith. Among her many important discoveries in *Women's Faith Development* is the weight of silence in many women's faithing, such that for example in apophatic faithing 'to resist and protest against what is inadequate or oppressive is already to pave the way towards fresh and more adequate forms of faith'.[29] Given its landmark status, it is not surprising that, to date, *Women's Faith Development* has led to further related volumes under the auspices of the Symposium on the Faith Lives of Women and Girls.[30]

As well as expanding the repertoire of the sources drawn upon, and the images and metaphors used in practical theology, Slee consciously expands the form practical theology takes. And liturgy, for Slee, is a distinctive expression of practical theology. In 2004, Slee published *Praying Like a Woman*, which is comprised of prayers – in various modes: litanies, confessions, collects, graces – and poems, and so akin to Janet Morley's *All Desires Known* (which Slee commends as 'the feminist theological text above all others against which any subsequent work has to be measured').[31] It gathers in and extends the compositions that Slee had contributed to a variety of non-official, reforming liturgical productions over time, such as those of the St Hilda Community, responsible for the germinal collection *Women Included*.[32]

Praying Like a Woman has been enormously fruitful in at least two directions. First, it inspired others to think about ecclesial roles in feminist perspectives. So Susan Durbur entitled her book in homiletics *Preach-*

ing Like a Woman, gratefully acknowledging Slee's impetus to her own thought.[33] Then Slee herself collaborated in a collection, *Presiding Like a Woman*, which raised feminist perspectives on leadership of Christian assembly. Undoubtedly, Slee's feminist convictions have shaped her ecclesial negotiations, even as she has nurtured many women (and others) in their call to ordination while embracing her own clear sense of vocation as a lay theologian – evident not least in her insistence that even as others focused on presiding in liturgy she would turn attention to presiding in the classroom, the context in which 'more than any other ... I have the experience of "sitting in front of the assembly", occupying the seat of authority, exercising superintendence, conducting and directing the company of learners', as she says.[34] Slee's *Faith and Feminism* grew out of her own 'presiding in the classroom' at Queen's,[35] in which she speaks in her own voice about a range of concerns: the Bible, religious language, sin, christology, salvation, the Spirit, and so on – thus being the closest thing she has attempted to a so-called systematic theology.

Second, *Praying Like a Woman* became the first of another informal trilogy, this time of Slee's own work and encompassing *The Book of Mary* and *Seeking the Risen Christa*. *Praying Like a Woman* is more diffuse in its range than the other two although characteristically in step with Slee's consistent attention to prayer and praise. The second and third, though, each have a particular doctrinal focus. All have strong elements of 'spiritual autobiography'[36] – so deepen the sense of the life making sense of the work – and, most notably, all three mix prose and poetry, marked by Slee's burgeoning confidence in writing theology as poetry. Such confidence has been encouraged by her fellow Diviners, the group of poet-theologians who produced *Making Nothing Happen*, to which Slee contributes in clear continuity with her trilogy of poetry books in her own name: '(W)riting Like a Woman: In Search of a Feminist Theological Poetics'.[37]

Both *The Book of Mary* and *Seeking the Risen Christa* are themselves highly innovative, her Marian foray placing Slee among a limited number of British Anglican women who have written on the mother of Jesus of Nazareth from a feminist perspective.[38] *The Book of Mary* is also the point at which Slee's voice in queer theology, then 'recently emerging',[39] begins to sound. This 'queer' trope finds remarkable expression in Slee's book on Christa, a bold move to destabilize, by re-gendering, the figure of Christ. Few if any other books have so carried forward the feminist insight that although Jesus is male, Christ isn't. *Seeking the Risen Christa* is astonishing, not only for being the first full-length 'monograph' on the Christa symbol, but for its significant development of the symbol beyond ways it had just peeped into view in the work of a handful of

North American scholars: Rita Nakashima Brock and Carter Heyward especially.[40] Their earlier constructs imagine Christa as community (particularly so, Nakashima Brock) and, in Heyward's case, as part of the dynamic of 'godding' in relation in a distinctive theological schema. More broadly, earlier portrayals tended to emphasize Christa as crucified, whereas the title of Slee's book gives the clue towards the new vistas in which Slee places her. The very opening poem in Slee's book marks the essential point she goes on to develop with courage and verve:

Why is the Christa always suffering, broken, dying?
Where is the risen Christa?[41]

Slee by no means ignores the crucified Christa, and indeed she was a key participant in 'The Christa Project' which celebrated the permanent installation in 2016 of Edwina Sandys's female Christ-figure on the cross in a reredos at the cathedral of St John the Divine in New York City, where it had been temporarily displayed and then removed in 1984.[42] What Slee's own work went on to do, though, was depict Christa in 'her risen forms', for which she took inspiration from another piece of art, Emmanuel Garibay's 'Emmaus' painting which graces the cover of Slee's Christa book and about which she has a poem, 'Christa of the Red Dress':

I want to sit with you for a long time
like your companions do ...
throwing back their heads and laughing
yet listening to each other too ...
in this unlikely inn of happiness.[43]

While *Praying Like a Woman* can be mined as a liturgical resource,[44] *Seeking the Risen Christa* is explicitly arranged around liturgical seasons, from nativity and incarnation through to a rich array of settings in which the risen Christa may be glimpsed: bathing in spas, dancing, laughing, running across the grass, pouring Pimms and tequilas, cooking up extra food for unexpected guests, 'in some bar ... a little drunk', hitch-hiking across borders, listening to those who cannot speak or are usually ignored, embracing anxious bodies, reaching across 'intolerable pain'.[45] Notably, in her more recent writing Slee finds Christa at another mysterious nodal point of the liturgical calendar, Holy Saturday.[46]

Slee's most recent work turns to the First Person of the Trinity, as she re-imagines 'the Father' as 'Abba, Amma'.[47] For example,

Amma. Mmmm.
Mouth-shaped nuzzle
at your breast.

Amma. Ahhhh.
Sigh of contentment
in your arms.

Amma. Ommm.
The originating sound,
wound of the world.

Amma. Am.
Assertion of basic existence,
Is-ness of each one.

Amma: source
of life, bliss,
truth, breath

From whom I come,
Toward whom I daily move.

Amen. Amen.[48]

In this particular 'improvisation on the Lord's Prayer', Slee begins with
an image of dependence on God of the most fundamental kind: a new-
born at the breast, itself an image with some biblical precedent (Psalm
131.2; 1 Peter 2.2).[49] It also invites connection to Slee's work over time
on a series of spiritual books for very young readers, centred on the figure
of Teddy Horsley.[50] Her work for children in turn resonates with Slee's
image of Mary reading – the under-valued tradition of Mary as Lady of
the Book, a woman of letters – and the associated idea that Mary taught
Jesus to read.[51] In *Abba, Amma*, we find Slee's keen interest in prayer and
praise is central, as ever.

There is much more of Slee's work to explore than has been mentioned
hitherto in this Introduction – notably her own large collection of essays,
Fragments for Fractured Times, to which this present volume is intended
as a kind of companion. The current collection explores the range of
themes on which Slee herself writes in *Fragments* and here engages others
in theological conversation that aspires to the kind in which Slee has
herself excelled.

So: welcome to the conversation. The writers in *From the Shores of Silence* are concentrated in the UK, but not limited to its islands. Indeed, as an editorial team split between England and Australia, our conversations journeyed back and forth over the oceans, as day turned to night and night to day. As editors, we were also conscious of the collection coming together through the waves of the coronavirus pandemic, which kept us further at a distance. We enjoyed how, as the pieces of the collection arrived, they made our conversation shift, and authors influenced our own thinking as they took up distinctive emphases from their own particular settings and experience. We sense and want this collection to convey difference with respect to the various tenors in feminist practical theology. And of course not all settings are represented, so we are aware too of gaps, not just of time and space, but of attention, even as interlocking forms of discrimination are acknowledged, while different personal intersectional realities are articulated, and in their place in the collection made adjacent to one another, and able to be seen in relation to one another.[52]

Whatever the unpredictable currents of our days and contexts, one centre that connects us is the Queen's Foundation for Ecumenical Theological Education in Birmingham, at which our friendships with Nicola Slee have been formed. Many of the authors in this volume are or have been associated with Queen's. No doubt, too, that shared institutional context is important for this collection as well as for Slee's own work.[53] It is a determinedly ecumenical setting and has carved out distinctive spaces in the British theological landscape for what Slee has sometimes called 'advocacy theologies'.[54] In doing so, it has generated a significant research profile, unusually so for a relatively small independent institution – and largely under Slee's directorship. Queen's has created ways to integrate research into the life of a theological college while also offering something distinctive to what it means, theologically, to research theology.

Slee has herself been instrumental in exploring feminist concerns at Queen's, and made it the centre of the aforementioned Symposium. The work of John M. Hull, Slee's colleague at Queen's, has been formative for disability theologies.[55] Above all, Queen's has been a significant location for Black theology in the UK, with the (latterly international) journal *Black Theology* finding a home there through the enterprise of two of the contributors to this collection, Anthony G. Reddie and Michael N. Jagessar, both of whom were colleagues at Queen's; and the further development of Black theology at Queen's through the work of Robert Beckford, Mukti Barton and Dulcie Dixon McKenzie. Queen's is a context where such perspectives have been and are to be found present together, able to be allied to one another.[56] As such, it has consistently sought to be a place where difficult conversations are possible, even if partial and faltering. In her poem 'Wrestler', Slee recalls the encounter of the one re-named 'Israel', who strives with God in Genesis 32.[57] Slee's poem emphasizes 'this place' as one in which 'love' may be sought, where a 'dar[ing] to look' in the face of the other finds a parallel to the courage 'to declare' which other poems impress,[58] and where blessing may be grappled for and grasped even if 'the wound will always show'. For many writers in this collection, perhaps, Queen's has been such an arena – and long may it continue to be, in company with Christa who:

> listens with her whole body
> to what others never even realize
> is there to be heard ...
>
> listens where others never bother ...
>
> hears the voices that never speak in the councils of
> the wise
> and the wisdom of their silence ...
>
> [and who]
>
> Out of her listening [ ] is readying herself to speak,
> if only anyone can be found ready to listen.[59]

In the shadow of such imagining, Nicola Slee would encourage her readers once more: 'It isn't far from the shores of silence to the boundaries of speech'. And so we turn to the chapters that follow.

* * *

The chapters in this book arrive in four waves pulled by the energetic rhythms of Nicola Slee's own writing. The first wave (Part 1) is the poetic. The Diviners is a group of poet-theologians who have gathered over 20 years to share in 'food and news' and to listen and critique one another's writing.[60] In Chapter 2, 'Nicola Slee as Poet-theologian', members of the group – Gavin D'Costa, Eleanor Nesbitt, Mark Pryce and Ruth Shelton – offer a taste of the conversations the group enjoys in person. As editors, we wanted to include a chapter that embodies on the page something of this book's conversational theme, and this chapter signals that. The Diviners' poems and their accompanying reflections in Chapter 2 are fragmentary, dialogical and collaborative – hinting at Slee's own theological sensibilities. The chapter takes the form of a series of poetic offerings selected because of their resonance with aspects of Slee's theology and poetry, the fifth member of the group present though absent in these pages. One of Shelton's poems invokes the figure of Mary (resonating with Slee's *Book of Mary*), D'Costa improvises on the liturgy of the mass (resonating with Slee's latest improvisations on the Lord's Prayer and with her own authorship of several eucharistic prayers), one of Nesbitt's poems bears the title 'Cat' in friendly acknowledgement of the feline companions that have accompanied Nicola along the way, and one of Pryce's poems evokes the streets of Nicola's Birmingham.

Then comes Rachel Mann – herself a poet – who in Chapter 3 invites attention to Slee's own poetry. Beginning with a story about Nicola donning a stole – the neckcloth worn by liturgical ministers that is supposed to recall the towel Jesus wrapped around himself to wash others' feet as a servant – Mann emphasizes the stole as a mark of authority bestowed on ordained priests. This action leads Mann to reflect on Nicola as a 'queer priest', a person adept at doing two basic things that priests do: teaching people to pray and preparing them for death. Mann suggests that one of Slee's major contributions is to remind readers that patriarchy is death-dealing. She twists, as it were, the priestly vocation; and she explores connections across Slee's poems and prayers, particularly in her books about Mary and Christa, to identify a number of sacramental dynamics. Mann points out how Slee's poems highlight quotidian tasks – not least ones that patriarchal societies have especially associated with women, such as baking or laundering – as contexts of prayer. As Slee's poem 'Mary Bakes Bread' has it: 'There was never an end to the baking ... the kneading ... my hands prayed the hunger', while her 'Madonna of the Laundry Basket' suggests that hanging out washing teaches the skills needed to 'unpeg' the corners of wide-open skies dappled with divine glory.[61] Slee's poems are rich in subversive ritual depictions, making many proposals about feminist liturgical practice that disrupt much of what passes for common prayer:

There is no seat of honour
for all are honoured

There is no etiquette
except the performance of grace

There is no dress code
except the garments of honesty

There is no fine cuisine
other than the bread of justice.[62]

Above all, Slee 'unveils women's serially excluded bodies as sacrament':

> We are the eucharistic feast
> This is the divine mystery
> of God made manifest in flesh.[63]

Poetry puts words under pressure, pushing writing to its limits. The task of writing has long been a concern of feminist practical theology, and is at the heart of Heather Walton's work.[64] In Chapter 4 in this book, Walton recalls her own and Nicola's desire to do theology differently, to write out of and into a rich, complex life of faith. It is from the embodied experiences of faith, health, relationships, out of faded and still fresh memories, that such theology emerges. Walton's chapter demonstrates what it means to attend to the particular: the rhythm of the school register; the gift of new languages and names alongside the loss of old ones; whispered prophecies and sacred stories of love – all these form a new theological language. As with Slee's work, this is theology that is form breaking. Drawing on Julia Kristeva's work, Walton divides her writing into two columns which stand apart but remain in dialogue. It is the gap between, the listening space, that is for Walton the space of revelation. Here the waves wash back and forth, connecting one thing to the other – broken and blessed; silenced and speaking; poetic and logic; joyous celebrations of life and unexpected death; glimmers of grief and glory. Memory and reflection ebb and flow, moving back and forth across the page, drawing the reader further into conversation.

The next wave of chapters (Part 2) begins with Anne Phillips's story of the Research Symposium on the Faith Lives of Women and Girls, synonymous with Slee's life and work and the creative energy behind numerous publications of the Symposium.[65] This chapter demonstrates the importance of creating and protecting long-term and long-lasting institutional spaces for the sorts of conversation that give voice to those often silenced and sidelined.

In Chapter 6, Jenny Morgans, a former doctoral student of Slee's, provides an example of the sort of generative feminist practical theology that has emerged from the Symposium. Through feminist qualitative research methods Morgans explores the faith lives of three Christian women students in the context of the 'multiple overwhelmings' of university life. Morgans focuses on the importance of friendship to the women's faith identities, experiences and practices, and on the way these women students attempted to craft home at university, nurtured by their shared experience of university chaplaincy. But this chapter is only in part an exploration of the research participants' experiences of university life, for Morgans also uses it to explore another of the integral features of practical theology: reflexivity. Morgans allows her research experience to help her devise a methodology that best matches the thematic focus of her research, which she terms 'a relational, reflexive method'. The result is a fascinating exploration of faith and friendship, gender and embodiment, university and home.

Deborah Kahn-Harris's Chapter 7 begins in 'a snow-covered Sarajevo' where she and Nicola Slee were part of a group meeting with women survivors of the Bosnian war. The act of bearing witness is costly, both for the teller and the hearer, and Kahn-Harris reflects on the importance of support and solidarity in such work. From the silence of the unnamed victims of the Bosnia war, the chapter explores two biblical texts concerning unnamed women subject to violence. Kahn-Harris here continues the task of feminist interpretation to uncover the violence present. From the book of Esther, she invites us behind the palace walls to encounter the young women who, like Esther, are trafficked and raped by king Ahasuerus. And, from the end of Judges, she amplifies the voices of the women of Jabesh-gilead and Shiloh who are taken into rape-marriage, asking how their trauma might linger for generations. Yet amid the violence of text and context, Kahn-Harris notes acts of resistance, and how, even when silenced, women continue to bear witness.

In Chapter 8 Karen O'Donnell intensifies what is already flowing in Slee's own theological imagination, covering similar ground but going further by discovering fresh dimensions as new ideas are uncovered. Entitled 'Mary the Crone', and drawing inspiration from Slee's preaching and poetry, this chapter dialogues with some of the distinctive themes found in Slee's writings: the figure of Mary, feminist hermeneutics, the faith and bodily lives of (in this case, older) women, gaps and absences and areas of inattention. O'Donnell explores these themes in conversation with the seventh-century text *The Life of the Virgin* by Maximus the Confessor, and in the process reveals something new of the older Mary. The chapter climaxes in the crafting of new prayers (the 'Liturgy of the Crone') and poetry ('Our Lady of Hot Flushes') as a way of reclaiming the place and voice of older women in the life of the church.

The third wave of chapters (Part 3) invites reflection on prayer, liturgy, power and privilege. Sharon Jagger's Chapter 9 explores themes central to Slee's work and feminist practical theology more widely: the faith lives of women, the revelatory nature of the female body and women's place within the church. Women-led rituals around the start and end of menstruation are common across cultures and religions. Yet this chapter is transgressive of the silence concerning menstruation that persists in ecclesial and theological contexts. As with *Women's Faith Development* and other feminist practical theology,[66] Jagger's theological reflection emerges out of conversations with women, on this occasion woman priests in the Church of England. Jagger explores how the female priestly body is both under intense scrutiny and yet often required to remain hidden beneath priestly robes. This tension is evidenced in the stories told by her interviewees who speak of both a refusal to acknowledge their presence and a surveillance rooted in fear of it. Jagger explores how female bodies are considered to have the power to pollute, even to deconsecrate the altar. In response, she detects among her interviewees a rebellious re-claiming of menstrual blood as symbolic of suffering, life and salvation.

Drawing on his Caribbean heritage as the 'place' in which he 'dwells' and from which he thinks even though a long-time resident in the UK, Michael N. Jagessar in Chapter 10 offers an 'island hermeneutic' of Christian worship. Here Jagessar shares with Slee the task of developing a 'renewed religious imaginary' while at the same time he calls on feminist and other liturgists and theologians to confront and move beyond colonial worship practices. Jagessar's vision is of liturgical practice that learns with postcolonial insight to unmoor itself from static notions of 'tradition' and launch out in a different mode – on what he calls a 'floating rib'. His advocacy of more 'carefree' or, in the language of the Caribbean Taíno people, *makabuka* worship reconsiders, not least, the possible exclusionary dynamics of making central the imagery of table, as well as asking questions of songs of praise, including world church music. Jettisoning versions of what many might presume key to Christian worship, Jagessar makes various proposals about the disruptive dance that the embrace of decolonial worship would entail.

In dialogue with critical Whiteness studies and critical masculinity, Al Barrett in Chapter 11 then considers what it means to pray as a White, straight man, bringing Slee's work into dialogue with a range of perspectives to seek out a theology of prayer beyond White normativity. Praying like a man, Barrett suggests, requires a process of unlearning, of resisting the dehumanizing effect of praying in 'the master's house'. To leave the house of male-dominated, White-privileged prayer must not leave it standing. Rather, this is a call to pilgrimage with those who have come to pray differently in the co-creation of new liturgies that energize anti-patriarchal and anti-racist ways of living and praying. It means being interrupted by and joining with the prayer of the praying Christa, becoming guests 'at the table of Christa' in the contemplative lands of others, standing together in solidarity with those called into the doxological work of dismantling the structures that uphold the idols of patriarchy, Whiteness and privilege. It means working tentatively but surely towards a very different kind of life.

The final wave (Part 4) pulls us further from the shore into the rips. In Chapter 10 in Part 3, Jagessar notes that a decolonial agenda for Christian worship is something that not only White Christians need to learn, but is needed also in 'Black theological discourse in Britain'. Here in Part 4, that discourse is central to Anthony G. Reddie's Chapter 12. While Slee's theology has often taken poetic shape, Reddie's own approach has emphasized drama as a means of liberation – a 'practice of freedom' that linked with Black theology must involve 'anti-racist discipleship'. If Jagessar's contribution to this volume invites reconsideration of the imagery of the table beloved in much feminist theology and liturgy, in Chapter 12 Reddie adds depths to another treasured feminist image, the circle, describing how one of the exercises he has developed in his pedagogical practice invites participants to think in concentric circles about aspects of identity, in ways that illumine what otherwise might remain unspoken about race, power and context. The circle here may create contact or conflict, unsettling as much as enabling. Reddie notes his own work in Black theology and education has resonances with Slee's feminist scholarship, as both are committed in their different and related ways to 'inclusivity, safe space and radical transformative models of teaching and learning'.

In a collection that progresses through various waves and moves in different modes – prose and poetry, singular and collaborative voices, and so on – the final chapter – Chapter 13 – is most fittingly given to that which remains mysteriously 'beyond words': silence. And, at the end of it all, points to a further journey, which its author, Alison Woolley, calls (after Virginia Woolf) the 'voyage out'. Woolley turns her attention to Slee's work on sabbath, identifying *Sabbath* as 'her most sustained work on contemplative spirituality'. Itself a meditation on Wendell Berry's *Sabbaths I*, Slee's book is concerned with 'essential *undoing*', 'being in a not-doing in a not-place'. If much of the imagery in this collection has been 'liquid', silence provides another alternative to '*terra firma*' – and Woolley invites readers to glimpse 'the abyss of silence', exploring the wisdom of mystics across the ages, from the medieval author of *The Cloud of Unknowing* to the likes of contemporary religious Maggie Ross. Apt given the impetus of Wendell Berry's poem which leads its hearers 'into the woods', Woolley thinks about 'rewilding' in an ecological age – which is itself a powerful reminder that contemplative spirituality has dimensions of action that reach beyond the 'topography of the mind'. This, though, is set within a much wider orbit of response to God, and Woolley's sensitive explorations of the possibilities of what she calls 'disposition towards kenosis' appropriately end with a reference to Slee's latest work. She gives the last word to lines from Slee's *Abba, Amma*, lines that praise the 'unknowable vastness of divine love' as both our 'longest journey' and 'final home'. If 'it isn't far from the shores of silence to the boundaries of speech', we are reminded, to quote the conclusion of 'Conversation with Muse', that 'you must be prepared to leap'.

Notes

1 Nicola Slee, 'Conversation with Muse', *Praying Like a Woman* (London: SPCK, 2004), 60.

2 Nellie Morton, 'Beloved Image', *The Journey is Home* (Boston: Beacon Press, 1985). See Nicola Slee, *Women's Faith Development: Patterns and Processes* (Aldershot: Ashgate, 2004), 7, with numerous subsequent references in the same text.

3 Slee, in *Women's Faith Development*, laid down this charge and in subsequent collaborative collections by Slee, edited with Fran Porter and Anne Phillips: *The Faith Lives of Women and Girls: Qualitative Research Perspectives* (Farnham: Ashgate, 2013); and *Researching Female Faith: Qualitative Research Methods* (London: Routledge, 2018).

4 Slee, 'Women's Silence: A Confession', *Praying Like a Woman*, 30.

5 Held in conjunction with her role as Director of Research at the Queen's Foundation for Ecumenical Theological Education in Birmingham and visiting professorship at the University of Chester.

6 The 'Explorations in Practical, Pastoral and Empirical Theology' series published by Routledge.

7 Slee supervised the following theses published in the series: Anne Phillips, *The Faith of Girls: Children's Spirituality and Transition to Adulthood* (Farnham: Ashgate, 2013) and Alison Woolley, *Women Choosing Silence: Relationality and Transformation in Spiritual Practice* (London: Routledge, 2019); and examined the doctoral thesis on which the following is based: Susan Shooter, *How Survivors of Abuse Relate to God: The Authentic Spirituality of the Annihilated Soul* (Farnham: Ashgate, 2012).

8 Slee, *Women's Faith Development*, 2.

9 Leslie J. Francis and Nicola Slee, eds, *A Feast of Words: An Anthology for Exploring Christian Worship* (London: Collins, 1983), which is pervaded by liquid images.

10 Slee, 'Coming to Water', *Praying Like a Woman*, 138.

11 Slee, 'Sea Song', *Praying Like a Woman*, 139.

12 It would take a very long endnote to chart this, but some signal examples include: the 'Feast' in *Feast of Words*; 'All Golden Peach', *Praying Like a Woman*, and not least that book's table graces (98, 120–1); her emphasis on Mary baking bread and as presider in communion in *The Book of Mary* (London: SPCK, 2007), 78–90; eucharistic prayers in *Praying Like a Woman*, *The Book of Mary*, and *Seeking the Risen Christa* (London: SPCK, 2011); the evocation of feminist imagery of the round table (after Letty Russell) in *Faith and Feminism: An Introduction to Christian Feminist Theology* (London: Darton, Longman and Todd, 2004), 83–94; her co-authored chapter (with Clare Carson) on eating disorders, 'Brokenness, Love and Embrace: Eating Disorders and the Eucharist', in *The Edge of God: New Liturgical Texts and Contexts in Conversation*, eds Stephen Burns, Nicola Slee and Michael N. Jagessar (London: Epworth Press, 2008); and the centrality of

the image of the table in *Fragments for Fractured Times: What Feminist Practical Theology Brings to the Table* (London: SCM Press, 2020).

13 Nicola Slee, 'Word', *Journey*, ed. Stephen Burns (Norwich: Canterbury Press, 2008), 36–61 (36).

14 See Slee, 'Word', *Praying Like a Woman*, 117. Note Slee's many years of compiling Bible Study notes (*Words for Today* produced by Christian Education Publications), quite apart from her early work on parables – on which see below.

15 Slee, 'Texts of Terror' and 'Veneration of the Cross', *Praying Like a Woman*, 36–8, emphasis original.

16 For the address to the Lesbian and Gay Christian Movement, see Slee, *Fragments for Fractured Times*, 108–20.

17 Slee, 'Letter to the Church', *Praying Like a Woman*, 31.

18 Daphne Hampson, ed., *Swallowing a Fishbone? Feminist Theologians Debate Christianity* (London: SPCK, 1996), ix.

19 Hampson, ed., *Swallowing a Fishbone?*, xiii.

20 Hampson, ed., *Swallowing a Fishbone?*, x, xiii.

21 Notably perhaps Sarah Coakley, whose essay 'Kenosis and Subversion' became the kind of keynote to her own first collection of essays, *Power and Submissions: Spirituality, Philosophy and Gender* (Oxford: Blackwell, 2002), and includes an indication of 'her next book', which did not appear until very many years later as *God, Sexuality and the Self: An Essay 'On the Trinity'* (Cambridge: Cambridge University Press, 2013).

22 'Parables and Women's Experience' is the second thing Slee had published. Included in Ann Loades, ed., *Feminist Theology: A Reader* (London: SPCK, 1990), 41–9, originally published in *Modern Churchman* 16, no. 2 (1984): 20–31.

23 Slee, *Women's Faith Development*, 12.

24 Slee, *Women's Faith Development*, 3.

25 Slee, *Women's Faith Development*, 9. See James W. Fowler, *Stages of Faith: The Psychology of Human Development and the Quest for Meaning* (London: Harper and Row, 1981).

26 Slee, *Women's Faith Development*, 9.

27 Slee, *Women's Faith Development*, 61–2.

28 Slee, *Women's Faith Development*, 79.

29 Slee, *Women's Faith Development*, 79.

30 In addition to the volumes referenced above, see also: Nicola Slee, Dawn Llewellyn, Kim Wasey and Lindsey Taylor-Gutharz, eds, *Female Faith Practices: Qualitative Research Perspectives* (London: Routledge, forthcoming).

31 Slee, *Praying Like a Woman*, viii. See Janet Morley, *All Desires Known*, 3rd edn (London: SPCK, 2006).

32 Monica Furlong, ed., *Women Included: A Book of Services and Prayers* (London: SPCK, 1991), with *The New Women Included* appearing in 1996 (London: SPCK).

33 Susan Durber, *Preaching Like a Woman* (London: SPCK, 2007). Durber had previously co-edited *Silence in Heaven: A Book of Women's Preaching* (London: SCM Press, 1994) which included Slee's own sermons among others.

34 Nicola Slee, 'Presiding in the Classroom', in *Presiding Like a Woman: Feminist Gesture for Christian Assembly*, eds Nicola Slee and Stephen Burns (London: SPCK, 2010), 156–65 (157).

35 Nicola Slee, *Faith and Feminism: An Introduction to Christian Feminist Theology* (London: Darton Longman and Todd, 2003), ix.

36 Janet Morley in the back cover-blurb for *Praying Like a Woman*.

37 Nicola Slee, '(W)riting like a Woman: In Search of a Feminist Theological Poetics', in Gavin D'Costa, Eleanor Nesbitt, Mark Pryce, Ruth Shelton and Nicola Slee, *Making Nothing Happen: Five Poets Explore Faith and Spirituality* (Farnham: Ashgate, 2014), 9–48.

38 Ann Loades, *Grace is Not Faceless: Reflections on Mary* (London: Darton, Longman and Todd, 2021) collects some of Loades's essays over time.

39 Slee, *The Book of Mary*, 131.

40 For its genealogy as it were, see Carter Heyward's entry on Christa in *Dictionary of Feminist Theology*, eds Letty M. Russell and J. Shannon Clarkson (Louisville: Westminster John Knox Press, 1993). See also Carter Heyward, *Speaking of Christ: A Lesbian Feminist Voice* (New York: Pilgrim Press, 1989) and Rita Nakashima Brock, *Journeys by Heart: A Christology of Erotic Power*, 2nd edn (Eugene: Wipf and Stock, 2008).

41 Slee, 'Christa, Listening', *Seeking the Risen Christa*, 144.

42 See the catalogue *The Christa Project: Manifesting Divine Bodies, October 6, 2016–March 12, 2017* (New York: Cathedral Church of St John the Divine, 2016), with an essay by Slee relating to her lecture 'Seeking a Risen Christa', 25–9. In between her Christa book and this event, Slee also published an important essay, 'Visualizing, Conceptualizing, Imagining and Praying the Christa: In Search of Her Risen Forms', *Feminist Theology* 21, no. 1 (2012): 71–90.

43 Slee, 'Christa of the Red Dress', *Seeking the Risen Christa*, 121. In retrospect, both *Praying Like a Woman* and *Presiding Like a Woman* hint at Slee's search for Christa, with a eucharistic prayer (123–6) in the former naming Christa and in the latter a poem – 'At the Table of Christa' – emphasizing an 'etiquette of grace', later to turn up again in *Seeking the Risen Christa*, 57.

44 See Slee, *Praying Like a Woman*, 148, for its liturgical season index. Note also Slee's work with her partner Rosie Miles, which focuses on alternative Advent and Christmas celebration, *Doing December Differently*, eds Rosie Miles and Nicola Slee (Glasgow: Wild Goose, 2007). Of course, at a fundamental level *Sabbath: The Hidden Heartbeat of Our Lives* (London: Darton, Longman and Todd, 2019) also connects into rhythms expressed in liturgy.

45 Slee, *Seeking the Risen Christa*, various allusions: 124 (bathing, cf. 48 and 101), 122 (dancing), 121 (laughing), 137 (running towards), 128 (with Pimms), 138 (cooking), 122 (drunk), 118 (crossing borders), 144 (listening), 120 (embracing), 131 (reaching across pain).

46 While *Seeking the Risen Christa* has a chapter titled 'The Feminist Gap: Holy Saturday', 94–108, her later work becomes more circumspect. See Part 6 of Slee, *Fragments for Fractured Times*, and especially 'Witnessing to What Remains, or the Power of Persisting: Power, Authority and Love in the Interim Spaces', in *Contemporary Feminist Theologies*, eds Kerrie Handasyde, Cathryn McKinney and Rebekah Pryor (London: Routledge, 2021), 21–32 (27).

47 Nicola Slee, *Abba, Amma: Improvisations on the Lord's Prayer* (Norwich: Canterbury Press, 2022).

48 Slee, 'At Your Breast', *Abba, Amma*, 29.

49 For its development in the tradition, see Teresa Berger, *Gender Differences and the Making of Liturgical History: Lifting a Veil on Liturgy's Past* (London: Routledge, 2011).

50 There are over 20 books in the series published by Christian Education Publications.

51 Slee, 'Mary Reading', *The Book of Mary*, 67, 134–5, in which Slee notes the 'inspiration' (cognates used twice) of an unpublished sermon by Margaret Hebblethwaite.

52 Gale Yee, *Towards an Asian American Biblical Hermeneutics: An Intersectional Anthology* (Eugene: Cascade Books, 2020) is a valuable text for making visible, and persistently enquiring about, intersectional perspectives.

53 *The Edge of God* collection comprised essays written by persons associated with Queen's.

54 Her chosen nomenclature in Nicola Slee, 'Speaking with the Dialects, Inflections and Rhythms of Our Own Unmistakable Voices: Feminist Theology as Public Theology', in *Public Theology and the Challenge of Feminism*, eds Anita Monro and Stephen Burns (London: Routledge, 2014), 15–34.

55 Frances Young, although never on the teaching staff at Queen's, has had a long-term and deep involvement, not least as a valued governor, and honorary research positions, and is honoured by a new building named after her. Her works on disability include *Face to Face: A Narrative Essay in the Theology of Suffering* (Edinburgh: T&T Clark, 1990), *Encounter with Mystery: Reflections on L'Arche and Living with Disability* (London: Darton, Longman and Todd, 1997) and *God's Presence: A Contemporary Recapitulation of Early Christianity* (Cambridge: Cambridge University Press, 2013). Jane E. Wallman-Girdlestone contributed an evocative essay entitled 'Blurring the Edges: Finding Community by Smudging Our Differences', in *The Edge of God*, eds, Burns, Slee and Jagessar, 104–16. John M. Hull himself, an Australian, has had a major role in British theology not only in adult Christian education, and latterly in challenging under-examined ideas about mission, but in theological reflection on his own experience of living with blindness, in *Touching the Rock: An Experience of Blindness* (London: SPCK, 1990) and *In the Beginning there was Darkness: A Blind Person's Conversations with the Bible* (London: SCM Press, 2001).

56 Michael N. Jagessar and Anthony G. Reddie, eds, *Black Theology in Britain: A Reader* (Sheffield: Equinox, 2007), a pioneering publication out of Queen's, importantly included the chapter 'What Are the Sistas Saying?', putting into print a number of Black British female theologians, and acknowledging that 'what can be construed as Black Christianity is tinged with (or even soaked in, if you prefer a more dramatic analogy) sexism and patriarchy' (109).

57 Slee, 'Wrestler', *Praying Like a Woman*, 51.

58 'Dare to declare' is the opening phrase of 'Conversation with Muse', *Praying Like a Woman*, 60.

59 Slee, 'Christa, Listening', *Seeking the Risen Christa*, 144.

60 D'Costa et al., *Making Nothing Happen*, 3.

61 Slee, 'Mary Bakes Bread', *The Book of Mary*, 82, 85.

62 Slee, 'Presiding Like a Woman', 178.

63 Slee, 'Charis', *Praying Like a Woman*, 110.

64 Heather Walton, *Writing Methods in Theological Reflection* (London: SCM Press, 2014).

65 The volume of material published under the co-editorship of Nicola only scratches the surface of the depth of conversation in the meetings themselves as evidenced by the wealth of yet unpublished material shared at Symposium events.

66 For example, Ellen Clark-King, *Theology by Heart: Women, the Church and God* (Peterborough: Epworth Press, 2004).

PART I

Poetry

Trapeze Artiste without Bird

after a Chagall lithograph

Nicola Slee

Bare breasted, arms triumphantly raised
she balances on her swing
high above the circus

Down below she can see the clowns cavorting
glistening horses pounding around the ring
a troupe of dancers in pink tutus

Up here, she is a long way
from the knife-throwers, flame-eaters
dangerous lions and tigers

There is no bird because
she is the bright-feathered creature
who has learned to soar and sing her heart out

swoop and dive without fear
she refuses to risk descent
she's not coming down off her perch

2

Nicola Slee as Poet-Theologian: In a Company of Voices

GAVIN D'COSTA, ELEANOR NESBITT, MARK PRYCE AND RUTH SHELTON

I'm not the same person at the end of a poem as I was at the beginning, even if I can't articulate what the poem has affected in me. I have learnt something, I have been moved, or comforted or been cleansed. I may have been shaken and disturbed, but in a way that leads me to a different place or awareness than before the poem started.[1]

One of the distinctive gifts of Nicola Slee's sensibility is to trace *patterns and processes* – the title she gave to her ground-breaking study of women's faith development, revealing what is implicit, unacknowledged or hidden in human experience.[2] Above, we see the same attentiveness to experience in Nicola's reflections on writing and reading poetry. In this chapter, we reflect on the experience of being members of the Diviners, the group of five poet-theologians of which Nicola is an integral part. We aim to trace something of the patterns and processes in our shared life as a community, and to reflect on what insights this reveals about the nature of poetic creativity.

The Diviners – a name hastily acquired, not without irony, when it was needed for a Radio 4 broadcast – have been meeting for over 20 years, three or four times a year, to talk about theological and spiritual issues arising from our poems, and to encourage and critique one another's writing. At the time of our founding, Gavin D'Costa, Eleanor Nesbitt, Ruth Shelton and Nicola Slee were working in theological and religious education, and this remains a common thread through the group, although before and since our theological backgrounds have taken us in a variety of directions. Rowan Williams was for a short time a member before his move to Lambeth Palace, and Mark Pryce joined subsequently.

We are an ecumenical group. Eleanor is a Quaker, Mark and Nicola are Anglicans, and Gavin and Ruth are Roman Catholics. In addition,

Eleanor's and Gavin's expertise contribute an interfaith dimension. The variety of theological perspectives and experience is an important element in the undoubted poetic development of the group members.

Our gatherings tend to have a regular pattern of travel to the meeting, a good lunch and conversation, then each poet presents two or three poems which are discussed and critiqued by the group. This may seem a simple model but at work is a perichoresis of entwined processes: an appreciative enquiry model, our critical reflexive responses, the learning to hone one another's poems while sensitively valuing their perspectives and the impact of each member's body of work on our own. While the journey away from day-to-day responsibilities and the hospitality offered at one another's houses are the gateway to a significant resource for us as poet-theologians, during the coronavirus pandemic and lockdown we found, as we met via Zoom, that our conversation and focused attention to one another's poems is the dynamic heart of our critical process.

Our intention in this chapter is to model something of the critical process of the Diviners group. First, we offer poems that each of us has selected as broadly representative of our work. We have made these choices with Nicola's work in mind; they are poems *for* Nicola rather than *about* her, chosen to resonate with our sense of dimensions of her writing and particular theological commitments. We then respond to these poems in conversation with one another, reflecting on the ways in which they seem to be significant as examples of the work of their author, and making connections between the poems and Nicola's distinctive approaches to poetry and theology. Many of the poems have been edited and changed through these earlier conversations in our meetings. In conclusion, we offer some reflections on what our process as the Diviners suggests for the practice of creativity and flourishing of the imagination.

The Sound of the Call

Ruth Shelton

Mary:
That morning, just pregnant
feeling off colour like the stones of my town
breathing judgements with the stale air,

I sat under the faux eaves
of the town hall, also a court,
'lacks imagination' says our tourist guide.

the air rattled and the red bricks shifted.
Time to go. Towards New Town
a young, pregnant woman walked beside me

My face, my gestures took on many colours,
glancing from the shop windows,
cloaking my companions like queens

Elizabeth:
That morning, six months gone
my bones spoke, sinews echoing
round the nameless square

of the New Town. I'd worn my age
like rags – now the years were raiment
Yes, you can hear me rise to meet her

stick ringing, my half-stifled laughter.
My body is speaking which has not spoken,
a square without a fountain has no story to tell.

Many old women stand beside me, waiting,
the background of many scenes, the rubble
of cities, the graves. Here she comes.

the lids of the drain holes lifted and women
who had died giving birth walked beside me.

the indifferent highway rumbled

We met in a piece of wasteland, unclaimed,
nothing growing but one self-seeded cherry tree.

As we embraced, our bellies bumping,
we stood among millennia of cherries,
the blossom like tears, the fruit ready to pick,
pick now.

Standing Stones

Ruth Shelton

for The Diviners

Strange to relate, the stones unseen,
sink to the ground or call to the sea,

mouths like shells, and ears
like caves, listen to me, listen to me.

Speaking together about the gaps,
the maps made by their related shapes

striped with earth, stained with blood,
made red by birth and green by death

or frayed with rain and written upon
by snails' traces of morning sun.

Waiting in the dark, the air-knives
whiten, whittling the unwritten

codes on sloping shoulders, keen
in the folds, making them lean

in, reach up for rain and nurture.
and bend to learn the other's nature.

How to make an arch: it only takes a
thousand years, or two, to search

the worlds between, to feel the braille
of the other's name, and breathe as breath

each other's warmth, to know as life
each other's deaths: in short, to touch.

The stones roll up their shadows and depart
made flesh by every answering heart.

A Mass for the Uncertain

Gavin D'Costa

Introitus

Kiyiya Vorna Insanlik[3]
Kiyiya Vorna Insanlik
Kiyiya Vorna n
Insanlik

Ad te omnis caro veniet[4]

Kyrie

April is the cruellest month:

Sayid pays off the man,
he holds Ayesha's hand;
roughly pushed into the boat
they crouch to stay afloat.

April is the cruellest month:
Will May ever come?

Her mother's escaped the trouble,
in Aleppo's choking rubble.
Her brother was buying sweets,
when the missile hit their street.

April is the cruellest month.

Moryo raheme'layn o'adarayn.
elfo hwoth maryam. w-te'nath
w-zayhath w-yaqar-theh.
l-haw qoo-bar-nee-tee
moro d-khul-heyn ber-yotho moryo.[5]

Gloria

Qui tollis peccata mundi,
miserere nobis.
Qui tollis peccata mundi,
suscipe deprecationem nostram.[6]

Still falls the Rain:
Ayesha's sodden breath
brings warmth upon his face,
he strokes her matted hair,
she trembles in his care.

Still falls the Rain:
drums hard upon his head
beats deep into her heart.
Sayid holds her tight
in this never-ending night.

Still falls the Rain:
that cares not for us,
swamps plains, rots grain,
sings its own song
carrying us along.

Still falls the Rain:
giving birth
to fertile earth.

Et in terra pax
hominibus bonæ voluntatis.[7]

Credo

Credo in unum Deum
factorem coeli et terrae,
visibilium omnium et invisibilium.[8]

la ilaha illa'llah[9]
la ilaha illa'llah

The sea is calm tonight:
the waves chorale the tide
the rhythms break and ride,
singing a gentler might
than the darkness of this night.

The sea is calm tonight:
drowning sleep will quell
the tears and fears of hell,
perhaps they will awake
with sun, the night will break.

The sea is calm tonight:
be true to one another,
see flotsam as our brother,
a stranger as our mother.
Be still. Behold the Other.

The sea is calm tonight.
   The sea is calm.
   Is calm tonight.

Credo in unum Deum
la ilaha illa'llah

Sanctus

Sanctus, Sanctus, Sanctus, Dominus Deus Sabaoth.
Pleni sunt coeli et terra gloria tua.
Hosanna in excelsis.[10]

Can we share the grape and grain?
Can we share this human pain?

Can we eat without our greed?
Can we drink the love we need?

She is a gift: give first;
   and then receive.

Afara-aytum maa tah'ruthoon
a-antum tazra-o'onahoo
am nah'nuz zaari-o'on.[11]

Benedictus qui venit in nomine Domini.[12]

Agnus Dei

Little Lamb who made thee?
Agnus Dei,
qui tollis peccata mundi,
miserere nobis.
Ayesha's bloated body floats
like a purple coloured boat
near the shoreline of Palermo

Agnus Dei,
qui tollis peccata mundi,
miserere nobis.
Little child who loved thee?
Agnus Dei,
qui tollis peccata mundi,
dona nobis pacem.[13]

Neither Virgin nor Venus

Eleanor Nesbitt

You and I never connected, Mary – virgin, mother,
obedience, miraculous conception, grief;
and 'virgin' not a word for speaking loudly
where I came from, except for olive oil
and snow, till it was everywhere on trains.

Venus, too, you did nothing for me either –
Aphrodite rising from spray, afloat
on Cypriot waves. Seductive, poised, knowing
you were so very beautiful. Venus, distant
evening star, your name hijacked by disease.

And Amazon – instant availability
of everything: tax avoidance, exploitation.
Amazon: fragile fecundity, primal forests
Torched or felled. Tribespeople on the edge,
planetary doom?

Yes, Amazons, fighters, women who fought,
women who won, though perhaps you were warriors
who only looked like women. However dubious,
your etymology, you brought resolve
and hope and courage when I faced the surgeon's blade.

Sirmione

Eleanor Nesbitt

O Catulle, it was then,
when I heard that perhaps
your girlfriend's sparrow wasn't a sparrow,
that I learned about men
and metaphor.

Today, in Sirmione, sparrows fly
from tumbling bougainvillea,
and three are pecking English cooked breakfast
beside the lake.

We explore a Roman villa, well what's left,
and marvel at portrait heads of beautiful young men
on frescoed fragments
under glass.

The place still rings with laughter,
giggles about selfies.
O Catulle, your songs out-selfie selfies
and Sirmio still pulls tired travellers home.[14]

Cathedral of Santiago de Compostela[15]

Eleanor Nesbitt

'Political correctness,' smiled our guide,
pointing to lilies, banked a metre deep
around the mounted warrior in a shrine,
to hide, he said the pile of Arabs dead,
defeated by the cheering victor on his steed.

There need to be so many, many lilies
in this pilgrim church. High on the
Romanesque façade a sculpted woman holds a skull.
'A woman meant temptation,' says our guide.
No doubt she's out of flower arrangers' reach.

Cat

Eleanor Nesbitt

The cat never lost its cool perhaps,
struggling for purchase on the plastic roof,
and sliding inelegantly sideways
down the polycarbonate, repeatedly.
Cats never fall or break their bones,
I told myself. Then, it disappeared
until I saw its grim unblinking stare –
two eyes smouldering in the narrow gap
below the wooden fence, locking their gaze
with mine, accusing me of doubting it,
or hypnotizing me to think it relished
skidding, no, skiing down plastic,
or, perhaps, angry at almost falling,
humiliated a human saw it almost
lose control, or challenging me
not to write this poem.

Behold the man

Mark Pryce

*The spoken testimony and music of a survivor of abuse, addressed to
Pope Francis and the conference of Bishops, Sala Regia, Apostolic Palace
Rome, 22 February 2019.*[16]

When he speaks
the words distil silence
to gaze at anger's stars
which like jewel-studs
stopper his once secret pain.

Before them his lips elevate
a miracle: true flesh known
by its damage,
the real presence of hurt

singing a litany of scars
in which every sorrowful heart
may trace the strange new shape
of a risen body dancing
on the sounds of his violin.

Turkish Magic Scissors, Bristol Road Selly Oak

Mark Pryce

In the eyes, flash of mirrors and lights.
To the ears, buzz-song of motors, clicking blades.
On the scalp, tug of deft hands shaping.
Up the nose, surge of rose oil and coconut.
For the lips, kisses finding a smooth new neck.

Waiata[17]

Mark Pryce

Having been given breath
we grow a forest of voices:
listen how your wind sings through our trees
under many stars.

When you blow, Lord Spirit,
across the vast plains of your realm,
the bush-land of language cries out
in ecstasy and suffering.
Burn in us, your dwelling of cleansed souls;
weave yourself a tent from our dry bones.

Gale-guided
you pull us into fresh harbours
or smash us on the rocks of endeavour.
The work is yours,
the energy is yours,
all is in you
unseen, yet driving.

You teach us the ancient truths in strange places,
uncovering treasure in harsh land
we learn to be poor in the deceitful palaces.
You give us words in dumb prisons.
Exquisite bird, your song calls to us:
hearing your beauty, we too are beautiful.
We welcome all you do,
witnesses of your Witness.

Find roots for the hungry as you go before us,
oils for the sick, leaves for the oppressed;
still us into watching and waiting for your path
as you place its bliss and service
in our hands, on our tongues.

Four Diviners Reflecting

In the light of these poems, the following contributions offer a series of
complementary reflections on the quality of our meetings as the Diviners
in shaping our work as poet-theologians.

Mark's Reflections

For many years I have thought of Nicola as a kind of theological fairy
godmother who sprinkles the stardust of transformative words, ideas and
places on my path through life. One of her most magical gifts has been to
introduce me to the Diviners.

An important dimension of Diviners' meetings as we rotate between
one another's homes – in times before Covid-19 – has been the travelling
to and fro. Each gathering is a kind of pilgrimage – a journey of celebration and discovery to the appointed place of meeting, each taking with us
the poems we plan to share with the group, and then the journey home
again at the end of the day, returning with the poems having been profoundly heard and critically appreciated, perhaps even enhanced, for the
change of a single word or the repositioning of one line can bring about
a transformation. A group of poets listening to one another's work has
a dynamic of deep encounter, a profound meeting of person with person
in their uniqueness that we see in Ruth's 'Standing Stones' or in 'The
Sound of the Call', her meditation on Mary's visit to Elizabeth. Eleanor's
encounter with creature in 'Cat' is one of sheer playful attentiveness.

Diviners also involve deep encounter with place. Each Diviner is located in a city that shapes and influences our work: Bristol, Coventry, Nottingham and Birmingham. Poetry anchors in place: Eleanor responding to Sirmione or Compostela, and Gavin's searing requiem on the shoreline of Palermo lamenting the washed-up body of Ayesha the child refugee. My poem 'Turkish Magic Scissors, Bristol Road Selly Oak' is a Birmingham poem, part of a sequence of poems celebrating Selly Oak, the vibrant student quarter close to the Queen's Foundation for Ecumenical Theological Education in Birmingham, and to the University of Birmingham, academic communities where Nicola has done much of her theology across the years. Like W. H. Auden, Louis MacNeice, Liz Berry, Rosie Miles and Benjamin Zephaniah, much of Nicola's work is written in Birmingham.

Yet Nicola's reach as theologian and poet – dare I say her *spell* as theologian and poet – is never confined to place and extends beyond the local to the 'thin places' of liturgy and contemplative prayer at Glasshampton Monastery or West Malling Abbey, the marquees of Greenbelt, the seminar rooms of the Vrije Universiteit Amsterdam and the American Academy of Religion, and to the wilder expanses of Australia and New Zealand. I have chosen '*Waiata*', a poem written at Vaughan Park Retreat Centre on the Pacific coast of New Zealand, North Island, to reflect on the power of place in Nicola's poems, particularly in relation to spirituality. It is a poem that celebrates the unboundedness of the Holy Spirit who is sacred adventuress and discoverer of uncharted places.

I see the illuminating power of this same Spirit in Nicola's work as a feminist theologian, uncovering hidden truths, breath that enables her, to use Adrienne Rich's powerful image, to dive into the wreck of patriarchy in a process of deep discovery, to forage there for fresh insight.[18] This fidelity to the partnership of poetry and theology has been an encouragement for my own work in practical theology as a discipline through which the unheard finds a voice,[19] not least in the validity of poetry as language in which to explore the liberative power of critical theological reflection on gender, sexuality and masculinities.[20] The poem 'Behold the man' celebrates feminist and queer liberative discourses in theology which give men space to articulate our personal, sexual and spiritual experience as gendered beings, even the deepest hurts and betrayals of sexual abuse within the churches.

Ruth's Reflections

The Diviners' meetings begin with a meal, always cooked with care and attention. This sharing of the meal is the gateway, through talking, listening and exchange of news, to the poems, the sharing of the bread and wine opening us to the sharing of the word.

The making and sharing of a meal is an everyday grace but, for some – especially those who are poor, displaced or imprisoned – it can be a costly one. Nicola's poems with their sensitive, strung-out sensibility walk on the brink of great cost. At times they mimic the tightrope walker's experience, teetering between falling and steadying; living a generous but costly life, supporting family members, struggling to follow Christ in an indifferent world, being a queer woman in an indifferent or hostile church and identifying with Mary as an ordinary woman who follows her son into wild and alien places. Whatever Nicola writes about, often with deceptively simple forms and vocabulary, she offers her own vulnerability and truthfulness, her witness. As in Mark's poem 'Behold the man', she sings 'a litany of scars'.

Eleanor chooses to speak of her scars as 'Neither Virgin nor Venus' but an Amazon warrior. The poem is brave and witty but recalls an experience involving emotional and bodily pain, at the same time asking us to consider whether the myths we live by, Christian or cultural, offer women resonant models of self in contemporary society. For many women this is a question involving loss and alienation. Gavin's 'Mass for Uncertain Times' breaks bread in the rubble of Aleppo, associating grape and grain with pain, with the radical sacrifice of displacement. Not so far away, in Mark's 'Turkish Magic Scissors, Bristol Road Selly Oak' a vulnerable neck, in a sensuous haze of rose oil, is offered to the blade.

One consequence of walking into a hospitable space is the willingness to be vulnerable and to share the cost of the others' vulnerability. The critiques that are shared and offered can demolish pretensions, identify tropes and tics, excise sentimentality and open up the element of self-regard that is part of any creative work into wider dimensions where the work may speak to all. When a poem is read out loud to the group for the first time something happens. It is no longer one's own little bit of the world but has taken on the listening presence of the others that it will always carry, even if the subsequent critique and practical suggestions are not fully implemented.

I chose to write two new poems for our contribution to reflect Nicola's academic and poetic concerns in an overt way. 'The Sound of the Call' was particularly difficult to write because Nicola has written a fine poem herself about this story in *The Book of Mary*.[21] However, it was the right poem, the only poem for me to write for this book. Nicola and I, many years ago, collaborated on an educational publication featuring Nicola's commentaries on my illustrations of Mary.[22] It is part of our friendship and our shared story. As a Roman Catholic, my spirituality has been enlarged by Anglican Nicola's connection to Mary, and her feminist approach to Mariology. I wonder how many other subjects, emotions, ideas and feelings shared between us over more than 15 years have shaped not only our poems but ourselves?

When we meet, we enjoy the grace of connection, often unexpected, always unplanned, as themes emerge, adding mysterious dimensions to our individual poems just as someone, unasked, might bring a dish for lunch, a dish that complements and contrasts with the dishes already there, the offering of the unique plateful that makes the whole a feast.

Eleanor's Reflections

With Mark's encouragement (thank you, Mark) I have allowed 'Cat' into my offering in acknowledgement of Nicola and Rosie's companions, Pumpkin and Tinkerbell. Cats are, I suspect, an unacknowledged presence in so much scholarly endeavour, and not least in Nicola's practical feminist theology. In their own ways, Pumpkin and Tinkerbell contribute to Nicola's theologically infused poems. They carry on the proud tradition of the monk's companion, Pangur Ban (white Pangur), and the (madly?) religious poet Christopher Smart's cat, Jeoffry. They too, like my anonymous 'cat', will have triumphed with feline aplomb at potentially embarrassing moments.

My other poems recall different moments, ones when I responded (unmistakably to myself) as a woman. One was approaching mastectomy, a rite of passage largely unremarked by poets; another was a loss of innocence through early exposure to a Latin poet, followed by moments of delight, five decades later, in visiting Sirmione, Catullus' idyllic 'almost-island' home. Visiting Santiago de Compostela was, by contrast, an experience of composite outrage – compounded of acute discomfort with the guide's words and discomfiture too with the crusading Islamophobia and biblically grounded misogyny that the pilgrim church enshrined.

Nicola's poems have helped give me voice and her eloquent vocation must have strengthened so many others in their faith lives and in their poetic enterprise. In her professorial inaugural lecture in Amsterdam, Nicola spoke of 'the ways in which women pray, preach, preside, protest and prophesy' and she observed, following Simone Weil, the related attentiveness of poet and ethnographer that can also be a preparation for prayer – that same attention (perhaps) that Pangur Ban's human companion had recognized in him.[23]

Gavin's Reflections

Nicola's 'religious' poetry has succeeded, for me at least, in bringing into focus a deep tidal connection between nature and the process of healing. It does this through maintaining a solemn rhythm – almost a liturgical one. Quite a magical mix. One could chant many of Nicola's poems, as an individual or in community, as prayers, as well as a preparation for prayer (as Eleanor notes). The experience of women is also central to Nicola's work. It is for all these reasons that I have chosen to celebrate her work with my own offering: 'A Mass for the Uncertain'. But the work celebrates many other collaborations.

'Mass' was commissioned by the BBC in 2018, with the music for this text composed by my friend John Pickard. He sculpted it into a heart-rending, powerful 16-part choral piece with no instrumentation except the human voice. The commission allowed me to take the appropriate form of the mass (the story of the crucified one) and fill into it the narrative story of tragic loss and innocent suffering. The mass is a narrative that is supposed somehow to include all our messy stories and broken dreams. Aware that I was writing from a European Christian context, while being a Kenyan Asian, about an imaginary Syrian Muslim refugee family (based loosely on a real one), I tried also to acknowledge the cultural and interfaith complexity of the subject matter and the location of the narrator's voice. In suffering, we touch one another across all sorts of boundaries. However, the shadow of cultural, like experiential appropriation, haunts every creative act – and I am not sure this question can be 'resolved'.

The 'Mass' was twice taken to the Diviners. They encouraged, criticized and praised and it was rewritten twice, so making something happen. We are a restorative community, as Ruth has it in her 'Standing Stones', 'whittling the unwritten'. And so, the 'Mass' slowly emerged. It was a sensitive subject, so I also tried it out with secular and Muslim friends – hoping to get it right. It took the current shape after nine versions. And who knows if it is right, if the 'sound' is appropriate? The music certainly is. When Mark writes so powerfully in 'Behold the man' of 'risen body dancing/ on the sounds of his violin', you just know the sound is right. Writing poetry is a bit of a gamble. I am fortunate that the Diviners like gambling – and do not mind losing at times.

Ruth's 'The Sound of the Call', like Eleanor's 'Cathedral of Santiago de Compostela', and Mark's 'Behold the man', wonderfully subvert any piousness in the idea of a group of 'religious' poets – which is the element that brought us together. I have learnt from and loved this quality of subversiveness in the Diviners: the woman who is out 'of flower arrangers' reach' in Eleanor's 'Cathedral', or those women in Ruth's 'Call' who are 'the background of many scenes, the rubble of cities, the graves'. Ruth's refusal to let them be invisible but to get them marching in columns, literally, regardless of what is thrown at them. Mark goes to the grand Apostolic Palace in Rome to speak about the 'real presence' in the body of a man abused by clerics. Churches, prayers and liturgies cry out for a touch of humanity – and thus divinity – to transfigure disfigured 'religion'. This is where we are in the messy story, where dreams are too often turned into nightmares.

While these last poems are sombre, I recall our meetings often being filled with raucous laughter. Eleanor's 'Cat' and Mark's 'Turkish Magic Scissors, Bristol Road Selly Oak', as well as Nicola's sheer delight in nature and its exuberance, display the sheer range of sentiment we might enjoy in a single sitting. The 'surge of rose oil and coconut' up the nose tells it all.

'Let us go to the School of Writing ...'

These words of Hélène Cixous reflect on the practice of writing as a dynamic enterprise, an art that requires continual critical reflection, refinement and renewal, a movement of effort and engagement in *work*, writing as striving onwards and upwards, like climbing a ladder.[24] A monologue of innate genius and unchallenged individual creative aptitude are insufficient in and of themselves to sustain authentic writing:

> I have talked about *school*, not *goals* or *diplomas*, but places of learning and maturing. Because even if there is, in the person writing, 'an aptitude for fairyhood', a relationship to legend, a state of creation – this is not enough. We must work. The earth of writing. To the point of becoming the earth. Humble work. Without reward. Except the joy. School is interminable.[25]

In our reflections on the experience of participating as poets in the Diviners group we have come to understand the pattern of gathering, eating together, engaging with the events of one another's personal and professional lives and ethical commitments, sharing poems in that context of deep listening and critical engagement, as a process of creative work. This shared work of community generates its own distinctive, dialogical and generative dynamic of *poiesis*.[26] Cixous' place of 'learning and maturing' in the work of making poems, a place of 'miracle' in the sense that hearing one another's poems, can make us 'see differently'.[27] The radical hospitality of exchanging poems impacts deeply and powerfully on our own writing and thinking.

Reflecting on her experience of Christian faith in relation to the significance of poetry and theology, Nicola concludes that both are necessary in dynamic relationality. In their distinctiveness and contrasting approaches to apprehending truth and constructing meaning, both dimensions 'need each other; feed off each other, scrutinize, correct and critique each other'.[28] It is the inter-relationship between poetry and theology that creates a dynamic in which faith may flourish. In a similar way, the sounds and silences of the poem in text on a page, once read out and spoken into the listening community and heard by others, becomes a voice in the company of voices.

Nicola has been a persistent and persuasive advocate for practical theology as a space in which a multiplicity of voices is to be encouraged through personal conversation, spoken and written word in the academy, and through the sharing of liturgy and prayer, poetry and art.[29] In a theological domain where 'conversation' has been a key methodological term,[30] Nicola's vigilance around power dynamics in that conversation, and her commitment to the empowerment of women, queer and other marginal voices, has been eloquent.

Conclusion

In this chapter we have celebrated Nicola's achievements and importance as poet and theologian, giving particular attention to the critical process of the Diviners poetry group of which she is a part. As a reflexive shared enterprise each co-author has presented a selection of their own poems which are indicative of our work as poets. In dialogue with one another we have explored how these poems resonate with Nicola's poetry and theology, seeking out the substantial meanings, connections and differences between us and Nicola as the fifth, absent/present member of the Diviners. This critical appreciation approach has generated a richer understanding of Nicola's significance to us as individuals. We have recognized how the generative quality of participation in a company of poets sustains a creative vitality of poetic creativity which nourishes us as individual public poet-theologians. This participative, dialogical and reflective dimension to the work of writing is crucial for sustaining and refining creative artistry and spirituality. The missing dimension in this particular dialogical reflection is, of course, Nicola's own responses to our interpretations and apprehensions. We look forward to those in person.

Notes

1 Nicola Slee, *Fragments for Fractured Times: What Feminist Practical Theology Brings to the Table* (London: SCM Press, 2020), 130–1.

2 Nicola Slee, *Women's Faith Development: Patterns and Processes* (Aldershot: Ashgate, 2004).

3 Turkish: 'Humanity washed ashore' – hashtag used in mourning the death of a three-year-old Syrian boy, Aylan Kurdi.

4 Latin: All flesh shall come before you.

5 Syriac: Lord have mercy upon us and help us. Mary, like a ship, carried, adored and honoured Him, the Helmsman and the Lord of all creation. From the *Syriac Orthodox Church Liturgy of the Divine Mysteries*.

6 Latin: Thou that takest away the sins of the world, have mercy upon us. Thou that takest away the sins of the world, receive our prayer.

7 Latin: And in earth peace to men of good will.

8 Latin: I believe in one God maker of heaven and earth, and of all things visible and invisible.

9 Arabic: There is no god but God (the first part of the shahada, the Muslim profession of faith).

10 Latin: Holy, Holy, Holy, Lord God of Hosts. Heaven and earth are full of Thy glory. Hosanna in the highest.

11 Arabic: Have you seen that which you sow? Do you cause it to grow, or are We the grower? (Qur'an 56. 63–64).

12 Latin: Blessed is he who comes in the name of the Lord.

13 Latin: Lamb of God, Who takest away the sins of the world, have mercy upon us. Lamb of God, Who takest away the sins of the world, have mercy upon us. Lamb of God, Who takest away the sins of the world, grant us peace.

14 'Sirmione' (Sirmio in Catullus' time) may benefit from some awareness of his poems 2 and 31. See http://rudy.negenborn.net/catullus/text2/e2.htm and http://rudy.negenborn.net/catullus/text2/e31.htm (accessed 9 September 2022).

15 Originally published as Eleanor Nesbitt, 'Cathedral of Santiago di Compostella', *Theology* 118, no. 4 (2015): 283. Reproduced with permission.

16 The spoken testimony can be found at: www.youtube.com/watch?v=oLdUQAx16Jo (accessed 31 August 2021).

17 A Maori word for *song*.

18 Adrienne Rich, 'Diving into the Wreck', in *Diving into the Wreck: Poems 1972–1973* (New York: W. W. Norton, 2013), 22.

19 Mark Pryce, *Poetry, Practical Theology and Reflective Practice* (London: Routledge, 2019), 24.

20 Mark Pryce, *Finding a Voice: Men, Women and the Community of the Church* (London: SCM Press, 1996) and 'Taking Form: On Becoming a Christian Poet', in Gavin D'Costa, Eleanor Nesbitt, Mark Pryce, Ruth Shelton and Nicola Slee, *Making Nothing Happen: Five Poets Explore Faith and Spirituality* (Farnham: Ashgate, 2014), 86–125 (102).

21 Nicola Slee, *The Book of Mary* (London: SPCK, 2007).

22 Nicola Slee, *The Remembering Mary Study Guide* (Birmingham: Christian Education Publications, 2000), 3–4.

23 Slee, *Fragments for Fractured Times*, 19.

24 Hélène Cixous, *Three Steps on the Ladder of Writing* (New York: Columbia University Press, 1993), 3.

25 Cixous, *Three Steps on the Ladder of Writing*, 156.

26 Eleanor Nesbitt, 'Where Poems Come From: Spirituality, Emotion and *Poiesis*', in D'Costa et al., *Making Nothing Happen*, 127–69 (128).

27 Gavin D'Costa, 'The Miracle of Poetry: Divine and Human Creativity', in D'Costa et al., *Making Nothing Happen*, 171–210 (172–3).

28 Nicola Slee, '(W)riting like a Woman: In Search of a Feminist Theological Poetics', in D'Costa et al., *Making Nothing Happen*, 9–47 (27).

29 Slee, *The Remembering Mary Study Guide*, 3–4.

30 Stephen Pattison, 'Some Straw for the Bricks: A Basic Introduction to Theological Reflection', *Contact* 99, no. 1 (1989): 2–9; James W. Woodward and Stephen Pattison, eds, *The Blackwell Reader in Practical and Pastoral Theology* (Oxford: Blackwell, 2000); Patricia O'Connell Killen and John De Beer, *The Art of Theological Reflection*, 2nd edn (New York: Crossroad, 2004); Elaine Graham, Heather Walton and Frances Ward, *Theological Reflection: Methods* (London: SCM Press, 2005).

3

The Poetry of Priesthood: Writing the Body of Mary, Christa, of You, and of Me

RACHEL MANN

If I can no longer remember the precise date or occasion; nonetheless I shall never forget what I saw. It was during a service in the chapel of the Queen's Foundation for Ecumenical Theological Education in Birmingham, where I was formed for ministry. Stephen Burns, our liturgy tutor, was presider and Nicola Slee the preacher. Stephen wore the simple garb of a priest – cassock/alb and that mark of priestly authority, a stole. Then, right in the middle of the service, it happened. Nicola, smartly dressed, but without cassock or other robe, got up from the body of the chapel to preach or pray (I forget which) and Stephen took off his stole and laid it on Nicola's shoulders. She stood there, lay woman, poet, scholar and preacher. And priest? Well, not in the canonical sense. However, as I shall argue here, for me, few have acted more clearly as an icon of Christ(a).

That moment in chapel was remarkable. It was a striking gesture. Perhaps I am inclined to overplay the power of symbol, but what I saw was Nicola – a lay woman with remarkable authority, a first-class theologian and a poet of rare gift – being recognized as holding priestly authority. Given that she had not received episcopal ordination, it felt such a transgressive gesture. It was strange and queer. It felt like the work of poetry, that most acute and often edgy wrestling with the work of the divine.

In this chapter I want to explore some of the intersections between poetry and priestly ministry as I find it in Nicola Slee's work. In doing so, I recognize that I shall be reflecting, in part, on her impact on me as poet and priest, as much as taking a theological dive into her writings. I should acknowledge, at the outset, that Slee's work as a feminist theologian and poet has been and is hugely influential on my own work as priest and poet. She supervised my studies through my second year at Queen's, where I was given permission to range widely as an emerging poet and theologian. She was, in effect, my first formal poetry tutor, as well as someone whose work and being has enabled me to grow as a feminist and queer theologian and be ready to be a braver priest than I might otherwise have become.

Slee has always struck me as a poet with an acute sense of poetry's liturgical horizons and rhythms.[1] I begin this chapter, then, by exploring what it means to speak of Slee as a 'liturgical poet' with a gift for speaking into the strangeness and queerness of priesthood. I shall attempt to do so by speaking of her work as poet as a work of 'Word' and 'Sacrament' located in the life of the Body. This is, of course, a conscious borrowing of the language of priesthood. In the vocational circles of which I am part, priesthood is often spoken of as a ministry of word and sacrament. While Slee is not an ordained priest, I discern in her feminist poetic disruptions something of the work of a priest: one who acts as an icon of Christ, making God available in the midst of the Body of Christ.

A Liturgical Poet who Dares to 'Write the Body'

'[Poetry] witnesses to the transcendent, to the beyond in our midst, to the "more than" that beckons human beings beyond the immediate, the functional needs of the moment.'[2] As an account of the mystical nature of poetry, Slee's claim is striking and crisp. I hear within it, consciously or unconsciously, echoes of Robert Graves' claim that poetry, in its essence, is 'a wild Pentecostal speaking in tongues'.[3]

Such a mystical, Spirit-infused poetics might seem to be far from 'liturgy' or 'the Liturgy'. When one uses such words such as liturgy one inevitably, if one is an Anglican, hears 'structure', 'order', 'repetition' and 'form'. Perhaps one pictures the gathered Body of Christ on a Sunday, what Robert Hovda called 'this assembly of believers'.[4] As a priest and liturgist, however, I am conscious of a number of fascinating resonances in Slee's claims for poetry. Note her use of 'our midst' – of whom does she speak? A generalized 'us'? A gathered community? Those at the margins? Slee senses that poetry moves human beings beyond functional needs of the moment. There is something profoundly liturgical in this conception of poetry: she suggests, I think, that it operates as part of a community (of human beings, of makers and poets, of searchers and so on) offering language as a response to mystery and, crucially, as a resistance to the utilitarian. She implies that poetry has, just like liturgy, a kind of holy uselessness.

Slee readily acknowledges this intersection between liturgical text and poem. 'Every poem or liturgical text is partial, provisional, incomplete.

It cannot do everything; perhaps it can do something.'[5] She understands, as I have certainly come to appreciate as a priest and poet, that poetry and liturgy work at the limit of what can be said and done. At precisely the moment that liturgical and poetic speech attempt to say something positive – cataphatically, as it were – it breaks in the face of the divine's mysterious silence. If the cataphatic discovers its limits in the wild and strange power of the apophatic, still the poet and liturgist is called to speak. Perhaps Slee's most acute appreciation of the beautiful problem, the glorious mystery at the heart of one's attempts to witness to the transcendent, is in her liturgical poem 'Litany to a Dark God'.[6]

At the heart of the poem is mysterious loving relationship. The speaker addresses a female-coded God as a lover, who nonetheless is beyond sight and touch. She is known in breath, as well as in speech that is beyond ready comprehension. Her ways are beyond understanding and yet are understood as love and dynamic relationship. Slee presents a divine lover who models tenderness and cradling and a darkness that is entered as if it has not been entered before. There is an implication that this darkness is that of the womb and what Julia Kristeva calls *Khora* – the space of unknowing which is also a making of (feminine) possibility. Slee reaches for sense and form – this is a poem that, after all, seeks to articulate something and yet knows that in the face of the glorious dark and wondrous mystery of the ultimate Other, God, language breaks. Yet, still the poet and liturgist speak. Why? Because the Other invites it.

Slee herself notes that 'Litany to a Dark God' draws on both the biblical Song of Songs and the Psalms, as well as the apophatic mystical tradition. She says, 'by deliberately employing the cadences, rhythms and formal features of archaic biblical and liturgical language, the litany implicitly claims the authority and dignity of scriptural speech for a contemporary, feminist community'.[7] I discern then a playful and subversive alignment of Slee's work with the scriptural speech traditionally associated with those who held priestly and levitical roles in Jewish communities. In aligning her work with the erotic speech of the Song of Songs, a section of the Bible that has commonly been used in Christian wedding services (a service in the Church of England always officiated by a priest), there is an intriguing adjacency between her language and the words of the marriage service presided over by a priest.

Equally, Slee recognizes that for all the disruptive, creative potential of the apophatic tradition, it has still been dominated by patriarchal ideas of God, commenting: 'The apophatic way was parasitic on the cataphatic and, to that extent, was limited by the patriarchal and dualistic assumptions of every positive affirmation about God.'[8] 'Litany to a Dark God' models a creative tension in its garrulousness about God – its endless determination to speak of God as she rather than he – as well as its dis-cretion. Slee recognizes that 'the dark god evoked in the poem is, in a very real sense, nameless and faceless, and her namelessness and facelessness are also, paradoxically, revelatory: revelatory and, strangely, a source of power … whatever is affirmed of her is immediately contradicted or negated'.[9] For me, Slee again speaks into the intersections between the life and work of a poet and that of a woman priest serving in an institution absolutely shaped by patriarchal or kyriarchal discourse. She reminds me of the extent to which ordained women and queer people like me always negotiate the undertow of patriarchy. The very fact that we are always known as 'priests' rather than 'priestesses' is a signal of taboo; 'priestess' (even as a joke) is the word that dare not speak its own name. There is no space even for the (questionable) joke made, when I was first ordained, when I was often called a 'vicarette' rather than 'vicar'. All women who are priests meet with a history that has erased women's (and other sub-alterns') histories.

In the next section I want to dive deep into this phenomenon of silenc-ing, a dive into what Adrienne Rich called 'the wreck' (of histories, memories, stories), as I examine Slee's attention to the figure from Mary, the mother of Jesus, as one way of interrogating the dynamics of speaking the word under conditions of erasure.

A Ministry of Word – Who is Permitted to Speak? Who Dares to Speak? Who Refuses to be Silent?

Not least among Slee's gifts is an honesty about the pressures and demands of occupying and speaking boldly into space that has tradition-ally been reserved for men. She says that 'poetry and theology have been arenas in which I've struggled to come to authentic speech as a woman'.[10] The practical theologian Brita Gill-Austern gives further shape to the theological challenges of finding a voice in male-dominated spaces: 'for persons who have lived under structures of inequality, domination, and control, the experience of feeling silenced is a common phenome-non'.[11] The queer theologian Elizabeth Stuart further suggests, 'Depriving people of language with which to make sense of their experience is a particularly effective way of keeping them silent and disempowered.'[12] For women poets – indeed for women priests – negotiating stereotypes of what women may be and may legitimately speak about, there has been deprivation not only in terms of words, but of cultural iconography. This phenomenon is brilliantly explored in Adrienne Rich's classic *Diving into the Wreck*, which pictures tradition as a mythic book in which the names

of women, and lesbians in particular, do not appear.[13] Slee, drawing on
Rich, says this about the poet-theologian's work:

> The female poet, like the political agent, is required to exercise 'radical
> imagination' – 'the radical imagination of the not-yet, the what-if' – in
> order to give birth to new forms of perception, new ways of speaking
> … feminist poets, like feminist theologians … have employed invective,
> lament, irony and humour to undo the assumptions of patriarchal texts
> and traditions, and feminist liturgies of denunciation and protest use
> such strategies.[14]

Slee's claim regarding the 'not-yet' and the 'what-if' is suggestive, indicat-
ing how 'subaltern' poetries can make new theological insight available.
She indicates how the poet's specific gift may speak into places that have
traditionally excluded women, including priesthood, and find ways to
queer the word. In this regard, *The Book of Mary* presents a truly striking work which reclaims Mary, the mother of Jesus, from the ecclesial/
dominant tradition's sentimentalized and oppressive representations.[15] In
poems such as 'In Praise of Mary's Hairy Arm Pits' and 'The Mansion
of Mary', Slee reveals both the provisional and particular power of a
contextualized, embodied Mary, but adds her voice to feminist and queer
traditions that claim that God is encountered in specific – often politi-
cized – contexts, through actual bodies and stories. It is in *The Book of
Mary* that Slee precisely and intentionally brings poetry and theologies of
Mary into sharp and revealing conversation with questions of ministry
and priesthood.

Slee reminds us that Mary is 'minister and priest par excellence'.[16]
She adds, 'As one who bore the Word and brought it to life and flesh,
as God-bearer, she exemplifies the work of all ministers and priests – yet
also, as Thomas Merton reminds us, of all poets and artists who also
labour to enflesh the Word.'[17] Slee's outworking of these powerful claims
entails, in the first instance, taking the quotidian seriously. In *The Book
of Mary*, poems like 'Madonna of the Laundry Basket' as well as 'Mary
Bakes Bread' – which meditates on the almost timeless, quiet rhythms of
domestic work and which suggest God's hands weave into Mary's hands
– show how Slee is unafraid to reclaim 'feminized' space as powerful, disruptive and dangerous space.[18] In 'An Artist's Litany to Mary', Slee takes
the familiar claim that Mary is 'Queen' and refracts it through unexpected
spaces: not simply Queen of Heaven, but the queen of poets, fools, clowns
and, ultimately, queen of all creativity.[19] This striking move re-centres
God's making on to the feminine: the Word who was from the beginning,
and through whom all things are made, is refracted through the figure of

Queen of all creativity. The one who carries God in her womb becomes the locus for poetic and priestly creativity. Slee reveals connective tissue that links Jesus' royal priesthood to Mary's queenly authority and creativity.[20]

Slee's interrogation of Mary as Queen of Poets and Priests does not rest there. As a poet, she is clearly drawn to the ekphrastic. Many of her poems respond to visual art and cues. The remarkable and transgressive 'Mary Celebrates the Eucharist' is a prayerful, poetic and disruptive response to a fourth-century catacomb fresco:

> She rises like a stern monarch from the sea,
> massive and fierce-eyed,
> her arms aloft in the gesture of prayer,
> her man-child like some shield across her breast.[21]

The Mary in this poem is no feminist 'con-celebrator' with her sisters but one who asks no permission and simply claims authority to herself.[22] She is source of blessing and judgement. This is a Mary who refuses the male gaze which would turn her into an object of beauty, of pity, or a plaything. This is Mary Pantocrator. Slee's vision of a woman occupying the space of 'ur-priest' is devastating and awesome and, ultimately, strangely empowering. She reminds women and other subaltern persons in ministry that their priesthood is not derived as some pale shadow of white, male, straight, middle-class authority. We dwell in our own authority, located in God's own dwelling in the world.

Writing specifically about women's relationship with poetry, Yopie Prins and Maeera Shreiber offer a helpful general observation about the etymology of the verb 'to dwell' which underlies the radical possibilities of women's poetry. They indicate that the notion of 'dwelling' gestures towards 'a process of perpetual displacement, [reclaiming] the wayward etymology of "dwelling" not as a hypothetical house to inhabit but as a verb that also means to go astray, leading us away and unpredictably elsewhere'.[23] They indicate how women poets' work almost necessarily 'dwells' in the tradition (and, one might argue, in the divine) in such a way that it goes 'astray' from ready-made meanings. Slee's work is iconic in this regard: she has a gift for going faithfully astray; if this work of departure might upset some, it promises to disrupt theological and cultural assumptions which have ossified into ready and exclusive doctrine and dogma. As John's Gospel reminds us, the Spirit of God carries out her work of creating no matter what box we wish to fit God into. 'The wind blows where it chooses, and you hear the sound of it, but you do not know where it comes from or where it goes. So it is with everyone who is born of the Spirit' (John 3.8).

A Ministry of Sacrament – Daring to Take the Breaking and Remaking of Christa's Body Seriously

If Slee's reworking of the figure of Mary as priest-poet reflects her willingness to stand within the tradition and discover the rich, surprising and subversive flex that tradition holds, it is her work on Christa that I suspect many find most challenging and liberating. In *Seeking the Risen Christa*, Slee acknowledges that 'to some readers, especially those versed in contemporary feminist theology, the idea of the Christa will not be new'.[24] Certainly, her searching for what one might call a language of location – of being able to situate herself in Christ and Christ in her lived identity – is very much part of an established tradition, yet finds its resonance in her own desire to know what it means for her to be feminist and a person of faith. Slee quotes that fabulous line of Karen Trimble Alliaume: 'As women have been told they do not resemble the saviour, we are in the process of "reassembling" that figure.'[25] However, for many – including many women of faith – the radicalism of coding Christ as female or feminine will be terrifying. Nonetheless, her poetic searching, written out of a desire to take particular, excluded and often traduced bodies seriously, makes, as we shall see, new christological visions available which powerfully speak into the lives of women and stretch the language of priesthood in liberative and exciting ways. For, not least among the titles and identity-markers that have accrued to Christ is 'Priest'. The search for the Christa, embodied, crucified and risen, is the search, in part, for the Priest(ess).

At the heart of *Seeking the Risen Christa* is an interrogation of the Triduum, that journey from Maundy Thursday through to Easter Day, a journey that, in turn, dynamically reads 'backwards' from Easter Day through the things that have been said about Christ. In her meditations on Maundy Thursday, Slee connects the domestic and servant/enslaved person work of Jesus – specifically foot-washing, but also meal-making – with the labours of women; once again one sees how in the queering of Christ into Christa, the divine horizons of previously demeaned intimacy and work is revealed. The servant-priest ministry of Christ is parsed into the priestly ministry of women and others who have been coded as subaltern. Thus, Slee writes a litany 'In Memory of Her' which centres both on the traduced figure of Mary, who anoints Christ's feet with costly perfume, but also – for those who have eyes to see – locates this work of anamnesis in the feminist theological tradition:

We will break open our gifts ...
  We will claim our prophetic powers ...
We will insist on saying our names
  in memory of her.[26]

Equally, as ever, Slee stretches biblical language of service and ministry. In 'Christa Gives a Mudwrap' one discovers God offering herself in the context of a spa.[27] It is quietly subversive, almost outrageous and yet deeply faithful. The speaker in this poem – who addresses Christa as divine lover – is made new by the ministrations of Christa.

Slee's understanding of intersections is both supple and – in a profound sense – simple. In the poem 'The Table of Women' – both an echo of that first eucharistic feast on Maundy Thursday and its own thing entirely – the model of priesthood is egalitarian and shared. Slee says that around the table of women bread is brought warm and eaten lustily and paradise is spoken of without restraint; around that table there is no priest because all are priests. The liturgy is life itself. She is radically inclusive, as in 'Litany for Messy Eaters', where real-life individuals are named (including me) for whom eating is deeply problematic, alongside those who are responsible for producing our food as well as those who are fearful of judgement at the eucharistic feast. The refrain takes us to the heart of the Body of Christ(a): we who are many are one body because we all share in one bread. This is Slee being queer priest to pilgrims both at the edge and at the centre. Christa's offer is liberation for all. In this radically equal vision of priesthood, there is – as we hear in 'At the Table of Christa' – no need for anyone to be instructed to 'remember' the gift of self-offering precisely because everyone receives the fullness of healing, an abundance of grace and the bread of justice. This is the lived promise of the kingdom.

Lest anyone see Slee's theological poetics as merely fantastical – they are certainly predicated on a vision sorely needed at such a time as this – ultimately they are grounded in the dignity and truth of lived bodies. I could explore this at great length, not least through her startling meditations on the Good Friday Christa, the 'feminist gap' of Holy Saturday and in the dynamic verbal energy of what she calls 'the Rising' rather than the 'Risen' Christa. It is sufficient here to draw attention to her long, quietly fierce and unapologetic poem 'Presiding Like a Woman'. The claim that the work of the priest is, in part, presiding at the eucharistic assembly is well-established. When one reads the poem's title one immediately is alert to the sacerdotal. However, Slee's unfolding and unpacking of the notion of (eucharistic) presidency is wide-ranging and disruptive. From the outset, Slee is clear on how 'we' women do it: in boardrooms and kitchens, at operating tables and on parliamentary committees, in bedrooms and at water pools; crucially this work of presidency is always in 'our own voices'. This encompasses every language given by God and in every accent and undertaken with elegant as well as rough words. This presidency is never alone and always the work of priests, whether acknowledged and recognized or not. It is undertaken in all places – in shanty towns and in grand palaces. It is simply done and it is done in and through real bodies with thanksgiving, in the face of the fracturing of hopes. This common work of priesthood transfigures wounds without lionizing them. The marks of Christa are carried in every woman's body, in:

> the bearing, the manifesting of the body of God,
>> the carrying in our bodies of the marks of the risen One;
>> seeing the light reflected in each other's eyes,
> seeing Her beauty mirrored in each one's softened face.[28]

This is heady and extraordinarily moving stuff. I am personally very moved when Nicola speaks, in this poem, of how 'we' speak in our own voices, recognized for the priests we are, or – and here is the biting honesty – 'mostly, not'. I have walked too far with women denied priestly authority or have found my own canonical priesthood demeaned or ignored too often not to be shattered by Nicola's honesty. However, it is her patient work of wider recognition and revisioning that is, finally, most moving, truthful and redemptive. In 'Presiding Like a Woman', as much as in any feminist poem I know, Slee unveils women's serially excluded bodies as sacrament. She writes the body exquisitely and honestly and reveals its sacramental horizons – how it is food, and wound and scar and a place of encounter with the wild love of God.

Teach us to Pray and Prepare us for our Death: Towards a Conclusion

Ahead of my priestly ordination as a youngish woman, a dear friend and spiritual director reminded me that in many ways the work of a priest is simple: it is to teach people to pray and prepare them for their death. In this concluding section, I want to draw Slee's priest-poet's work together. I want to do this by focusing on how she inhabits, as a poet, this vocation of teaching people to pray and preparing them for their death. As we have seen in previous sections, her priest-poet's gift is to undertake this work of pedagogy and formation through an astute and acute attentiveness to particular, fragile and wonderful bodies; it is by being attentive to death and resurrection in the midst of specific communities and lives.

In *Praying Like a Woman*, Slee acknowledges that the work of 'praying like a woman' entails 'struggle, anger, lament, exhaustion, contemplation, waiting, wondering, discovery, delight, passion, sensuality, sexuality, politics and theology, both shared and solitary, not necessarily in any order at all'.[29] Such a list is almost a prose-poem itself, and captures the wide-ranging need, if we are to be feminist poets, prayers and priests in a kyriarchal/patriarchal world, never to dismiss the seemingly irrelevant. Too often theology has been treated as philosophical and cerebral; Slee invites our whole selves and actual bodies into the centre. The long, titular prose poem that begins the book is all the more moving because it emerged simply out of Slee's own need to write it. In an era when poets have become afraid of 'we' and of imperative, her use of 'we must' as the refrain and anchor throughout the poem feels especially bold. In doing so, she not only adds her voice to those whose bodies and concerns have been excluded and marginalized, but empowers (through her personal honesty) others to pray through their rage, silencing, lament and longing. She reminds minoritized and marginalized people that we cannot expect others to bring new life to us; we must, as she puts it, 'open our own graves' and help one another to clamber out.

Slee's priestly vocation, then, is to teach us to pray – in part by example, in part in solidarity, and in part by a refusal to lie down dead in the face of the death-dealing patriarchal world. She grants us permission to shout aloud with the truths we know in our bones. She prepares us for our 'death' through a determined attention to the facts of the body and, well, by reminding us that patriarchy is already killing/has killed us. 'Writing the Body' is a poem that exhorts its readers to undertake the work of attention required to face the facts of a world riven by patriarchal traces. The reader is asked to write every cell and nerve, every bodily curve, work her mouth into the words that articulate truth; she is asked to become a kind of poetical chiropractor 'righting' the body's twists and contortions that have been foisted on it by the world's distortions. Finally, the reader will be ready to 'rite' the body – that is, to dance with abandon in sacred space, where she is unbounded and is impossible to stop. This invitation into an arc of rebirth – from the recognition of the truth of the body, of the violence and death-dealing that is done unto it and on into new life unfettered by patriarchal control – is a key marker of Slee's priestly-poetic work.

Lest this sound relentlessly austere or lacking in tenderness, Slee's queer, lesbian sensibility grounds her poetic invitation into prayer. The outstandingly lyrical 'Making Love With You', a paean to Nicola's lover and partner Rosie, is both cosmic and intimate as she reveals how the human body in loving relationship is prayer itself.[30] When the speaker of the poem makes love with her partner she is being born again and the experience is heaven come on earth. These cosmic resonances build to include the silence of holiness and prayer; however, this is earthed in the body's softness and wetness. Ultimately, the intimate Other – both distinct from the speaker and one with her – is holy sacrament and divine food. Together this couple constitute the eucharistic feast. Finally, together they are 'fecund god' and holy goodness. As Slee puts it in another poem, 'Charis', an intimate, fearless, loving relationship constitutes the 'caress of grace'.[31]

It is out of this work of thanksgiving – not least among the marks of priestly ministry – that celebration and praise come. Slee reminds us that 'praise is a willed, intentional activity to bless, to honour and to sacralize in the blessing, some person or activity and, above all, God who is the source of all blessing and goodness'.[32] What is repeatedly refreshing about Slee's work is her willingness to discover the edges of blessing and hope, the dream and hope of liberation, beyond the structures that conform canonical priests like me to the church's authorized ways of going on. This does not mean her poetry or her specific forms of priestly authority lack discipline or formal constraint. Rather, she is simultaneously attentive to the wildness of the Spirit and the weightiness of the body.

There is a wrestling that is deeply biblical. It goes back to the truth that God's world was made, in the first instance, in and through blessed speech. For, in the beginning, God spoke and the world was. This language of hope, praise and blessing that makes and remakes the world still holds good despite the fact that patriarchy and kyriarchy messes things up. As Slee reminds us,

> I want to say that every act of thanksgiving or praise is intrinsically eucharistic insofar as it realizes the very blessing it invokes. Whenever we take words of praise and blessing upon our lips and utter them aloud, we not only express our existing joy and pleasure, we also make more joy and pleasure to abound in the world, both for our own, for others' and for God's greater delight.[33]

Finally, then, one can begin to see how Slee's priestly poetry is an invitation into the deep self-revelation of God: that in daring to speak the words of love and blessing and promise and praise we participate in God's making and God participates in our making. It is a holy vocation indeed.

Notes

1 For example, see 'Cloister in the Heart', in Nicola Slee and Rosie Miles, *Doing December Differently* (Glasgow: Wild Goose, 2006), 201.

2 Nicola Slee, 'The Public Use of Poetry', *Audenshaw Papers* 215 (2006): 1.

3 Robert Graves, *The White Goddess*, ed. Grevel Lindop (London: Faber and Faber, 2010), 50.

4 Robert Hovda, 'Environment and Art in Catholic Worship', *Bishops' Committee on the Liturgy* (Washington: United States Catholic Conference, 1977), para. 28, 18.

5 Nicola Slee, 'Writing the (Feminine) Divine: Reflections on the Practice of Contemporary Feminist Liturgy', in *The Edge of God: New Liturgical Texts and Contexts in Conversation*, eds Stephen Burns, Nicola Slee and Michael N. Jagessar (London: Epworth Press, 2008), 187–201 (190).

6 Nicola Slee, *Praying Like a Woman* (London: SPCK, 2004), 140–1.

7 Slee, 'Writing the (Feminine) Divine', 193.

8 Slee, 'Writing the (Feminine) Divine', 196.

9 Slee, 'Writing the (Feminine) Divine', 197.

10 Nicola Slee, '(W)riting like a Woman: In Search of a Feminist Theological Poetics', in Gavin D'Costa, Eleanor Nesbitt, Mark Pryce, Ruth Shelton and Nicola Slee, *Making Nothing Happen: Five Poets Explore Faith and Spirituality* (Farnham: Ashgate, 2014), 9–47 (9).

11 Brita Gill-Austern, 'Pedagogy under the Influence of Feminism and Womanism', in *Feminist and Womanist Pastoral Theology*, eds Bonnie J. Miller-McLemore and Brita Gill-Austern (Nashville: Abingdon Press, 1999), 151–99 (153).

12 Elizabeth Stuart, *Daring to Speak God's Name: A Gay and Lesbian Prayer Book* (London: Hamish Hamilton, 1992), 10.

13 Adrienne Rich, *The Facts of a Doorframe: Poems Selected and New 1950–1984* (New York: W. W. Norton, 1984), 164.

14 Slee, '(W)riting like a Woman', 20.

15 Nicola Slee, *The Book of Mary* (London: SPCK, 2007).

16 Slee, *The Book of Mary*, 79.

17 Slee, *The Book of Mary*, 79.

18 Slee, *The Book of Mary*, 82, 85. Slee adds her voice to a now well-established tradition of poets and feminists reclaiming traditional female space as feminist space. For example, see Kathleen Norris, *The Quotidian Mysteries: Laundry, Liturgy and 'Women's Work'* (New York: Paulist Press, 1998).

19 Slee, *The Book of Mary*, 86.

20 In biblical terms one can begin to see how Mary – the one who sings Magnificat – is the one who teaches Jesus to speak the Beatitudes.

21 Slee, 'Mary Celebrates the Eucharist', *The Book of Mary*, 88.

22 In Catholic and some anglo-catholic practice, concelebration involves a number of priests joining the priest presiding at a eucharist to perform some liturgical gestures and speak words ascribed to Jesus.

23 Yopie Prins and Maeera Shreiber, *Dwelling in Possibility: Women Poets and Critics on Poetry, Reading Women Writing* (Ithaca: Cornell University Press, 1997), 1. In Old English, 'dwellen' means 'to lead astray', developing into 'tarry, stay in place' in Middle English.

24 Nicola Slee, *Seeking the Risen Christa* (London: SPCK, 2011), 3.

25 A rewording of Karen Trimble Alliaume, 'The Risks of Repeating Ourselves: Reading Feminist/Womanist Figures of Jesus', *Cross Currents* 48, no. 2 (1998): 198–217 (205). Quoted in Slee, *Seeking the Risen Christa*, 7, emphasis original.

26 Slee, 'In Memory of Her', *Seeking the Risen Christa*, 46. *In Memory of Her* is, of course, the title of one of Elisabeth Schüssler Fiorenza's seminal works.

27 Slee, 'Christa Gives a Mudwrap', *Seeking the Risen Christa*, 48.

28 Nicola Slee, 'Presiding Like a Woman', in *Presiding Like a Woman: Feminist Gesture for Christian Assembly*, eds Nicola Slee and Stephen Burns (London: SPCK, 2010), 7–8 (8).

29 Slee, *Praying Like a Woman*, 4.

30 Slee, 'Making Love with You', *Praying Like a Woman*, 111.

31 Slee, 'Charis', *Praying Like a Woman*, 110.

32 Slee, *Praying Like a Woman*, 115.

33 Slee, *Praying Like a Woman*, 116.

4

Registering:
Theology and Poetic Practice

HEATHER WALTON

Registering: Marking down as present (or absent); conveying recognition; ascribing identity; claiming a place, position, benefit or entitlement; noting a presence.

Registering: Making it official; notifying the authorities; putting it on record; stating an opinion; marking forgotten lives, histories and experiences; exercising dangerous memory.

Registering: Feeling a touch; sensing an attraction; showing an emotion; revealing the marks of experience; being struck by grief, suffering and loss; knowing in the body.

Registering: Experimenting with the range of an instrument; exploring the capacities of a voice; employing different modes of expression; writing that exceeds genres.

Registering a Moment

I am sitting in the bar at Westminster College with Nicola. I know her and I don't know her. There are not so many of us: feminists who are engaging with theology. I can recite every name. We gather in supportive groups but we are now also finding ways into the academy. We share information – where the back door is unlocked and how you might enter through an open window. We invite one another into the pages of our publications and we provide each other platforms on which to speak. So, of course, I know Nicola. I have long registered her presence and she has noted mine. The chords that connect all of us vibrate constantly with news of work, writing, campaigns and conferences, but also with lives and loves and losses. Yet this is different. I am not reading something she has written, or waving across a conference hall. Here we are sitting in the bar together with our drinks in our hands. We don't need any introductions but we need to register a friendship already formed.

We speak of our childhoods in the chapel: 'Tell me the stories of Jesus I love to hear.' Cups of tea, cake and the kindness of aproned aunties. We discuss our studies, intellectual passions and the obstacles we've faced working towards registration in the guild. We talk of years of frustration, personal conflict and sacred callings that seem impossible to fulfil.

And because it is in the bar, and I can say things with my eyes looking into my glass instead of directly into the eyes of my friend, I begin to admit to fragile hopes. Nicola does also.

I don't just want to be recognized as a clever girl.
I don't only want to write well.
I want to do the whole thing differently.

So I said it and she said it too and then it was said and it could not be unsaid.

Registering Conflicts of Interest

In a brief poetic memoir and manifesto, '(W)riting like a Woman', Nicola Slee describes the circumstances and processes that formed her as a poet and theologian.[1] When I read it, I am reconnected to the conversation that took place between us some 25 years ago in which we spoke together of the challenges we faced and the hopes we cherished. We both had had childhoods in the faith, encountering the wonder of words in the King James Bible and Wesley hymns, and knowing the grace of women poured out from huge enamel chapel teapots into endless cups of loving kindness. We were both enthralled by literature and were seeking to create theological reflections that were generative and rich. But things had become complicated for us. We had struggled to find ways to express our insights within male-centred theological conventions and to find a place for our academic work among the competing demands of personal, political and faith commitments. Despite years of theological labour neither of us had yet gained our doctorates and both of us had experienced challenging embodied conditions that seemed to mirror our vocational struggles. I had experienced many years of infertility, with its debilitating cycles of hope and despair, and the sense of failure that accompanied being unable to conceive and carry what I longed to bear. Nicola was facing many health challenges that entailed periods of forced inactivity when she longed to be producing new work. Both of us confessed to a sense of inadequacy that despite living in such 'exciting' feminist theological times we were not quite making the contribution we felt called to make.

Struggles are easier to admit to than hopes are to own. But amid the challenges we faced both of us had begun to find that our writing practices were becoming increasingly important to us. As Nicola was to reflect later, 'Looking back now, I can see that the flourishing of my writing emerged out of that time of stripping down, of illness, joblessness and homelessness.'[2] The compulsion to write seemed to represent something more than a therapeutic form of self-expression and to be integrally bound up with the theological vocation we had set out to follow. However, there seemed to be little possibility of uniting creative and theological work. Nicola describes this conundrum with painful clarity:

> I was deeply engaged in both, but sometimes inhabited them as if they were separate compartments, coming from different parts of me: the rational versus the affective, the professional versus the personal, the academic versus the spiritual. Theology was associated with the former, poetry with the latter … There was, for a long time, a huge split between these different parts of myself, and the tension created by this produced enormous paralysis … I was working – or trying to work – in two modes, two forms of writing … both were essential and yet I experienced them as pulling in different directions, and it was almost impossible to keep both alive at the same time.[3]

As this passage indicates, the felt conflict between the theological and the poetic is bound up with other tensions, including those between theological thinking and spiritual affect and the abstract and embodied ways of knowing. Beyond these it speaks of the cultural separations made between an unutterable sublime and the everyday domestic sphere with its intimacy and household gods as well as a theological divide between the perfections of the divine economy and life in this dear, damaged world that we call home. Traditionally such divisions have been seen as the generative expression of an ordered creation which places theology eternally in a masculine realm of ideal forms and locates poetry in a fleshly, female sphere. As Jacques Maritain categorically states, both theology and poetry may be understood as spiritually productive but their characters are quite different:

> Metaphysics snatches at the spiritual in an idea, by the most abstract intellection: poetry reaches it in the flesh … Metaphysics enjoys its possession only in the retreats of the eternal regions, while poetry finds its

own at every crossroad in the wanderings of the contingent and the singular ... Metaphysics gives chase to essences and definitions, poetry to any flash of existence glittering by the way.[4]

Maritain may view these distinctions with benign equanimity. He flourishes in the bright clarity of the eternal regions but is enriched (even enchanted) by the feminine wiles of the poetic. However, for the woman theologian who is a writer this (deeply gendered) divide is problematic. When there is enforced separation between the spheres the division separates her from her very self. There must be a living communication between them.

Frequently in her work Slee refers to Julia Kristeva's distinction (without separation) between the archaic maternal semiotic, an embodied sphere of rhythms and sensations that is imaged as the ground of poetic utterance and the symbolic realm of logocentric discourse and the father's law. The symbolic abjects the semiotic and yet continues to be both nourished and disrupted by it. It is a powerful, if not unproblematic,[5] way of imaging an ongoing subterranean relationship that endures between bodies and words. In one of her most powerful works, 'Stabat Mater', Kristeva gives textual form to this relation.[6] She writes in two columns. One articulates her own sensual experience of motherhood in rich, evocative, fragmentary and poetic terms. The other reflects on Western culture's sacralization of maternity and this column is written in conventional prose. What is very interesting to me is that while both sides contain insight it is in the unarticulated connections or conversations between the two columns that are revelatory.

I will employ a similar device to reflect upon the tensions that Slee has articulated between the realms of creative expression and theology – as well as how vital communication must persist between them. In doing so I employ my own creative practice. I am a life writer, not a poet. My registering is done through muddier and more makeshift means than those a poet employs – although I use them to respond to similar challenges as those Slee articulates in relation to her poetic work. I also seek a form of speech 'that pierces through the superficial ... and arrests the hearer, awakening desire and awareness, compelling us to attend to the concrete particular yet, at the same time, leading us beyond the particular to some larger vision of things'.[7]

Registering: Marking a Presence

My first classroom was painted yellow and there was a picture of a girl in a yellow dress on the wall above the nature table. There was a sandpit and a hamster in a cage. A tame jackdaw called Constable perched on the windowsill and tapped loudly on the window with his beak. And the teacher took the register in the morning first thing. Often we were late. My mother was pregnant and sick. Mornings were difficult, but it was not good to be late and miss the register: 'Adams, Ackroyd, Braithwaite, Bosomworth ...'. So many names and mine was the very last: 'Walters ... Walton'. 'Here, Miss' I shouted as I flung my coat over the peg that had a picture of a red balloon taped above it.

At Sunday School there was no register but you took your little green star card to be stamped each week with a purple star which showed you had attended. If you asked, then you could have a pretty star stamped on the back of your hand also. When there were five stars in a row on your card you could choose a postcard, with an animal picture and a verse from the Bible on it to take home. There were kittens and puppies and baby rabbits to choose from.

Consider these conditions:

1 There is no section in the library for feminist theology. The handful of books on this subject are filed in the seminary library under 'doctrine of man' and in the university library between 'magic' and 'folklore'.
2 To teach this subject you must order textbooks from the United States. The bookshop is owned by Quakers and is based in Boston. The package, when it arrives, is very discreetly wrapped in brown paper as if the books might offend.
3 No woman has lectured in theology here before. Not one woman. Not ever.

There are many challenges to be faced but the most difficult is how to account for yourself. The female theologian in her work as 'writer' must carefully consider how she will register her presence. Spaces have always existed in ecclesial contexts and spiritual discourses for feminized modes of participation and expression. These appear to be welcoming, bright and warm. They may become, however, infantilizing, parochial and confining. Slee writes:

> The struggle for the woman writer, the woman thinker, is how to inhabit patriarchal discourse without doing fundamental violence to her

In the last class of junior school the teacher did not recite our names at all. She was cross and her long face never smiled. We all had numbers that we chanted in quick succession and nobody dared to be late and miss the moment where their number must be called out. I was still last but there were fewer of us now. Some had left to go to the new school that had been built opposite the Co-op. 'Thirty one', I shouted when my turn came.

The sharp and angry teacher took away our names but I should be very honest and say she also gave us new ones. She began to teach us French. She said our Yorkshire accents were a terrible problem – but less so when we were singing French songs. Frère Jacques. Sur le Pont d'Avignon. The name she gave me was Colette and she wrote it in special, curly letters on a lilac card that I must place on the desk in front of me for every French lesson. 'Je m'appelle Colette.'

Colette was not a very pretty name, like Angeline or Michelle, but I liked it. The teacher said in her cross voice, but quietly and just to me, 'You should be Colette. She was a writer.' She said aloud so everyone could hear, 'You are a clever girl – it is a shame you will make nothing of your life.'

sense of self, without reinforcing her very absence and silence or positioning herself as stereotypically 'feminine' – passive, receptive, occupying the affective domain.[8]

Facing this dilemma you may seek to become fluent in the discourses of the academy. Able to say, 'I have learned your language it cost me dearly but I have mastered it well.' Proficiency is exhilarating at first but there is sadness at the sacrifice of the mother tongue. There is no easy way to mediate between these opposing spheres and moving beyond both of them is not a pleasant process of discovery – it entails loss. You have lost your birthright in seeking the ability to 'pass' without suspicion in your adopted country.

Registering in new terms involves becoming, at least for a while, inarticulate. This is painful to the self and puzzling to others.

In order to speak or think at all, the woman writer has to find a new language, make new maps … exercise 'radical imagination' … in order to give birth to new forms of perception, new ways of speaking.[9]

Registering: Putting on Record

I dressed my wee daughter in the little suit that I had chosen for the occasion. It was cute but not girly. The trousers had narrow, navy-blue and white stripes and the top had the same but with cherry red pockets and a wee red hood. It was the first time she had worn it and she looked both sweet and sassy. 'Oh my beautiful darling'.

We had left the whole thing very late for two reasons. First, because to register her birth seemed to be tempting fate. Saying everything was all right now. Here we were, safe and sound washed up upon the shore. Bruised and exhausted maybe, but rescued from the waves. The years of infertility, the probing and invasive medical procedures, the almost-losing-her-right-at-the last-moment, all over now and the baby safe in the cradle. Except the situation did not feel secure at all. So much more to lose now than ever there was before and so dangerous to inscribe all those years of hope and longing in pen and ink on a paper form.

The second reason we waited was to find a special date. And there we had it. Our mothers shared a birthday: 1 October. That seemed a good day to register her in the maternal lineage from which she came.

Julia Kristeva wrote in two columns down the page. Adrienne Rich wrote two separate works on the same theme that are invisibly co-joined. Her celebrated essay 'When We Dead Awaken'[10] is about the work of cultural revisioning through which women (in all spheres) must wrestle with a cultural heritage in which the records of their presence are systematically and perpetually obliterated. How to sift through this pile of stuff and what to make from it?

Its twin is the poem 'Diving into the Wreck'.[11] In this the poet makes the perilous journey to the depths of the ocean where dead forgotten faces 'sleep with open eyes'. They carry as totem and unreliable guide a book of sacred stories in which their 'names do not appear'. The quest is both 'to see the damage that was done/ and the treasures that prevail'. It is not a simple process of reclamation leading to regeneration. The journey acknowledges that cultural gestation often takes place in the womb space hollowed out inside the 'ribs of the disaster'.

Judy Chicago reclaims women's history in her iconic 'Dinner Party' where a grand table is set for 39 women of historical distinction and ceramic tiles celebrate the lives and contribution of 999 others. The work is important. It forges 'an

Her Dutch Oma and her English Grandma evoked as invisible witnesses in the Manchester Register Office.

Which was a rather blank and uninspiring place on a rainy autumn morning but, as her father said, quite a bit better than the Birmingham Registry Office in which we had been married. That had to be done as quickly as possible because of the deportation order which stated his presence in the UK would not be 'conducive to the public good'. The first available appointment had been at nine o'clock in the morning (is it even legal to get married at that time of day?). Two shocked but determined people making political promises to each other while my parents watched in sad silence. No cake and no confetti.

'Yes, we had to get married but not for the usual reason'. This 'making it official' thing is clearly difficult for people like us but the forced registration left us free to mark our partnership in the way we wanted. Non-juridically. In a marriage service in which there was no 'signing on the dotted line' and in a party afterwards in which my father's sparkling apple wine came out late in the evening when the shop-bought bottles were finished. It was Cana in Galilee.

alternative tradition of repressed and neglected female lives'[12] as well as staging a 'recovery and retrieval of a feminine symbolic imaginary rooted in the female body and ancient archetypes of the goddess'.[13] But, says Slee, there is something oddly static and formal about this important work. Missing from it are the lives of ordinary women. Which are not ordinary at all. Also excluded from this formal setting are representations of the ordinary things the extraordinary ones were doing and making when they weren't being poets and prophets, mystics and martyrs. They have been separated from the worlds that shaped their stories.

The sphere of the everyday is gradually reclaimed in feminist theology. It is the place of reproductive labour, so long dismissed as the unproductive 'housework' of human culture, but in truth the material from which the garment of culture is woven. It is also the place of struggle out of which transformation is born. Our lives, our loves, our intimate and personal experiences, cannot be registered in the dominant categories but, sacred to us, we will speak them, celebrate them, perform them anyway. This is resistance to oppression.

For this registration there were papers to be presented and I held up my wee girl-child to present her too. The registrar was nice and said she was a very lovely baby which was clearly true. 'Father's occupation?' Nurse – very conducive to the public good. No space on the form in those days for mother's occupation but I wanted it recorded as well. I was absurdly adamant this should be done. The wonderful man squashed in the word 'Lecturer' in a no-box place on the form next to my name. 'Thank you so much. Is that it?'

'Yes – that's it. All done.'

We went out into the street. It was still raining. And I thought at just this time last year I was barren and today I am blessed. But it is not really like that at all. I am truly both at the same time. Now and for ever.

But the question still remains how to register this submerged history. Slee employs two ways of writing from the ordinary into the sacred. She works as a qualitative researcher transcribing the faith experiences of women that otherwise pass unmarked and from the same material that constructs her poetry.[14] These processes increasingly intermingle and interact. She has become a poetic researcher and a recording poet. Her work may take place in two voices but both are incorporated into one process of making and remaking. Life becomes-word-becomes-life. 'As soon as it is set down, it is gone; yet by being made into something – a poem, a research paper, a lecture – it is lifted up for attention, and has the capacity ... to become part of a larger poesis.'[15]

Registering: Knowing Through the Body

There was a notice read out in our church that next Saturday, the day before our Harvest Festival, that anyone who wanted to could join a group going to Ilkley Moor to gather heather. We met at Leeds station early in the morning and set off. The weather was grand for our short trip and we sang songs on the train and played cards. My Auntie Dorothy passed round a paper bag of pink and yellow pear drops. Uncle Arthur shared his wicked 'wine gums' (choose from port, cider, gin, claret, brandy, sherry and champagne). But it was all right, because they were fruit flavours really and the man who invented them was a Methodist.

My special friend on this trip was Zanna. She was the minister's daughter. A year younger but several inches taller than me with long, curly, dark gold hair – that always escaped her plaits. She could run very fast. I was always trailing along behind her out of breath. When we saw the hill rising up before us, where the huge stone cow stood looming over her smaller rocky calf, she grabbed my hand and said, 'Let's get to the top first!' And we did. We found a very good spot to begin our harvest. We used old hessian potato sacks and faded, flowered pillowcases to gather

A distinctive feature of biblical poetics is parallelism. Two phrases are closely related to each other in some way. The relationship can take many forms. There may be an actual repetition of a key word or sentiment. Sometimes the second line emphasizes or explains what the first was expressing; at other times it adds to or expands upon the first. A parallel phrase makes the original meaning clearer or, alternatively, more mysterious and strange. In all cases what biblical parallelism achieves is to entangle the reader more deeply in a density of sensations and affects. This propensity is deepened by the poetic deployment of concrete nouns. Words denoting objects. Common things of substance. The Bible is not a book of spiritual equations. It is a book of stones and seeds, wine and water, clay and blossom, tree and bird. Meaning arises out of the tangible relations between these material forms.

When teaching creative writing one of the hardest challenges is to enable participants to move beyond language they understand to be literary (that is, archaic or abstracted) and find ways to grasp the 'thingyness' of things. To craft work using words with heft and to recognize that such words share the stubborn and intractable features of material things.

in the sprigs of purple heather. While we worked and because it seemed right to do so, I told Zanna my special story:

> When I was born my grandad and grandma got on the train to come and see me. But when they were halfway there my grandad made my grandma get off at a station in the middle of nowhere and they went out on to the moor and picked some heather to bring to my mum and me – because my name was Heather. There is a photo of me lying on a white blanket and I am only a few days old and the heather is all around me.

'Oh that's lovely,' Zanna said and I knew I had been right to tell her. She was quiet for a little while and then she said 'Let's pick bilberries.' And so we did, our fingers stained purple with their sour-sweet juice.

We got back to Leeds in the late afternoon and went straight to the church. Some of the older ladies, who did not hold with galivanting on moors and picking heather and bilberries and such like, had been preparing a pie and peas supper. We ate the hot pork pies from bowls with the mushy peas poured all over them. Then we decorated the church. The heather was arranged on the altar table and threaded through the communion rail. It was placed

Writing that is concretized produces embodied and sensual responses. The reader not only feels themselves related to the text but to the living world of which they are part; all the receptive faculties are engaged. A quantum response is engendered of inseparable connection.

Christina Rossetti's poem 'Goblin Market' generates its sensuous appeal from multiple parallelisms and references to fruits that are good to eat:

> Rare pears and greengages
> Damsons and bilberries
> Taste them and try[16]

From these simple resources Rossetti crafts a fable of longing, love and loss that is also a tale of sacrifice and redemption. The reader is tempted by fruit the poem bears. The reader can taste the words.

It would be a mistake to think that either theology or poetry has the work of turning earthy stuff into something different, something spiritual. The spiritual emerges by entering more deeply into the common substance of existence and that substance is revelatory. Transcendence is manifested not in distance or separation but experienced through the flaring light of haecceity, the 'thisness', through which things manifest in their particularity an irreducible aspect of glory.[17] The larger poesis around the pulpit and what was left over was intertwined between the harvest fruits and flowers. Allotment cabbages, plums and big Bramley apples. Huge bronze chrysanthemums, scarlet, spikey dahlias and purple Michaelmas daisies. It was glorious and glorious and glorious. The heather made everything that was common-home-and-garden place become wind-and-wide-open-skies special. I felt honoured that my own name flower was doing this wonderful thing. While the grown ups drank tea and ate Battenberg cake in the fellowship room, Zanna and I commandeered the youth club's record player and organized the children to play statues and musical chairs in the church hall. After that the adults came through and we danced. Zanna and I together, and the little ones running around shrieking and playing tig between the dancers. Because she was taller than me I rested my head upon her shoulder and her arms met around my back.

And that was the last time I danced with Zanna. She had a birthday coming and she begged her parents for a new bike.

Zanna rode too fast. Zanna was always going too fast.

Zanna with her dark golden hair too thick to be bound in plaits.

of which Slee speaks is a sacred-making that is 'pledged to the ordinary'.[18] This does not mean that it is bound to the trivial or banal. Rather, that it is on the terrain of the ordinary that glory flickers.

Henri Lefebvre viewed the everyday as generative of intense moments. 'Sometimes profundity and beauty can be born from … [an] unexpected combination: an encounter … they become moments, combinations which marvellously overturn structures.'[19] Paradigmatic of these moments are festivals that occur when those elements that constitute the everyday (intimacy, eating, sharing, working with the seasons) come together with explosive force. Festivals present to us a world as it might be, for a 'moment'. Bathed in brightness.

Alongside the festival is the tragic through which we encounter 'a different kingdom which is the kingdom of darkness … [we] traverse daily life under the flash of the tragic'.[20] No refuge from anguish and the destruction of our known worlds. But making is to be done here too. Poesis does not 'shy away from the horror of the world, the darkness, but looks it straight in the face'.[21] It is both the memorializing and metamorphosis of grief, 'through action and works, hence through thought, poetry, love'.[22]

Registering Between Worlds

Mayra Rivera describes theological work as 'passionate engagement, indeed of true com-passion, with the beauty and the pain, with the joy and the suffering of the world'.[23] It is labour that attends to the halo of glory that encompasses: 'life in all its fragility and ambiguities'.[24]

> Displaying both light and darkness ... [reflecting the] luminosity of ordinary things, neither irresistible nor self-sufficient, but incessantly alluring. It is often barely perceptible, yet sometimes disconcerting – even terrifying. The apparent aberrations of its depictions do not diminish a theologian's zeal to convey its varying, hazy radiance. Drawn by passion to the glory that flickers in the midst of everyday life ... theologians persist in our weak attentiveness ... in our attempts to describe it, however inaccurately and distortedly. We seek, with feeble words and images to express the inexpressible, in a multiplicity of voices, languages, and genres.[25]

I have evoked in this chapter the many tensions between different forms of expression, language use and genres and the struggles that women, in particular, have had in finding voice and being heard. There is no doubt that these conflicts have powerfully shaped the construction of theology and have often been the source of painful divisions among theologians themselves as they have sought to 'express the inexpressible' through the weakness of their words.

A fault line runs right through the centre of this chapter but, as I have indicated, it serves both to highlight a divide and as an invitation to undertake the imaginative work of moving between, across and beyond genres as traditionally understood. Through the work of poet-theologians our registers are becoming more expansive and we are increasingly able to engage in fluid and creative processes of 'registering' that refuse the separation of discrete spheres. Spanning old divides is absolutely necessary as we seek to register the ambiguity and fragility, the glory and the terror at the heart of things. Our theology must concretize and engage and our poetry school us to recognize the startling everyday sublime. As this happens territories will be redrawn and new terrains emerge.

Does this mean that tensions will ease and all boundaries disappear? I do not think so and nor do I even wish so. How then could we play between worlds? In her reflections on this theme, Slee speaks of acknowledging that rifts and chasms may be generative; creating new landmasses and fertile valley territories. It is the fissures opened up by seismic pressures out of which 'something extraordinary is born'.[26] Crucially, while tensions remain, we can never lose a sense of the provisional, shifting and unstable nature of our theological work. There is no synthesis, no realm of idealized absolutes in which all are reconciled. There is movement, there is forming and unforming, and behind it all something that does not itself take shape but shapes all things.

Poets and theologians are incessant form-makers but our vocation is also to be form-breakers. There is, as Slee reminds us, a need to recollect that all our work unravels and that wisdom is to be found at the point of rest when working becomes praying, and we let formlessness be:

> permitting the unmaking
> of thoughts and lines and words
> and the grasp of and the hold on things
> over and over to slip.[27]

This is the best and last challenge to the theologian and the poet: not to resolve 'the tensions or ... [tie] up all the ends neatly'.[28] We do not so much need to discover a way to bind things firmly together, but instead to find the words that bless our own undoing.

Notes

1 Nicola Slee, '(W)riting like a Woman: In Search of a Feminist Theological Poetics', in Gavin D'Costa, Eleanor Nesbitt, Mark Pryce, Ruth Shelton and Nicola Slee, *Making Nothing Happen: Five Poets Explore Faith and Spirituality* (Farnham: Ashgate, 2014), 9–47.

2 Nicola Slee, *Fragments for Fractured Times: What Feminist Theology Brings to the Table* (London: SCM Press, 2020), 99.

3 Slee, '(W)riting like a Woman', 17.

4 Jacques Maritain, *Creative Intuition in Art and Poetry* (London: The Harvill Press, 1954), 235–6.

5 The distinction and relation Kristeva posits between the symbolic and the semiotic offers ways of imaging and exploring differing spheres of subjectivity and culture. These can be helpful and creative. However, as a revisioning of Lacanian psychoanalytic categories, I do not find it helpful to essentialize them as if they were states of being. Similarly, I do have significant problems about the gendered binaries at play in her schema.

6 Julia Kristeva, 'Stabat Mater', *Poetics Today* 6, no. 1/2 (1985): 133–52.

7 Slee, *Fragments for Fractured Times*, 125–6.

8 Slee, '(W)riting like a Woman', 19.

9 Slee, '(W)riting like a Woman', 20.

10 Adrienne Rich, 'When We Dead Awaken: Writing as Revision', *College English* 34, no. 1 (1972): 18–30.

11 Adrienne Rich, 'Diving into the Wreck', in *Diving into the Wreck: Poems 1972–1973* (New York: W. W. Norton, 2013), 22.

12 Slee, *Fragments for Fractured Times*, 16.

13 Slee, *Fragments for Fractured Times*, 16.

14 Slee, *Fragments for Fractured Times*, 205–18.

15 Slee, *Fragments for Fractured Times*, 19.

16 Christina Rossetti, 'Goblin Market' (1862).

17 For a celebration of 'thisness' in literature and theology, see, for example, Richard Kearney, 'Epiphanies of the Everyday: Toward a Micro-Eschatology', in *After God: Richard Kearney and the Continental Turn in Contemporary Philosophy*, ed. John Panteleimon Manoussakis (New York: Fordham University Press, 2006), 3–20.

18 Nicola Slee, 'Faithfulness', *The Book of Mary* (London: SPCK, 2007), 17.

19 Henri Lefebvre, *Critique of Everyday Life, vol. 2: Foundations for a Sociology of the Everyday*, trans. John Moore (London: Verso Books, 2002), 66.

20 Henri Lefebvre, *Critique of Everyday Life, vol. 3: From Modernity to Modernism (Towards A Metaphilosophy of Daily Life)*, trans. Gregory Elliott (London: Verso Books, 2005), 171–2.

21 Lefebvre, *Critique of Everyday Life*, vol. 3, 171.

22 Lefebvre, *Critique of Everyday Life*, vol. 3, 165.

23 Mayra Rivera, 'Glory: The First Passion of Theology', in *Polydoxy: Theology of Multiplicity and Relation*, eds Catherine Keller and Laurel C. Schneider (New York: Routledge, 2010), 167–85 (170).

24 Rivera, 'Glory', 167.

25 Rivera, 'Glory', 167.

26 Slee, *Fragments for Fractured Times*, 105.

27 Slee, *Fragments for Fractured Times*, 100.

28 Slee, *Fragments for Fractured Times*, 105.

PART 2

Faith and Feminism

Christa Ignored

Nicola Slee

In the chapel with the rattling windows and white-washed walls
we sat with the wounded one in our midst,
unremarked, unremarkable.

She had her arms lifted over her head
her eyes closed in a gesture
we could not read as pleasure or pain.

We milled and drifted about
circling her body, not touching.
Some arrived late,

without language or a reason to be here.
Some spoke often, rehearsing their anxiety,
asking many questions.

Some knew the story, others only a name
or a hint of a name that may
or may not have been hers.

All the time, she kept silence at the centre
absorbing the way we ignored her
without resentment or blame.

She kept her own counsel, a body of wisdom
to which we might still reach out,
a saving deliverance we yet might choose.

5

The Faith Lives of Women and Girls: An Expanding Story

ANNE PHILLIPS

I do not stand alone
but with others to support me
I will stand my ground.[1]

Lodged deep in my personal archive lie these words from a poem Nicola Slee sent me years ago when I was holding together a full-time teaching post in a theological college, part-time doctoral research, and family life.

It captures the journey through the many years during which I have worked, periodically, alongside Nicola as ecumenical colleague, writing companion and editorial collaborator. For several of those years, Nicola also acted as a wise and patient doctoral supervisor. The poem's paean to interdependence describes the experience of many other women whose paths have crossed with Nicola's, to which this chapter bears testimony. She has offered us support to break down our research isolation and the opportunity to flourish in the interdependence of networking. As a whole, the poem sums up the purpose of Nicola's ongoing work within the Research Symposium on the Faith Lives of Women and Girls, expressing its ethos and echoing the high value participant scholars have placed on it. In the years since its inception, it has contributed substantially to the many ways Nicola's pioneering work on women's and girls' faith development has been expanded, critiqued and nuanced since the publication in 2004 of *Women's Faith Development*.[2]

Building on the growing (largely White Western) corpus of feminist theology and the varied writings on women's spirituality, Slee's book offered something new, an empirically based qualitative 'examination of the patterns and processes in women's spirituality and faith development',[3] crucially in critical conversation with the work of James Fowler.[4] By the end of the twentieth century Fowler's *Stages of Faith* had become the key text by which academy and church were categorizing faith development. His stage theory aimed to provide 'a formally descriptive and normative model' applicable 'within the particularity of each faith tradition'.[5] In her dialogue with Fowler, Slee both suggests ways his theory illuminates women's faith development, and in the light of her own findings posits 'what theoretical revisions would ... better account for women's faith'.[6] Drawing on cognitive, psychodynamic and dialectical theories of development, Slee built on the newly gendered theoretical base that women were developing, especially in the USA where they had begun to grow 'a new stage of consciousness in women's collective spirituality', although at the time this was mainly through anecdote and personal testimony.[7] What scholars lacked was a thoroughgoing empirical and contextual study of women's faithing within the disciplines of feminist theology, challenging the unacknowledged androcentric normativity among the overwhelmingly male scholars in the field, who held that developmental growth was consistent and unchanging across diverse cultural contexts, echoing Fowler's claim to universality.

The doctoral research on which Slee's book was based generated UK-sourced data from women inhabiting a variety of contexts 'belonging to, or on the edges of, Christian tradition'.[8] While not setting out to 'test the validity of [Fowler's] faith stages as such', and affirming basic coherence between her findings and Fowler's understanding of faith,[9] analysis of her data revealed 'aspects of my findings that seem to demand different interpretation, which push against the grain of Fowler's theory, or for which Fowler does not seem to offer an appropriate or adequate account'.[10] She then offers four key findings that challenge Fowler particularly in the crucial maturational move between his Stages 3 and 4 and the achievement of an owned faith.[11] In the first two, she highlights respectively women's tendency towards 'apophatic faithing operating at the edges of rational and critical thinking',[12] and the dominance of relational faith consciousness embedded in a strong sense of connectedness to the other in harmony rather than in competition with 'the preservation of one's own selfhood'.[13] In the third, she stresses the importance of employing a methodology, mainly a semi-structured interview process, by which the way each woman chooses to shape her narrative becomes intrinsic to the data, and contributes to her expression of, and the researcher's understanding of, her faith. Finally, Slee concludes that her analysis challenges the relentless emphasis in Fowler on progress through a sequence of linear stages, moving 'towards the next, "higher" level of consciousness or pattern of behaviour'.[14] Not only her data but many models drawn from mystical traditions evidence periods of paralysis and impasse, often expressed creatively in poetry or in women's fiction. The placing of cognition so prominently in Fowler's staged faith development eclipses the more multi-faceted and nuanced ways by which women travel the faith journey.

The Loneliness of the Long-Distance Researcher

By the time of the book's publication, Slee had found a home in the hospitable academic environment of the Queen's Foundation for Ecumenical Theological Education in Birmingham, specializing then, as now, in the work of its research community. She brought with her the legacy of many years' networking with other feminist scholars in formal and informal settings, building on her recognized skill as theological educator and spiritual guide, especially of women. Slee was all too aware, both from her own history and from those of other women she met in diverse academic contexts, of the difficulties women researchers experienced. Chief among these were finding supervisors with sufficient knowledge of – and sympathy with – feminist theology and qualitative research methods, and the scholarly isolation and loneliness of pursuing research that was little understood or valued by the academy whether for its subject matter (female experience) or its qualitative methodology and creative methods. Although the number of women researching female faith is growing, many still feel isolated in institutions that offer no academically informed context within which to fit their work: in their own words, too frequently their peers and staff 'don't get it'. These women live in a variety of contexts. Those researching at master's level may be training for ordained or lay ministries, or undertaking 'refresher' study; others, mainly at doctoral and post-doctoral level, will already be in academic or ecclesial posts but aiming for professional advancement or careers as scholars. Academic posts carry high expectations of research measured by quantity of publication. For many, though, their research will be part time, their empirical and analytical work undertaken alongside professional commitments and personal and family responsibilities and relationships, which have been shown still to impact more heavily on the lives of women than men. This broadly mirrored my own situation, one that Slee well understood in supervising my doctoral research into the faith of girls,[15] an area her own work had included only nominally, but to which my data and analysis gave complementary (as well as challenging) content.

Expansion through the Symposium

Since publication, *Women's Faith Development* has become a landmark text for women of faith, for feminist researchers and for faith communities.[16] Nothing matching Slee's academic rigour had hitherto been published. She places her book within an evolving process of learning, expanded by a growing community of women who share a common aim, to give voice to women's distinctive experience of doing and living faith in an ever-widening variety of contexts. 'Expansion' is her chosen metaphor for this process. Her published research opened a door. Women researchers who crossed its threshold gained the tools to widen their perspectives as they gazed on women's faith lives. The horizon continues to expand with every new area subjected to their scholarly gaze. In opening up this wider horizon to critical view, it is also worth noting the validity feminist researchers are bestowing on women's and girls' everyday experiences by studying them ethnographically in their lived contexts, in contrast to the laboratory-style or clinical settings typical of the research of Fowler, his predecessors and contemporaries. Although academic validation for qualitative research is still more difficult to achieve through the perceived lack of precise comparability within the data-gathering process, a different analytical epistemology has emerged. Greater transparency is achieved through the growth of, for example, reflexivity and triangulation,[17] permitting author-constructed narratives of 'ordinary' life to be heard within the academy. Thus theory is grounded in the narrated experience of women and girls.

As Slee attended conferences, acted as external examiner and received correspondence, she encountered more women engaged in qualitative research into female faith, often spurred on by her writing but working in isolation in their respective institutions. From among the many examples shared with me in private correspondence while researching for this chapter, I cite this from Gwen Henderson, one of the first doctoral students for whom Slee acted as external examiner, and in whose work among women from a conservative evangelical background Slee recognized an important critique:

[Slee's work] profoundly shaped my own frame of reference for exploring the constantly changing, dimensional nature of women's relationships in their 'multiple worlds' ... It opened my eyes to the importance of 'embodiment' through the relational and conversational strategies women might use as an essential expression of faithing change, particularly with regard to the changing nature of their relationship *with* God, not simply beliefs *about* God. This was an area of research I particularly wanted to explore as it seems, in theological circles, it is seldom seen as a valid or substantial area of exploration, despite the Christian experience being an embodied and relational rather than simply a cognitive phenomenon. This is particularly the case when women's preference for relational over abstract, propositional and analytic faithing styles alienates them in Western academic and ecclesial contexts: where their speech about faith and description of their experiences of God are often misunderstood, dismissed or judged theologically inadequate. Nicola ... argues the opposite – that women's habitual linguistic and non-linguistic ways of articulating their relationship with God through activities from painting, sculpting, gardening to wordless contemplative prayer actually constitutes a substantial theological language. Her understanding of the 'embedded' nature of female theology in the fabric of women's life narratives gave me, as a researcher, a deep attentiveness to participants' frequently meandering, occasionally repetitive stories which implicitly concealed substantial insights into the nature of women's relationships with God.[18]

Henderson further comments: 'I began to believe I might, in fact, have a voice ... and something unique to contribute to our understanding of women's ways of navigating and embodying faith.'[19] This would be echoed by many women inspired by *Women's Faith Development*, but none of them knew one another. Thus was sown in Slee the seed of the idea that blossomed into the Symposium, initially conceived as a one-off gathering, but which immediately generated an energy that has sustained it up to the present, going online through the coronavirus pandemic.

The symposium format is fundamental to the concept: distinct from a 'conference', the term suggests not only a common theme (feminist qualitative research into the faith lives of women and girls) but also an element of informality stemming from its ancient Greek roots in the combination of quality hospitality and serious conversation, both of which are given attention. Participants have commented on this, drawing comparison with the destructiveness of competitive engagement felt elsewhere in academia. As one put it, 'so many research-based conversations are awash with egos', whereas here there are 'no competitive or critical academic power dynamics'. An independent researcher's sense of loneliness dissipated as 'ideas were respectfully listened to and commented on without any sense of hierarchy or being made to feel insignificant'.

At the first meeting, held in November 2010, 16 women postgraduate scholars responded to Slee's invitation to gather at Queen's in Birmingham for a two-day meeting, each sharing a short paper outlining for discussion her recent or current research. This constituted the formal part of solid relationship-building which continued informally 'after-hours' as, being residential, we were sharing college accommodation facilities.

The format of that meeting set a non-hierarchical pattern consistent with Slee's own personal and scholarly values based on participation and mutual regard, one that has been maintained. All women are valued as of equal status, whether researching at master's or post-doctoral level, college students, local ministers, lecturers or professors. One participant commented on how that ethos makes it 'as supportive an atmosphere as possible while retaining the edge of professionalism'. A horseshoe arrangement of tables ensures all can make eye-contact. Presentations normally of 20 minutes, in sessions of two or three papers broadly linked, are followed by discussion. Time-keeping as well as academic critique is rigorously applied, but in a constructive spirit of mutual up-building and respect. Chairing of sessions is shared among participants, a valuable learning experience for some. The seminar room holds a focal point of inspiration – 'an "altar-like" space' – filled with symbols of our temporary shared life together, variously through colour (fabric, flowers), movement (candles) and hospitality (comfort snacks). Optional times of reflection/worship in the chapel are also scheduled at residential events. Date, duration and timing of each subsequent Symposium are chosen taking account of predictable commitments to study, work, family and travel.[20] Women's commitment to faith practice on Holy Days is honoured too.

Attention to aesthetics and faith's affective side is intrinsic to the Symposium's identity, and distinctive of its academic positioning. In her opening paper to the first gathering, Slee mapped out feminist qualitative research into the faith lives of women and girls as spiritual practice, aligning its developing stages with aspects of faith's practice such as prayer, or handling sacred text.[21] This enables all conducting research in this field to occupy with authenticity the liminal space they inhabit[22] – on one side, objective observers of others' practice as they work towards the creation of new knowledge and on the other, subjective participants in relational growing while sharing a common pilgrimage journey with their subjects towards mutual spiritual transformation, within a faith tradition or none.[23] Although most of the Symposium's participants are faith practitioners (predominantly Christian but increasingly multi-faith), it is neither a presumption nor a prerequisite. There is, however, an understanding that all researchers hold as authentic and precious the spiritual dimension of female faith lives, and can broadly assent in non-confessional ways to the thesis Slee proposes.

These factors combined in that first meeting to create a synergy such that the consensus at its close was twofold: that the Symposium should continue, and 'wouldn't it be good to share this more widely and publish the papers!' Both desires materialized. By 2021, 17 gatherings had been held, usually biannually, with two books published. The first collects some of the early papers from wide-ranging contexts, the second focuses on varieties of feminist methodology.[24]

Describing the Symposium's format in some detail illustrates the serious attention we pay to ensuring every aspect models collaborative learning and empowerment for women scholars. Those experienced in making their voice heard at all levels of academia, institutional church and beyond come alongside, in an informal mentoring capacity, those beginning the journey to help grow their expertise and confidence to operate in the public square. Through workshops on preparing and presenting a paper to shaping a journal article or book chapter, from practice in asking good questions to receiving critique constructively, the Symposium has provided a safe space in which to own vulnerabilities, to share and to gain experience, and above all to grow the confidence to bid farewell to 'impostor syndrome' which muffles many women's voices. The Symposium's working principles are maintained through its small size, attendance limited to around 25, and low running costs which ensure its accessibility to all. It has no external funding.[25]

Symposium participants have confirmed that for many the aimed-for safety, acceptance and mutual understanding is met. Comments record the feeling of 'joy and relief' that 'my presence was welcome and mattered', that it was 'invigorating', and 'exciting and encouraging to be a part of such a diverse and enthusiastic group'. It was 'truly a safe space … warm and inclusive', and 'an unfailingly welcoming space'. These factors not only strengthen the women involved, but also contribute to developing more confident and creative researchers and research outcomes, as narratives below illustrate.

Organization of each Symposium was at first ad hoc with Slee taking the lead but drawing in trusted others as sounding boards and support colleagues. Thus when the idea of publication took root, Fran Porter and I joined her as co-editors of the first two volumes. Symposium leadership has remained with Slee as has its core base at Queen's, but once it had become a sustainable research forum, a planning group was established to share vision and organization with Slee: the aim of its composition is to embody inclusivity, its membership representing women from varied social, ethnic, academic and faith contexts.

This chapter is neither the place to offer a full analysis of the Symposium's work, nor to critique the extent and quality of the 'expansion' of understanding of women's and girls' faith lives that Slee's book has inspired, although there is sufficient in the body of material for such a research project in its own right. In the remainder of the chapter, however, I offer a few examples of the shape of Slee's research 'legacy', both for the general-interest reader and to offer resources for those engaged in or contemplating research in this field.

Symposium Communities

While the formal research stages – particularly data transcription and analysis – are solitary and isolating activities, each project begins in community, in the lived experience of women and girls across most age groups and many cultures.[26] In the design, piloting and execution of our projects we gather individuals and groups. In semi-structured interview, in focus group conversation or through other creative methods, we record data drawn from the heat and heart of real lives as girls and women reflect individually and together on their beliefs and behaviours in favourable or inhibiting circumstances. With the increasing use of technology, a pilot research study into qualitative data-gathering using social media platforms has also been undertaken,[27] a further tool that could be of advantage to research undertaken within restricted circumstances such as imposed during the pandemic. Innovation and flexibility are hallmarks of participant women's research.

When we gather for each Symposium bringing with us the products of this activity, we create with one another a community, fresh each time but with a continuing core ensuring continuity and facilitating welcome. As together we share and deliberate on the papers, we participate intentionally in the 'expansion' of Slee's work. At the time of writing, presentations number over a hundred, alongside ten workshops, and there is no perceptible diminution in research volume or scholarly activity, even through the pandemic which may itself become a future area of research for its effect on women's and girls' faith lives.

Scope of Research

The scope of the contexts represented is broad. It encompasses age groups from pre-adolescent to old age. Among the predominantly Christian-based research, many denominations and ecclesial traditions feature.[28] That variety is reflected too in the increasing participation of Muslim and Jewish scholars. Cultural diversity is extended through studies conducted in the four nations of the UK including the effects on women of Northern Ireland's recent turbulent history.[29] The ethnic diversity, although not yet as broad as we would like, includes Black women (mainly Christian), women of South Asian (mainly Muslim) heritage and women from Korea and Hong Kong studying in the UK. Some researchers have worked overseas and brought to the table the experiences of women and girls from Ireland, the Caribbean, North India, Argentina and Aotearoa/New

Zealand. Life choices including motherhood/childlessness, and career/ family balance, together with contexts urban and rural, contribute to the rich mix for our learning and interaction.

Interviewing as Shared Learning

In line with Slee's strong advocacy of qualitative research methods, much attention is given in the Symposium to issues of methodology and the practice of semi-structured interviewing that feature regularly in papers and conversation. This inspired the second Symposium publication. These interviews where power is shared with the interviewee place huge demands on the researcher. For many interviewees it will be a new experience, providing a first, maybe unique, opportunity for reflection on faith in an unaccustomed person-centred encounter. The encouragement and permission both to explore their faith and to voice nascent doubts and struggles may take them into sometimes fearful territory, but more often it is a liberating one, thereby creating new knowledge for and about themselves, as well as for the researcher. When the conversation lags, it is tempting for the researcher to change role to teacher or counsellor especially with young or vulnerable people. Strong reflexivity and adherence to good ethical practice as demanded by university policies help to maintain focus for the researcher. Silences, however, may signal that the interviewee is reflecting deeply, and possibly lengthily, on the topic. Thus her silences may prove to be crucial turning points: indeed, 'chosen' silence, and its use more widely in women's spiritual practice, has itself been the subject of research presented.[30]

Expanding Understanding of Girls' and Women's Faith Development

In *Women's Faith Development*, Slee identified from the analysis of her data six processes and three patterns of faith. Abundant examples can be found in the Symposium papers of the six '*processes* … significant and recurring linguistic strategies which the women used, within the context of the interview, to shape and pattern their faith experience'.[31] With her three patterns, alienation, awakenings and relationality, 'generative themes which … reveal core *patterns* in women's faith development', particularly strong links were evident, and for each of these an organic image emerged as I reviewed each paper and my personal notes.[32] I use these as thematic symbols to offer some organization of the diversity of research in this limited overview. Boundaries between each pattern are fluid, however: movement is not one-way towards awakenings and growth, supporting Slee's critique of Fowler's model. Slee recognizes too a qualitative difference in her third generative theme in that 'relationality appears to represent not so much a moment or a phase within a developmental sequence of faith as a more fundamental epistemology which underlies and undergirds the whole of a woman's spiritual journey'.[33] Relating to others and to God is intrinsic to each pattern.

With exploration of each image, I include a narrative that describes an individual researcher's engagement with Slee and her work, as they contribute to the researcher's holistic growth.

Chrysalis

Although as a process of nature this image is not literally appropriate for the pattern of '*alienation*' Slee identifies, its metaphorical use by Sue Monk Kidd in a spiritual context – introduced to the Symposium by Gwen Henderson – usefully symbolizes the organic process of 'developmental diapause', a period of animal dormancy entered in response to adverse environmental conditions.[34]

Through her research into spiritual dissonance already cited, Henderson uncovered 'symptoms of constriction, paralysis and impasse' as women's lives and the rigid teachings of the churches they inhabited diverged. Through their narratives she found that the women tended to use 'psychological "splitting" to conform with their faith communities', becoming '"internal leavers", physically present but emotionally detached from the church'. Drawing on this 'developmental diapause', her exploration of these women's faith narratives 'assesses the potential of faith development theory to help women interpret their symptoms as growing pains in the context of healthy faith development and explores the challenges this presents to the evangelical community'.[35] Yet the tension of living with 'long periods of isolation or "splitting" ... rarely resolved' could have traumatic consequences for women and their mental as well as spiritual health where they lacked 'the resources, mentoring or companionship to help them negotiate the transition into new seasons of growth'. Their faith development was blocked. Henderson recalls that Slee recognized here an important critique of her work 'especially the ways it might *not* apply to women from particular contexts or experiences'.[36] A comment from my own research by a pre-adolescent girl expressed early signs of such a tension. Musing over the duality of faith as lived out between church and self, she said: 'it's like having two things, one that you've been taught to believe and one that you do [believe]'.[37] Not all women or girls gain or are given the 'courage to leave the place whose language you have learned'.[38]

The cocooning image applies to other examples within the papers of dissonance between women's development and ecclesial conservatism dominated by patriarchy, whether through male-dominated charismatic worship and theology 'deeply divorced from ... very earthly experience of motherhood and child care',[39] androcentric language leaving women 'voiceless and their experiences not valued',[40] or Bible teaching privileging male role models resulting in intelligent young women's tendency towards 'self deprecation and negative self esteem with regard to their biblical literacy'.[41] In a study among Orthodox Jews, exercise of male control and power over women's adaptation of traditional ritual practice uncovered areas of contestation in a synagogue too.[42]

Sexism or patriarchal 'norms' cloaked by contested theologies and biblical hermeneutics are also exposed. These range from expectations, even policing, of a certain kind of 'femininity' in behaviour and body shape,[43] opposition to menstruating women presiding at the eucharist and other examples of sexism targeting women in ministry,[44] to sacrificial models of Christian marriage that increase the risk of domestic violence.[45]

Womb

This image serves as a symbol of the gestation that takes place in the growth of faith, a process of *awakening* to a new phase that cannot be rushed, but can be nurtured in health-giving ways. It is ideally both an amniotic holding environment and a nourishing and protecting liminal place fed by its 'parent' body while growing an independent identity.[46] Its hospitable space allows the self to stretch and experiment as it grows new 'wings' (mixed metaphors alone comprehend the depth and breadth of the transformation process).

The 'wombing' image, implicit or explicit, reflected in the research papers is correspondingly multi-dimensional as Slee recognized in her plural, *awakenings*.[47] It can be applied to many studies around the transition to motherhood. One project explored from a pastoral perspective the rites of passage women created, either in preparing for, or from within their new status after, childbirth.[48] Another, from a psychological standpoint, studied first-time mothers' 'potential for deep spiritual transformation' alongside 'the potential for stagnation, depression and giving up'.[49] Rituals to mark this profound rite of passage also featured, such as reintroduction of 'churching' to counter the dominant focus on the child at baptism,[50] and a critique of a baptismal liturgy 'devoid of feminine symbolism in which the womb is excised'.[51]

Girls and women traverse a sequence of liminal spaces at each new stage of life, leading to a variety of other awakenings. Research papers have featured examples uncovering, often through thick description, their varied journeys towards the birthing of new identities. One common experience of liminality is at the interface of faith and society. Through the mixed ages of the Symposium's participants from young graduates to seniors, many personal as well as research resonances can be found – for example, in girls' isolation as Christians in school,[52] women making career choices in line with faith's urge to seek a 'calling',[53] and older women's contribution to worship and service.[54] Members of this last group, an irreplaceable cohort on which many churches are still reliant, are found to be largely disregarded, hence little known, in their multiple transitioning towards life's conclusion. A further valuable research exploration brings us full circle in a study connecting the liminal nature of both birth and death positing the 'relevance of a theology of natality for a theology of death and dying and pastoral care'.[55]

The hospitality of the womb, our originating home, nurtures awakenings in other ways. Examples include how its homing profile symbolizes 'emerging Christian women's transitions at university';[56] and even within the trauma of sexual abuse a growing transformative knowledge that 'God's timeless presence ... equips [women] to become God's agents for the transformation of others'.[57]

It is also a space for creativity, revealed in the methods employed to generate data and to engage in its analysis. Thus the arts (poetry, visual arts, literature and the drama of ritual) have inspired new methodologies to stimulate faith's search among girls and women, to create experiences that transcend mundane prose and touch the affective side, treading holy ground. Slee likens the visceral nature of our research journeys to an artist's sketch book or poet's journal.[58] The holistic nature of the Symposium's format has generated and affirmed these creative endeavours as women engage with the ineffable in their own lives as well as those of their research subjects through word and worship.

So to the individual narrative to accompany this section. It describes a particular awakening through the ethos established in the first Symposium, offered by Abby Day who, not then fully embodying her role in the academy and feeling an outsider as sociologist not theologian, was keen to 'present myself as a proper academic' – until she realized to her horror that she had forgotten to pack her presentation. However, as Slee delivered her opening paper with its 'message ... of empathy, enthusiasm and nuance', Abby recognized within it clear resonances with her own research experience. Her 'problem' then became transformed 'into a new opportunity to practise, engage and reflect', so with confidence newly birthed she invited us into 'more of a conversation than a lecture' – and no one guessed her dilemma! With the 'constructive feedback at the symposium', Day then worked her forgotten paper into a chapter for *The Faith Lives of Women and Girls*, and later into her own publication.[59] She described the experience in retrospect as 'invigorating'.

Web

Feminist theologians are familiar with the use of the 'web' image in debates about women's healthy growth in connection(s) that foster self-identity rather than in the separation and autonomy imposed upon them by male-authored developmental theories, although the reality is more nuanced as Slee argues in the introduction to her third pattern, *relationality*.[60] It is therefore unsurprising that 'web-weaving' focused on making and sustaining spiritual meaning through varied attachment-points features strongly in Symposium women's research. Projects already cited often include strong relational elements, with God and others, once more in diverse social and cultural contexts.

Relations with friends who join or form faith communities both official and fringe, and less frequently relations with family members who share faith, all show the richness of mutual support. Other opportunities for relationships of discovery and growth, as well as resistance to unwholesome patriarchal structures, are through spiritual direction, collegial relations and the research itself. Faith is not always expressed within an institution. Many women in today's society are 'de-churched', often the consequence of patriarchal and sexist alienation; others identify as spiritual, relating in alternative ways to the divine (by whatever name) within groupings that forge religio-spiritual lives in complex ways, often emphasizing practice and an 'ethic of care'.[61]

Ethical teaching and values affect lived-religion in community, and attitudes to ethical issues have also been of concern as women wrestle with faith in the face of relationships human and divine. Patterns of sexual relating among evangelicals, and abortion discourses within Roman Catholic communities, are both under scholarly scrutiny.[62]

Bible and theology feature in many projects. In my own work, I reflected on girls' God-talk to illustrate how church teaching is being processed by young minds,[63] a form of 'ordinary theology' evidenced in other studies that attend to the voices of the 'taught',[64] to investigate how relationships with God are being understood and lived.[65] The role of women preachers plays a part here, where the word spoken and the word heard must relate to women's experience to grow their faith.[66] For women to develop their own subjectivity, a new imaginary in relation to God without taking up masculinized subject positions (Christ and humankind as Sons of Father God) is an area also wrestled with. Mother and midwife link symbolically with creator God, and with Mary whose story reinterpreted in a conservative tradition can subvert idealistic but oppressive models of 'the good mother' and help create for these women new relational attachments.[67] My own ongoing theological reflection explores how a 'daughter-imaginary', rooted in biblical daughter narratives, might open up a richer more inclusive experience of relating to mother/father God and for appreciation of all that the female mind, body and spirit contribute to as well as receive from relationship with God.[68]

It is evident that there are still many barriers to break through for every woman to flourish in faith, ceilings often made of more impenetrable material than glass. Yet there are many grounded acts of courage by women offering constructive contributions to academic discourse, theological/scriptural debate and spiritual awareness that together chip away at these oppositional forces.

My final story demonstrates how Helen Collins, as a feminist researcher within a charismatic evangelical tradition, has grown in the Symposium both personally and professionally, and adapted feminist methodologies that habitually start from women's experience to a version more consistent with her tradition where authority lies in scripture and the inspiration of the Holy Spirit. 'Weaving the Web' is the title of her chapter in *Researching Female Faith*, in which she develops a novel web-based method for her doctoral research,[69] with scripture and tradition as anchor points alongside reason and experience, to encourage evangelical feminists to engage in research 'faithful to both identities' and others 'boldly to pioneer new methodological approaches' more fitting to their context and theological identities.[70] Helen has been a member of the Symposium throughout her Anglican ordination training, curacy and progression into diocesan and now academic posts, and the relationships established despite the 'very different theological circles I seem to move in' have helped her 'grow as an academic' through giving papers and chairing sessions. Exposure to 'worship and reflection far outside my tradition' gave her the courage to 'lead a feminist act of worship at my theological college, ... controversial ... but important for many people who participated'.

Conclusion

The above reflections, examples and narratives bear testimony to Nicola Slee's contribution to the understanding of the faith lives of women and girls. Her encouragement of researchers through whose efforts a more nuanced understanding is growing promotes women's empowerment and justice-making, 'attuned to the marginalized ways of knowing and faithing ... repressed and denied, both in academia and in the churches'.[71] When she published her book, I doubt she could have imagined how important it would become in the research lives of women who, through the Symposium,[72] live by her 'statement of interdependence':

I cannot master all skills
but with others who will lend their accomplishments
I can do enough.[73]

Notes

1 Nicola Slee, 'With Others: A Statement of Interdependence', *Praying Like a Woman* (London: SPCK, 2004), 66.

2 Nicola Slee, *Women's Faith Development: Patterns and Processes* (Aldershot: Ashgate, 2004).

3 Slee, *Women's Faith Development*, 1.

4 James W. Fowler, *Stages of Faith: The Psychology of Human Development and the Quest for Meaning* (London: Harper and Row, 1981).

5 Fowler, *Stages of Faith*, 293.

6 Slee, *Women's Faith Development*, 163.

7 Slee, *Women's Faith Development*, 33.

8 Slee, *Women's Faith Development*, 4.

9 Slee, *Women's Faith Development*, 164.

10 Slee, *Women's Faith Development*, 165.

11 Slee, *Women's Faith Development*, 3; Fowler, *Stages of Faith*, 151–73.

12 Slee, *Women's Faith Development*, 165.

13 Slee, *Women's Faith Development*, 166.

14 Slee, *Women's Faith Development*, 167.

15 Anne Phillips, *The Faith of Girls: Children's Spirituality and Transition to Adulthood* (Farnham: Ashgate, 2013).

16 Literature popularizing the concept of faith 'development' is rife, now overtly incorporating gender differentiation. For example, in constructing his own 'stages', McLaren includes an 'integration' with 16 others' stages, including Slee's. See Brian D. McLaren, *Faith after Doubt: Why Your Beliefs Stopped Working and What to Do About It* (London: Hodder and Stoughton, 2021), 305–6.

17 Methodologies that feminist researchers and theologians are continually evolving have featured strongly in Symposium papers and publications, with extensive bibliographies. See Slee, *Women's Faith Development*, 43–60; Nicola Slee,

Fran Porter and Anne Phillips, eds, *Researching Female Faith: Qualitative Research Methods* (London: Routledge, 2018).

18 Gwen Henderson e-mail to author (21 February 2021). All quoted comments in this section are from participants' e-mails to author between February and March 2021.

19 Following Nelle Morton's classic 'hearing into speech' text, Slee is a strong advocate of women 'finding or claiming a voice', a principle the Symposium embodies and practises within and to academy and faith communities. Hence it features strongly in many chapters of *The Faith Lives of Women and Girls: Qualitative Research Perspectives*, eds Nicola Slee, Fran Porter and Anne Phillips (Farnham: Ashgate, 2013); *Researching Female Faith*, eds Slee, Porter and Phillips; and Nicola Slee, *Fragments for Fractured Times: What Feminist Practical Theology Brings to the Table* (London: SCM Press, 2020), 193–4.

20 Participants come from all parts of the UK and Ireland. Zoom gatherings through the coronavirus pandemic have extended its reach.

21 Nicola Slee, 'Feminist Qualitative Research as Spiritual Practice: Reflections on the Process of Doing Qualitative Research', in *The Faith Lives of Women and Girls*, eds Slee, Porter and Phillips, 13–24 and Slee, *Fragments for Fractured Times*, 205–17.

22 Slee discusses feminist theology as 'marginalized discourse' in Slee, 'Feminist Qualitative Research as Spiritual Practice', in *The Faith Lives of Women and Girls*, eds Slee, Porter and Phillips, 16 and Slee, *Fragments for Fractured Times*, 208.

23 This applied especially where rituals were created in which the researcher was also a participant.

24 Slee, Porter and Phillips, eds, *The Faith Lives of Women and Girls* and Slee, Porter and Phillips, eds, *Researching Female Faith*.

25 However, a small grant from the Lincoln Theological Institute facilitated a novel departure, a wider conference held in 2019; selected papers from it form the basis of a further collection. See *Female Faith Practices: Qualitative Research Perspectives*, eds Nicola Slee, Dawn Llewellyn, Kim Wasey and Lindsey Taylor-Gutharz (London: Routledge, forthcoming).

26 Papers delivered at the Symposium represent both research completed, for which I give access/publication details, and studies still in progress where I give the author, paper title and date delivered.

27 Kim Wasey, 'Using Social Media for Feminist Qualitative Research', in *Researching Female Faith*, eds Slee, Porter and Phillips, 113–24.

28 These are Anglican, Baptist, United Reformed, Methodist, Church of God of Prophecy, as well as independent churches: among all are traditions loosely described as 'high', 'low' 'evangelical' or 'charismatic'.

29 Fran Porter, '"In-the-Middle" God: Women, Community Conflict and Power in Northern Ireland', in *The Faith Lives of Women and Girls*, eds Slee, Porter and Phillips, 91–101.

30 Alison Woolley, 'Wholly Sound: A Feminist Reframing of the "Problem" of Interview Silence as a Methodology for Discovering New Knowledge', in *Researching Female Faith*, eds Slee, Porter and Phillips, 155–70, and *Women Choosing Silence: Relationality and Transformation in Spiritual Practice* (London: Routledge, 2019).

31 Slee, *Women's Faith Development*, 61, emphasis added. The faithing processes are: conversational, metaphoric, narrative, personalised, conceptual and apophatic.

32 Slee, *Women's Faith Development*, 8, emphasis added.

33 Slee, *Women's Faith Development*, 160.

34 Sue Monk Kidd, *When the Heart Waits: Spiritual Direction for Life's Sacred Questions* (New York: HarperCollins, 2006), 102–4.

35 From her Symposium paper, drawn from her doctoral work, see Gwen Henderson, 'Evangelical Women Negotiating Faith in Contemporary Scotland' (University of Glasgow, 2008).

36 Henderson recounts embodying this blockage herself. E-mail to author, March 2021.

37 Phillips, *The Faith of Girls*, 106.

38 Carol Lakey Hess, *Caretakers of Our Common House: Women's Development in Communities of Faith* (Nashville: Abingdon Press, 1997), 58.

39 Helen Collins, 'Intimating the intimate: A practical theology of the experience of motherhood and charismatic spirituality', Symposium paper (26 November 2011).

40 Deseta Davis, 'The Use of Patriarchal Language in the Church of God of Prophecy', in *The Faith Lives of Women and Girls*, eds Slee, Porter and Phillips, 121–8.

41 Ruth Perrin, 'Searching for Sisters: The Influence of Biblical Role Models on Young Women from Mainstream and Charismatic Evangelical Traditions', in *The Faith Lives of Women and Girls*, eds Slee, Porter and Phillips, 111–19.

42 Lindsey Taylor-Guthartz, *Challenge and Conformity: The Religious Lives of Orthodox Jewish Women* (Liverpool: Liverpool University Press, 2021).

43 Manon Ceridwen James, 'Fat Chicks, Blue Books and Green Valleys: Identity, Women and Religion in Wales', in *The Faith Lives of Women and Girls*, eds Slee, Porter and Phillips, 103–9, and *Women, Identity and Religion in Wales* (Cardiff: University of Wales Press, 2018); Hayley Matthews, 'Power and pantyhose: Exploring the *habitus* of female priests', Symposium paper (20 October 2017); Hannah Bacon, *Feminist Theology and Contemporary Dieting Culture: Sin, Salvation and Women's Weight Loss Narratives* (London: T&T Clark, 2019).

44 Sharon Jagger, 'The Dialectic of Belonging: Resistances and Subversions of Women Priests in the Church of England' (University of York, 2019).

45 Rachel Starr, *Reimagining Theologies of Marriage in Contexts of Domestic Violence* (London: Routledge, 2018).

46 These are images I developed from my own research findings into the faith of girls. See Phillips, *The Faith of Girls*, 141–57.

47 Slee, *Women's Faith Development*, 109–34.

48 Jill Thornton, 'Moments Marked: An Exploration into the Ways in which Women are Choosing to Mark Aspects of their Rite of Passage into Motherhood' (University of Manchester, 2016).

49 Noelia Molina, 'The Liminal Space in Motherhood: Spiritual Experiences of First-time Mothers', in *The Faith Lives of Women and Girls*, eds Slee, Porter and Phillips, 207–20.

50 Dawn Llewellyn, 'Churching: Remaking a ritual for mothers in the Church of England', Symposium paper (27 November 2019).

51 Gill Hill, 'Return to the womb: Baptism from a female perspective', Symposium paper (20 October 2011).

52 Phillips, *The Faith of Girls*, 124.

53 Shaheen Akhtar, 'The factors and influences that affect the career choices of

Muslim women in Coventry', Symposium paper (19 October 2017); Kate Massey, 'Listening for the "I": Adapting a Voice-Centred, Relational Method of Data Analysis in a Group Interview to Examine Women's Faith Lives', in *Researching Female Faith*, eds Slee, Porter and Phillips, 141–54.

54 Abby Day, 'Understanding the Work of Women in Religion', in *The Faith Lives of Women and Girls*, eds Slee, Porter and Phillips, 39–49 and *The Religious Lives of Older Women: The Last Active Anglican Generation* (Oxford: Oxford University Press, 2017).

55 Jennifer Hurd, 'The Relevance of a Theology of Natality for a Theology of Death and Dying and Pastoral Care: Some Initial Reflections', in *The Faith Lives of Women and Girls*, eds Slee, Porter and Phillips, 195–205.

56 Jenny Morgans, 'Home-ing: Emerging Christian Women's Transitions at University' (Vrije Universiteit, Amsterdam, 2020).

57 Susan Shooter, 'How Survivors of Abuse Relate to God', in *The Faith Lives of Women and Girls*, eds Slee, Porter and Phillips, 221–31 and *How Survivors of Abuse Relate to God* (Farnham: Ashgate, 2012).

58 Slee, 'Feminist Qualitative Research as Spiritual Practice', in *The Faith Lives of Women and Girls*, eds Slee, Porter and Phillips, 21; Slee, *Fragments for Fractured Times*, 212.

59 See above, note 54. E-mail to author, March 2021.

60 Slee, *Women's Faith Development*, 1–14 and 135–62; my own analysis favours a helical developmental model proposed by Robert Kegan, which offers a 'theory to allow each gender to operate both autonomously and relationally' as identity evolves. See Phillips, *The Faith of Girls*, 29–31. For a brief fully referenced summary of the history and use of the web image in feminist research, see Helen Collins, 'Weaving a Web: Developing a Feminist Practical Theology Methodology from a Charismatic Perspective', in *Researching Female Faith*, eds Slee, Porter and Phillips, 58–9.

61 Janet Eccles, 'Living Religion: Collapsing (Male-Constructed?) Boundaries between the Religious and the Spiritual', in *Researching Female Faith*, eds Slee, Porter and Phillips, 70–9, drawing on Kristin Aune, 'Feminist Spirituality as Lived Religion: How UK Feminists Forge Religio-spiritual Lives', *Gender and Society* 29, no. 1 (2015): 122–45.

62 Ruth Perrin, '"Not what I would have wished for": Exploring the experiences of young unmarried heterosexual women within an Evangelical context', Symposium paper (19 October 2017); Sarah-Jane Page, 'Abortion discourses, Catholicism and women's faith lives', Symposium paper (26 October 2018).

63 Phillips, *The Faith of Girls*, 103–33.

64 For example, Francesca Rhys, 'Understanding Jesus Christ: Women Exploring Liberating and Empowering Christologies', in *The Faith Lives of Women and Girls*, eds Slee, Porter and Phillips, 185–92.

65 See Jeff Astley, *Ordinary Theology: Looking, Listening and Learning in Theology* (London: Routledge, 2017), and Jeff Astley and Leslie J. Francis, *Exploring Ordinary Theology: Everyday Christian Believing and the Church* (London: Routledge, 2016).

66 Liz Shercliffe, *Preaching Women: Gender, Power and the Pulpit* (London: SCM Press, 2019).

67 Helen Collins, *Mary the Worshipping Mother: Reclaiming Mary's Motherhood for Contemporary Mums* (Cambridge: Grove Books, 2019).

68 Anne Phillips, '"I am H/her daughter": Reclaiming daughterhood as an inclusive image for women relating to Mother/Father God', Symposium paper (14 February 2015).

69 Developed in Helen Collins, *Reordering Theological Reflection: Starting with Scripture* (London: SCM Press, 2020).

70 Collins, 'Weaving a Web', 67.

71 Slee, *Women's Faith Development*, 181.

72 At publication, The Research Symposium on the Faith Lives of Women and Girls is still meeting regularly. For more information and application go to https://www.queens.ac.uk/the-faith-lives-of-women-and-girls.

73 Slee, 'With Others', *Praying Like a Woman*, 66.

6

Faithing, Friendship and Feeling at Home: Three Women Encounter University Chaplaincy

JENNY MORGANS

Whether or not a person feels at home in her context has implications for her wellbeing, sense of self and interaction with the world. In my research, Christian women students made both intentional and subconscious attempts to craft home at university.[1] Away from the familial home and living in a liminal new setting, these students prioritized spaces, relationships and activities that contributed to their sense of 'home'. Crafting home involved relational processes of belonging and becoming, and often included negotiation of their multiple identities, requiring both freedom and safety at university. Understanding the complexity of the interrelated factors influencing students' crafting of home requires more scope than this chapter affords. What this chapter provides is a snapshot into three women's processes of crafting home: embedded in their friendship and faith, and fostered by their university chaplaincy. It places these processes under the scrutiny of feminist practical theology through the lens of these women's close friendship.

This chapter is based on research undertaken for my doctorate, completed in 2020 and supervised by Nicola Slee. The research emerged partly from a challenge offered by Slee in arguably her most influential text, *Women's Faith Development*.[2] Despite overwhelming evidence that 'female faithfulness [is] at the core of living Christian tradition', she writes, 'women's faith lives have generally not been accorded significance'.[3] In fact, women's experiences have often been denied or ignored by both churches and the academy, perhaps as a result of the assumed androcentric norm established in their patriarchal structures. In response, my research investigates the Christian faith lives of young women studying at university, all living away from home for the first time. As Zoë Bennett and her colleagues argue, 'theologies and research projects don't emerge from thin air'. Rather, they are grounded 'in the thickness of practice, commitments, bodies, attachments and emotions'.[4] Embedded in an intimate friendship, this chapter adds *relationships* to this list. It demonstrates the importance of the friendship to the women's faith identities, experiences and praxis, and to their crafting of home.

Semi-structured interviews with three Christian women are at the heart of this chapter. All undergraduates at a Russell Group university, I first interviewed Alexis, Melissa and Stephanie individually in their first semester.[5] A year later, having learned that they had developed a deep friendship, I interviewed them together as I describe below. I was interested in the women's experiences of faith and gender away from home and amid multiple transitions. I asked how their Christianity influenced their university experience – and vice versa. The data produced was analysed using grounded theory and thematic analysis,[6] in accordance with the principles of feminist qualitative research.[7]

This chapter begins by introducing Alexis, Melissa and Stephanie using their own words as much as feasible, then discussing their experiences and perspectives in theoretical context. Next, I detail the method I developed in interviewing the friends together, which I term a 'facilitated gathering'. Finally, I discuss the relational faithing processes shared by the women in their crafting of home in the two contexts of safe friendships and encounters with difference. Throughout the chapter, I engage with further works of Slee, including her article 'A Spirituality for Multiple Overwhelmings'.[8] A theological auto-ethnography, this article depicts human 'overwhelmings' that can either debilitate or release, demanding space for an 'engaged, embodied spirituality' that recognizes that 'the overwhelming overflow of the Spirit can never be quashed'.[9] I demonstrate how this work speaks directly into the three friends' experiences.

Introducing Alexis, Melissa and Stephanie

Alexis, Melissa and Stephanie met in their first week at university. Alexis and Melissa were flatmates in halls of residence and they encountered Stephanie at a Christian student society based at the university chaplaincy. The women were all white, middle-class, cisgender and aged 18 at the time. Two studied humanities, while Stephanie was an engineering student.

The women described feeling in 'limbo' and 'in-between' in their first year at university, sharing an insecurity and uncertainty that hindered their ability to feel at home. Alexis felt 'all over the place', including being 'really overwhelmed with work' and 'acclimatizing to university standards'. Two of her grandmothers sadly died in her first year, which she described as 'probably the worst thing about being at uni'. She also worried, 'I'm sort of missing out a bit because everyone else seems to be in, like, friendship groups already'. Melissa was also worried about her academic work, saying: 'I've got lots of essays and I don't understand what I'm meant to be writing.' She 'went through a pretty bad patch around my exams, um, just stress and panic'. Moreover, 'one of the harder things of coming to university' was missing her old friends and not having 'someone I could talk to about it', which meant she 'got very homesick'. She realized, 'when you get here you just have to talk to people or you're going to be miserable'. Stephanie had 'always had issues' with insomnia, but at university 'it just got quite bad'. Partly this was as a result of her flatmates who kept her awake. They 'were all very, sort of, clubby, party, get drunk, most nights, stay out 'til like 3 a.m.'. She 'did have a few low points where I'd sort of go for very long walks by myself and go and cry somewhere', including in a local church. She was 'struggling' with her new living environment so much that she moved into a different flat in her second semester.

The women had differing previous experiences of Christianity. Attending Anglican churches with their families, Stephanie had belonged to a large liberal church and Alexis a conservative 'high' church. Melissa participated in an evangelical youth group despite her family rarely attending church. Both Alexis and Melissa arrived at university rejecting conservative teaching that they had encountered regarding LGBTI+ inclusion and what they termed 'medieval' and 'misogynistic' theologies rejecting women's leadership. Such theologies resulted in Alexis not wanting 'to associate myself with Christianity' while Melissa resented other Christians 'spreading hatred'. The Christian student society that the women attended at the university chaplaincy was in the liberal Anglican tradition. Activities included social events and discussions as well as a weekly eucharist led by the Anglican chaplain. While at first Alexis also explored a larger, conservative evangelical student society, she critiqued its overt approach to evangelism involving 'shoving [Christianity] in people's faces'. She returned to the chaplaincy after a few weeks, attracted by its inclusive theology as well as her close friendship with Melissa and Stephanie. Alexis committed to the chaplaincy society despite finding the hymns somewhat 'dull' in comparison to singing more 'active' worship songs at the other society.

In their second year, the women attended the society weekly. All three had moved from halls of residence into private accommodation in the local community. They described the experience of moving as a further step towards independence and maturity – something both positive and 'scary'. Stephanie said that in the second year, 'people expect you to be a bit more adult, but that could just be, also, going from being a kid to an adult, the general transition'. Melissa added that the second year was still not 'the terrifying prospect of going into the real world [of] a job and debt', which was thankfully further down the line.

When I interviewed the women together, the friends were dressed similarly with matching hairstyles, and they joked about owning the same clothes. Alexis described them as 'attached'. They discussed the importance of female friendship, agreeing that most of their close friends were female. They each described themselves as feminist, and the significance of their gender in their everyday lives was something that they regularly discussed. They described experiencing 'hatred against femininity' while noticing that 'our perception of strong is masculine'. Melissa discussed how 'incredibly damaging' she had found the media's dichotomy between 'femininity' on the one hand, and 'being intelligent' and 'wanting to climb trees' on the other. They discussed the 'wider societal problems' involved in the terms 'girl' and 'woman'. Being a 'woman' involved 'being taken seriously', while '"girl" tends to be frowned on a lot in society as, sort of, seen as inferior to masculinity'. However, they liked the term 'girly', referring to 'that sort of conversation' where 'you're not holding anything back'. Stephanie compared her different identities as an emerging woman in transition. She said, in 'private or with friends I tend to be more like a girl, like: "girls' day out", "girly talk", "girls' house"'. However, on her (male-dominated) academic course, she had to be a 'grown up' woman, with 'responsibilities' in 'an adult environment'. She said, 'it is harder as a woman to be taken seriously … like, "I am professional … I do know what I'm talking about"'. In comparison, with friends, 'you don't have to be grown up, you don't have to sort of prove yourself'.

The Women in Context

Away from home, Alexis, Melissa and Stephanie were in a new environment where they initially knew nobody and were negotiating a new way of life. The women experienced arriving at university as somewhat traumatic, describing what David F. Ford terms 'multiple overwhelmings'.[10] Expanding on Ford's terminology, Slee argues that such overwhelming 'can be terrifying, life-threatening, a force of destruction'.[11] These women felt alienated, unhappy and out of their depth. All were facing a kind of bereavement – not just Alexis.[12] They were struggling with making new friendships and renegotiating previous ones. Their faith identity, to which this chapter returns below, provided both a means of fitting in and crafting home. As Damon Mayrl and Jeremy E. Uecker demonstrate, rather than students rejecting faith at university, they often join a multiplicity of 'moral communities' such as Christian student societies and churches where they practise and perform their faith.[13] For Nick Shepherd, such communities act as 'plausibility shelters', reassuring young Christians that their faith is valid and that they are not alone in believing.[14] The women's allegiance with the chaplaincy rather than the conservative evangelical society demonstrates broader trends in student Christian subcultures. For example, Mathew Guest and colleagues note that such 'rigorously conservative' societies 'may irritate or embarrass, offend or alienate other Christians'.[15]

The women's narratives are congruent with societal trends of 'emerging adulthood' and post-feminism. Emerging adulthood identifies the delay of traditional maturity markers into the thirties, or being dismissed altogether.[16] Post-feminism demands that gender equality has been achieved, emphasizing essential difference between women and men and normalizing the sexualization of women's bodies. While recognizing their transition away from adolescence, the women were ambivalent or even dismissive of their status as adults, including celebrating the term 'girly'. Yvonne Tasker and Diane Negra argue that in post-feminist media culture, girlhood is centralized and idealized 'for everyone'.[17] The three friends adopted practices of 'girling', including expending time and energy on their appearance and dressing similarly. Their tribal appearance can be easily critiqued: amid the uncertainties of emerging adulthood and multiple overwhelmings, the women found safety in potentially over-relying on one another to the loss of their own individuality.[18] Such 'girling' is undoubtedly detrimental to assumptions about women's abilities and worth, as well as to their everyday experiences. However, it also enabled the women to resist the responsibilities and commitments of adulthood, and to remain relatively safe in the transitions at university. Phillips observes a discriminatory attitude towards girls in the work of some feminist authors, resulting in women acquiring power at the expense of girlhood.[19] For Slee, a theology of girlhood must involve imaging Christ as a girl. Such a work of imagination, she argues,

> is an invitation to perceive God incarnate among us in new ways and to glimpse anew the sacral nature of human flesh; specifically, it is an attempt to lift up the bodies and lives of girls as holy and precious, capable of imagining and reflecting the incarnate God.[20]

Slee plays with a joke that Christ was first incarnate as a girl, yet no one took the slightest bit of notice, in a poem entitled 'Come as a Girl'. In the final verse, Christa is *still* the ignored and unwanted girl two millennia on:

Come as a girl.
I will. I am still arriving among you,
looking for a safe place to be born,
a welcome, a home.[21]

Being girls offered Alexis, Melissa and Stephanie an opportunity to be wholly themselves with one another on the cusp of adulthood. Slee continues that: 'The symbol of the Christa who comes as a girl affirms the girl as a symbol of the becoming God' and insists that girls be regarded 'as theologians who might teach us'.[22] As well as the students being encouraged into womanhood, the potential of their girlhood must be considered a sacred and necessary step in crafting home at university.

Finally, it is important to note that the women's racial and class identities facilitated unquestioned access to social capital and resources, and to some extent their 'habitus' enabled subconscious navigation of their university environment.[23] However, I say this unapologetically, and suggest that the women's experiences are no less valid despite their societal advantages. Elisa S. Abes argues that a failure to explore dominant groups 'reinforces their normativity' and ignores the intersectionality of privilege and oppression. Moreover, Abes continues, privilege 'does not guarantee agency in negotiating relationships among identities'.[24] The women recognized their marginalization as a result of their gender, and its negative impact upon their university experiences.[25]

A Relational, Reflexive Method

Slee consistently insists upon rigorous examination of methodology in researching questions of feminism and faith. Together with Anne Phillips and Fran Porter, she argues that 'the means of research must be commensurate with the topic of research and the core values of the researcher', ensuring 'a fundamental coherence and compatibility between research aims, questions, epistemology, methodology, methods and outcome'.[26]

Inspired by such imperatives, I was keen to integrate method and content. Interviewing Alexis, Melissa and Stephanie together in their second year fitted this paradigm and was in keeping with the 'experimental and creative nature of feminist research'.[27] As long as the research was consistent with my own methodological guiding principles and informed by the wealth of experience of other feminist researchers, I was encouraged to trial this underexplored method. Moreover, interviewing the friends enabled me to test early conclusions based upon previous interviews regarding the importance of relationality and quasi-familial friendships in the processes of crafting home.

Uwe Flick terms a collective interview with a 'real group' (such as a group of friends) a 'group discussion'. According to Flick, group discussions correspond more closely to the ways opinions are produced, expressed and exchanged in everyday life, whereby '[t]he group becomes a tool for reconstructing individual opinions more appropriately'.[28] While Flick warns that among friends the 'level of things taken for granted ... tends to be higher', this method is somewhat less contrived than a one-to-one interview, giving space for participants to interact together.[29] Yet Flick's use of the word 'discussion' is problematic, suggesting a free and unstructured conversation.

The data produced in this environment was quite likely different from interviewing the women separately, adding a further level of richness and triangulation to my research. The method enabled me to see the women in their own context (in their friendship) rather than in isolation, since the friends had a history of shared interactions. During the interview, the women's narratives were both influenced by and negotiated through one another, creating what Jennifer Coates calls a 'collaborative floor'.[30] As with Kate Massey, the communality of this method meant that while I could not delve deeply into individual stories 'the *group voice* that express[ed] their shared experience and communal discovery was key'.[31] The interview developed with layers of mutual prompting and encouragement. It was not that the friends always agreed, but rather that even in disagreement their words were couched in 'communal wisdom'.[32] Unlike one-to-one interviews reliant upon self-reflective monologue alone, knowledge was produced through dialogue, co-created in deep listening and what Patrocinio P. Schweickart calls 'really talking'.[33]

In their friendship, Alexis, Melissa and Stephanie had shared their everyday experiences as well as their biggest challenges with one another. The confidence they gained through this sense of being known and understood enabled them to grow in self-knowledge and maturity, which was not only described but also *embodied* in their conversation. One example of this relational embodiment and its impact involved a discussion about their favourite university experiences:

Melissa: [W]e just go [shopping for] fancy ball gowns (all laugh) ... and just like try on six! ... That's one of my favourite things 'cos like you [Stephanie] were talking about being able to be a bit more childish and I think it's just the friendship group here has been so wonderful, um, and sort of exemplified by trying on ball gowns!

Stephanie: I really like how, like, with you guys I feel, like, really comfortable ... you're not judging me for it, you may laugh but
not in, sort of, a bad way (laughs).

Melissa: My friends at home think I've got a lot weirder, and what it
is is, I've just stopped holding it back ...!

Alexis: Yeah, I think the best moments were just, like, when we're
all just hanging out as friends so, like, dress shopping and,
when we, so (laughs) like, we had this box (all laugh).

Stephanie: Yes! That was amazing!

Alexis: This is gonna sound, like, so weird ...

Here, Melissa begins by remembering a highlight (dress shopping), comparing it with an earlier story Stephanie told (about 'childish things').
For Melissa, these outings 'exemplify' their friendship. In agreement,
Stephanie expands on her original point, naming the friendship as
'comfortable' and without judgement. Melissa adds encouragement by
including other friends' similar opinions. Alexis then shares Melissa's
highlight. She expands Stephanie's understanding of 'childish' to include
Melissa's 'weird' by beginning another story (about hiding something in
a box). Stephanie offers affirmation in her brief interjection when realizing the story that Alexis is about to tell, which Alexis introduces by
again repeating Melissa's 'weird'. There is much laughter as the layers of
the conversation develop. This method demonstrated that for the three
women their friendship was not just one of the most significant aspects
of their university experience so far, it was the lens through which they
made meaning of that experience, and of their identities in that place.
This played out as they explored together what it meant to be gendered,
embodied women at university. The friendship became their new, shared
home.

Some of the most animated parts of the interview were similar to this
in that they involved all three women wanting to tell collective stories.
In another example, laughter grows as one of my questions prompts the
sharing of an encounter at a chaplaincy event.

Alexis: Can we tell the story?

Stephanie: Please can we tell the story!

Melissa: Yeah! Um, when we met [him], we definitely think that
(pause) I know *I* do and I think it goes for the others, please
correct me if I'm wrong ... [S]o, me and Alexis went along –

Alexis: Well, Stephanie went along and then she had to leave –

Melissa: Yeah, Stephanie went along at the start but you [Stephanie]
had a lecture ...

Alexis: ... so, Melissa said [to him that] she didn't wanna be a teacher, I mean I said I didn't wanna be a teacher as well but like –
Melissa: He really liked Alexis so – (laughs)
Alexis: Well, he didn't seem to dislike me so much (laughs) ...
Stephanie: And actually, like, but I think for all of us ...

First, agreement is sought about whether to share the encounter at all. Melissa clarifies that she will tell the story from her perspective, inviting the others to join in with their versions. As she begins, Alexis is quick to include Stephanie. In fact, despite Melissa's caveat that she is only giving her own opinion, it is striking how often the women repeatedly name one another, drawing one another into the conversation. Finally, Stephanie summarizes by tentatively offering a group opinion. The story develops in layers, bursts of text that consistently include the others and build upon what's already been said without assuming agreement, utilizing hedges and tag questions: 'so', 'well', 'yeah', 'I mean', 'I think'. For Massey, such linguistic features 'are a means of avoiding the expert role in sharing the task of discovery'.[34] The women collaboratively owned their story while ensuring it represented each of their experiences.

As Slee demands, I must state with clarity 'the conditions of production under which knowledge is pursued'.[35] As the researcher, it was a privilege to 'eavesdrop' upon the women discussing their thoughts and experiences with one another. However, conversational shifts such as these two examples involved the women together addressing *me*, rather than one another. Clearly, there was joy for the friends at the retelling of such stories to an attentive, listening outsider – a 'friendly stranger'.[36] Shared narration enabled the women to rehearse and reaffirm their friendship, their relational identities. Reflexively, I was aware that my own presence changed the nature of interaction between the three women as they performed these identities for my benefit. Slee, Phillips and Porter continue: 'The researcher shapes, probes, reads and interprets the field of research even as she interacts with it.'[37] Thus, rather than a 'group discussion', this method might more appropriately be called a *facilitated gathering*. This denotes my own active role as facilitator and listener, as well as the nature of the friendship as intimate and multiple. While the women's words were the rich content of the interview, my promptings and even my own embodied presence were the context for what we together co-produced.

Faith and 'Home' at University

As Christians, *home* is both origin and destination. It is also a calling; an invitation of belonging. Reflecting on the parable of the prodigal, Henri Nouwen writes that God is 'longing to bring me home' with a love that 'always welcomes home and always wants to celebrate'.[38] Wendy M. Wright emphasizes the earthly home as much as any eternal home. She argues that churches often focus on metaphors of journeying while ignoring Christians' ordinary dwelling places. She writes, '[W]e people who inhabit homes, who live among and with a people who give us identity, whom we serve, by whom we are served, need to turn to our experience.'[39]

Home is often messy, and can be permanent, temporary or occasional. Regardless, it is the place where our identities make most sense. Students away from home are in a new place, unfamiliar and often strange, and their relationships are the anchor in the crafting of home – or not. The challenges of making new friends require courage and resilience in a sea of unknown faces, yet the multiple overwhelmings of everyday reality can act as barriers to investing in new relationships, including mental illness, loneliness, bereavement and stress. Comparing their second year of study to their initial arrival at university, Alexis, Melissa and Stephanie correlated the sense of feeling at home with the depth of their new friendships:

Alexis: Yeah, I feel much ... more, like, secure at uni, so, I have a group of friends ... so, I feel like a lot better this year. I feel, like, more like, I belong here.

Melissa: [I'm] a lot more comfortable with friendship[s], like Alexis ... I feel happier.

Stephanie: Certainly ... I feel a lot more confident, and comfortable, sort of, with myself as I was quite worried about finding friends, and ... [I] have done! (laughs)

Relationships amid Overwhelmings

Slee's faith development theory holds a 'sophisticated account of relationality' as a 'fundamental epistemology which underlies and undergirds the whole of a woman's spiritual journey'.[40] She demonstrates that close relationships are often a context for Christian women in '"coming home" to themselves, to truth and to God'.[41] In particular, '[f]riends were those who, perhaps more than any other, represented a freely chosen commitment of love and availability'.[42] It is this *chosen, loving commitment* to one another at a time of increased freedom that enabled Alexis, Melissa and Stephanie to explore their faith with confidence. In particular, attendance at the chaplaincy society was a primary site for identity growth, both together and with God, and these relational processes were woven together in enabling and resourcing their crafting of home at university. Perhaps particularly because she did not need to resolve the theological questions shared by Alexis and Melissa, for Stephanie attending the chaplaincy 'was as much [about] the people as the faith'. She continued, 'I've become more myself ... [H]aving people who just like me as I am has really helped with that'. She described the community as:

> [T]he most welcoming [student society] that I've been to ... they were very good at making you feel included even though you are just a random new person they've never met before, and yeah, that's what I like about the church is the community.

The women found the chaplaincy society to be 'safe' and 'somewhere that feels like home'. This included 'really lik[ing]' the chaplain, with whom they spoke for 'advice' and support. In other, unfamiliar contexts, the women admitted to being 'quite intimidated in big groups of people', saying, 'I'm scared of people' because 'people judge you'. Alexis felt 'lonely' at the large evangelical society she briefly attended, saying 'I'm very bad at making friends when I'm thrust into a big group'. In contrast, the small chaplaincy society facilitated 'building the community quite quickly'.

Liz Carmichael offers a theology of friendship immersed in scripture and the Christian tradition, highlighting Jesus' friendship with his disciples as equal to that with 'tax collectors and sinners', as well as his friendship with God (Luke 7.34 and John 15.14–15, 17.22). Drawing upon literature from the biblical era to current authors, she concludes that '[t]he love of friendship ... sets people free to be and to become in their own individual uniqueness, and ... invites reciprocal love and the joy of fulfilment in mutual relationship' inspired by God's friendship with humanity.[43] She relates many examples of such friendships between Christian women, including some with explicit feminist values. For example, while Julian of Norwich referred to God as 'our friend' and Teresa of Ávila promoted spiritually supportive friendships,[44] Sallie McFague's model of God as friend emphasizes 'mutuality, respect, acceptance of differences, cooperation, solidarity, attraction, perseverance, tolerance, gift-giving, delight, sacrifice, constructive criticism'.[45]

As well as the friendship between the women, significant for Melissa was the society 'helping you facilitate a relationship' with the divine, enabling her to develop 'an actual connection with God'. Comparing it to her previous Christian community, she now 'realized ... all you need to do is believe in God'. Alexis and Melissa reported that their deepening relationships with God were influenced by sermons at the society, reminding them that 'you can't make God love you any more' because 'God loves all of us' and 'wants you to enjoy life not necessarily just follow all these rules'. A developing relationship with God also resourced their ethics and horizontal relationships. They connected a theology of love with having inclusive 'views on gay marriage', believing 'it's okay to be gay'. They began to see Christianity as 'having been impacted by a very misogynistic society', arguing that their feminist perspectives were 'based on what Christ said'. Carmichael points to many theologians who have similarly argued that friendship with God and love of neighbour 'is identical with justice' and human solidarity.[46] Melissa described something akin to a eureka moment: 'Having the sermons that sort of seem to talk more about modern life in relation to God, were, they've sort of confirmed how I felt ... It was like everything I'd sort of been thinking but not been able to vocalize was suddenly being said, and I thought "yes that's it!"'

Ford suggests three imperatives in positively navigating multiple overwhelmings: naming, describing and then attending to them.[47] The women's friendship and engagement with their faith society created space and support in all three, providing escape from their multiple overwhelmings while resourcing their ability to negotiate them. *Naming* involved acknowledging the complexity and difficulty of student life, a process that 'links our experience to others'. Being overwhelmed 'can be the most isolating of experiences',[48] thus the resulting process of *describing* both countered isolation and became easier in conversation with friends also engaged in the task of description. Finally, for Ford *attending* involves the 'whole shape of living' in which 'the main task is to stretch our minds, hearts and imaginations',[49] facilitated for these women by their closeness and their deep faith. The women affirmed one another, and all grew in confidence and intimacy together and with God. Practising, discussing and exploring their Christianity together meant the women felt more 'comfortable' in their faith and in their selves. Such loving commitment as embodied by Alexis, Melissa and Stephanie was a reminder to the women, as Slee argues, 'that God is present and at work in the overwhelming'. The chaplaincy facilitated 'a safe space in which experiences of overwhelming can be examined, explored and entered into', and provided 'soul-friend[s]' with which to do this 'work'.[50] In such a context, the women were able to accept that overwhelmings were in fact 'normative' and even 'something which defines our humanity'.[51] The friendship then became the primacy location of attending to their overwhelming, including their deepest fears, most cherished selves and their exploration of faith. Slee continues by stating that overwhelmings 'can also be marvellous, wonderful, uplifting and transformative ... we also speak of being overwhelmed by music or art or natural beauty, by the love of God or of friends'.[52]

Engaging with Difference

Carmichael emphasizes the need for friendship to guard 'against group selfishness and fear of other groups'. Instead, '[f]riendship is love between diverse people in dynamic interaction'.[53] The crafting of home through navigating multiple overwhelmings was apparent in the women's friendship. Yet it was also impacted by encounters with *difference* that were often facilitated by the chaplaincy. In building community, the women recognized the importance of encountering strangers and embracing friends with whom they disagreed. Stephanie appreciated having 'discussions on what we believe', saying: 'I like having friends with a range of views because it helps broaden your mind, and ... it helps me feel more secure in my own faith because ... it forces you to go "actually why do I believe this?"'

The women began to critique previous exclusionary teachings about other denominations and faiths being 'wrong' or 'battling' together. Rather, they valued multi-faith activities and volunteering with an ecumenical foodbank. Stephanie described the latter as 'what I think religion should be about: it's not about "I'm right and you're wrong", it's sort of working together to improve people's lives'. It was important for her to recognize that 'I'm part of this much wider community', including people of other faiths and of none. Belenky and her colleagues argue that for women in their first year at university, '[i]f one can discover the experiential logic behind [alien] ideas, the ideas become less strange and the owners of the ideas cease to be strangers'.[54] For Sharon Parks, '[y]oung adult meaning making and faith is steeped in questions'. She refers to such encounters with difference as 'conscious conflict', which can include: 'increasing curiosity, a devastating shattering of assumptions, vague restlessness [and] intense weariness with things as they are'.[55] She continues: 'When faith itself is being reordered ... a community of rapport is especially crucial ... Communities that remain resilient in the face of both doubt and wonder can profoundly serve the processes of imagination and the development of faith.'[56]

The chaplaincy society provided such a community for Alexis, Melissa and Stephanie. It contributed to their sense of being at home, which for

Parks is 'a place where we are comfortable; know that we belong; can be who we are and can honour, protect and create what we truly love'.[57] Through attending the chaplaincy, the women discovered a theology that made them 'a lot more comfortable in saying I'm a Christian [and] speaking about my faith', resourcing them in being 'able to talk about it and vocalize it more'. Melissa explained that this confidence also influenced her faith outside of the society: '[I]t's the first time I've really been in a community where I can talk about it and I'm like, well, if I can talk about it to [Alexis and Stephanie], I may as well talk about it to everyone else as well (laughs).'

Sonya Sharma and Mathew Guest find that student Christian societies become 'a means of coping with the novelty and abnormality of student life ... where students' imaginaries of family extend, where they experience and cultivate intimate ties that become "home"'.[58] However, they find that students seek 'familiarity' and 'continuity' in choosing a Christian society at university.[59] This was not the case for Alexis and Melissa who intentionally adopted a faith identity at odds with their past Christian communities in which they had felt distinctly un-home. The three women's engagement with their university chaplaincy reflects its place as 'refuge' away from often depersonalizing and destabilizing effects of university life;[60] a place where they could 'let go and let be ... find[ing] nurturing and rejuvenation' without being a 'hideaway'.[61] Although often relatively few in number,[62] chaplaincy can be profoundly transformative for those students who engage with its services.

Conclusion

Alexis, Melissa and Stephanie's experiences of community, support and resourcing at their chaplaincy-based society demonstrate the related processes of faithing, friendships and the crafting of home at university for student women. Such processes occurred amid post-feminist social trends that diminished women, and a transitional university environment causing multiple overwhelmings. 'Home' was found in relationship: with one another and the other members of their student society; through growth in their relationship with God; and through encounters with difference. This home in turn resourced the women in negotiating their multiple overwhelmings, in critiquing Christian theologies that they saw as harmful, and in engaging as women in the world. Bennett and her colleagues argue that '[t]he process and journey of practical theological research is as important as any final results, findings or insights'.[63] In keeping with feminist methodological ideals, the facilitated gathering with Alexis, Melissa and Stephanie integrated method and content, embodying these conclusions.

The comprehensive and inspiring work of Slee provided the initial challenge with which this research began, and enabled Alexis, Melissa and Stephanie's narratives to be heard. These women's experiences must be taken seriously. While I do not claim that they are representative or even commonplace, they undoubtedly have implications for university chaplaincies and all engaged in student ministry. I encourage practitioners working with Christian women students to provide safe spaces in which friendships thrive, home is crafted, injustices named, theologies expanded, and overwhelmings described and attended to. Equally important, women's voices and experiences must continue to be researched as central to the mission of the church and its understanding of everyday faith and praxis.

Notes

1 For an in-depth discussion of my doctoral research, part of which forms the basis of this chapter, see Jenny Morgans, 'Home-ing: Emerging Christian Women's Transitions at University' (Vrije Universiteit, Amsterdam, 2020).

2 Nicola Slee, *Women's Faith Development: Patterns and Processes* (Aldershot: Ashgate, 2004).

3 Slee, *Women's Faith Development*, 2.

4 Zoë Bennett, Elaine Graham, Stephen Pattison and Heather Walton, *Invitation to Research in Practical Theology* (London: Routledge, 2018), 5, 11.

5 Pseudonyms are used throughout.

6 For example, see Kathy Charmaz, *Constructing Grounded Theory: A Practical Guide Through Qualitative Analysis* (London: Sage Publications, 2006).

7 For a discussion of the principles of feminist qualitative research, see Slee, *Women's Faith Development*, 46–52.

8 Nicola Slee, 'A Spirituality for Multiple Overwhelmings', *Practical Theology* 10, no. 1 (2017): 20–32, republished in *Fragments for Fractured Times: What Feminist Practical Theology Brings to the Table* (London: SCM Press, 2020), 81–95.

9 Slee, 'A Spirituality for Multiple Overwhelmings', 28, 31.

10 David F. Ford, *The Shape of Living: Spiritual Directions for Everyday Life*, 2nd edn (London: Fount, 1997).

11 Slee, 'A Spirituality for Multiple Overwhelmings', 21.

12 For more on student bereavement, see David E. Balk, 'Grieving: 22 to 30 Percent of All College Students', *New Directions for Student Services* 121 (2008): 5–14.

13 Damon Mayrl and Jeremy E. Uecker, 'Higher Education and Religious Liberalisation Among Young Adults', *Social Forces* 90, no. 1 (2011): 181–208.

14 Nick M. Shepherd, *Faith Generation: Retaining Young People and Growing the Church* (London: SPCK, 2016).

15 Mathew Guest, Kristin Aune and Sonya Sharma, *Christianity and the Univer-*

sity Experience: Understanding Student Faith (London: Bloomsbury, 2012), 148, 157.

16 Jeffrey J. Arnett, *Emerging Adulthood: The Winding Road from the Late Teens Through the Twenties* (Oxford: Oxford University Press, 2004).

17 Yvonne Tasker and Diane Negra, 'Introduction', in *Interrogating Postfeminism: Gender and the Politics of Popular Culture*, eds Yvonne Tasker and Diane Negra (Durham: Duke University Press, 2007), 1–26 (18).

18 See Erik H. Erikson, *Identity: Youth and Crisis* (London: Faber and Faber, 1968) who argues that this is a common dilemma for turbulent young people.

19 Anne Phillips, *The Faith of Girls: Children's Spirituality and Transition to Adulthood* (Farnham: Ashgate, 2011).

20 Slee, *Fragments for Fractured Times*, 222–3.

21 Nicola Slee, 'Come as a Girl', *Seeking the Risen Christa* (London: SPCK, 2011), 33.

22 Slee, *Fragments for Fractured Times*, 228–9.

23 Pierre Bourdieu, *The Logic of Practice* (London: Polity Press, 1992). See also Amy A. Bergerson, 'Exploring the Impact of Social Class on Adjustment to College: Anna's Story', *International Journal of Qualitative Studies in Education* 20, no. 1 (2007): 99–119.

24 Elisa S. Abes, 'Constructivist and Intersectional Interpretations of a Lesbian College Student's Multiple Social Identities', *The Journal of Higher Education* 83, no. 2 (2012): 186–216 (207–8), and Susan R. Jones, 'Constructing Identities at the Intersections: An Autoethnographic Exploration of Multiple Dimensions of Identity', *Journal of College Student Development* 50, no. 3 (2009): 287–304.

25 For more on this, including a discussion of faith and lad culture at university, see Jenny Morgans, 'Emerging Christian Women at Uni: Intersection of Gender and Faith Identities on Campus', *Research in the Social Scientific Study of Religion* 32 (2022): 147–62.

26 'Introduction', in *Researching Female Faith: Qualitative Research Methods*, eds Nicola Slee, Fran Porter and Anne Phillips (London: Routledge, 2018), 1–19 (15–16).

27 Slee, Porter and Phillips, 'Introduction', 15.

28 Uwe Flick, *An Introduction to Qualitative Research*, 4th edn (London: Sage, 2009), 114.

29 Flick, *An Introduction to Qualitative Research*, 121.

30 Jennifer Coates, *Women, Men and Language: A Sociolinguistic Account of Gender Differences in Language*, 3rd edn (London: Routledge, 2016), 90.

31 Kate Massey, 'Listening for the "I": Adapting a Voice-centred, Relational Method of Data Analysis in a Group Interview to Examine Women's Faith Lives', in *Researching Female Faith*, eds Slee, Porter and Phillips, 141–54 (151), emphasis original.

32 Massey, 'Listening for the "I"', 151.

33 Patricinio P. Schweickart, 'Speech Is Silver, Silence Is Gold: The Asymmetrical Intersubjectivity of Communicative Action', in *Knowledge, Difference and Power: Essays Inspired by Women's Ways of Knowing*, eds Nancy Goldberger, Jill Tarule, Blythe Clinchy and Mary Belenky (New York: Basic Books, 1996), 305–31 (309).

34 Massey, 'Listening for the "I"', 150.

35 Slee, *Women's Faith Development*, 52.

36 Gayle Letherby, *Feminist Research in Theory and Practice* (Buckingham:

Open University, 2003), 109, 129. For a longer discussion of reflexivity and 'friendly strangers' in my research, see Jenny Morgans, 'Reflexivity, Identity and the Role of the Researcher', in *Researching Female Faith*, eds Slee, Porter and Phillips, 189–202.

37 Slee, Porter and Phillips, 'Introduction', 17.

38 Henri Nouwen, *The Return of the Prodigal Son: A Story of Homecoming* (London: Darton, Longman and Todd, 1994), 106, 109.

39 Wendy M. Wright, *Sacred Dwelling: A Spirituality of Family Life* (London: Darton, Longman and Todd, 2007), 14–15.

40 Slee, *Women's Faith Development*, 159–60.

41 Slee, *Women's Faith Development*, 123–4.

42 Slee, *Women's Faith Development*, 72.

43 Liz Carmichael, *Friendship: Interpreting Christian Love* (London: T&T Clark, 2007), 200.

44 Carmichael, *Friendship*, 130–1.

45 Sallie McFague, *Metaphorical Theology: Models of God in Religious Language* (London: SCM Press, 1983), 182.

46 Carmichael, *Friendship*, 169.

47 Ford, *The Shape of Living*, xvi–xix.

48 Ford, *The Shape of Living*, xvii.

49 Ford, *The Shape of Living*, xix.

50 Slee, 'A Spirituality for Multiple Overwhelmings', 27–8.

51 Slee, 'A Spirituality for Multiple Overwhelmings', 21.

52 Slee, 'A Spirituality for Multiple Overwhelmings', 21.

53 Carmichael, *Friendship*, 198, 200.

54 Mary Field Belenky, Blythe McVicter Clinchy, Nancy Goldberger and Jill Mattuck Tarule, *Women's Ways of Knowing: The Development of Self, Voice, and Mind*, 10th Anniversary Edition (New York: Basic Books, 1997), 114–15.

55 Sharon Parks, *Big Questions, Worthy Dreams: Mentoring Young Adults in Their Search for Meaning, Purpose and Faith* (San Francisco: Jossey-Bass, 2000), 109.

56 Parks, *Big Questions*, 111–12.

57 Parks, *Big Questions*, 34.

58 Sonya Sharma and Mathew Guest, 'Navigating Religion Between University and Home: Christian Students' Experiences in English Universities', *Social and Cultural Geography* 14, no. 1 (2013): 59–79 (59, 70).

59 Sharma and Guest, 'Navigating Religion Between University and Home', 66–9.

60 Christopher Moody, 'Students, Chaplaincy and Pilgrimage', *Theology* 89, no. 732 (1986): 440–7 (445). See also Guest, Aune and Sharma, *Christianity and the University Experience*, 114.

61 Jane Speck, 'King's College London', in *Being a Chaplain*, eds Miranda Threlfall-Holmes and Mark Newitt (London: SPCK, 2011), 34–6.

62 For example, see Peter McGrail and John Sullivan, *Dancing on the Edge: Chaplaincy, Church and Higher Education* (Chelmsford: Matthew James Publishing, 2007); Simon Robinson, *Ministry Among Students: A Pastoral Theology and Handbook for Practice* (Norwich: Canterbury Press, 2004).

63 Bennett, Graham, Pattison and Walton, *Invitation to Research in Practical Theology*, 31.

7

Reading for the Roar: Recognizing Sexual Violence in Esther 2 and Judges 21

DEBORAH KAHN-HARRIS

Nicola Slee and I first met on a trip to Bosnia-Herzegovina organized by the charity Remembering Srebrenica, which organizes trips to the region to help promote remembrance of the recent genocide on European soil. Our trip was for women only, with the express aim of focusing on violence against women and girls during the Bosnian War (1992 to 1995).[1] It was booked for the end of March, a time when the weather should be warming up and the trees coming into leaf. But instead we hit a late winter storm, our flights were delayed, my luggage was lost in transit, and we were met with a snow-covered Sarajevo upon our arrival. Nicola was the most supportive of companions, but one who was not afraid to share her own vulnerabilities and needs. We held each other's hands as we witnessed the bones of yet to be identified victims of the Srebrenica massacre.[2] We sat together fully engaged in the act of listening to the women who were there to tell us their first-hand accounts of surviving rape and sexual assault at the hands of men who had once been their neighbours and, they thought, friends. We took deep breaths together in the fresh mountain air to try and reconcile the horror of what we heard and learned with the beauty of the mountain passes we travelled through. Nicola, too, was the one who, on our last day in an all too brief final stop in the worsening snowfall, very literally extended me a helping hand to get up and down the steep incline to the Jewish cemetery and stood beside me while I whispered the words of the mourner's *kaddish*, the Jewish prayer for the dead. And, of course, it was Nicola who immortalized the whole experience for us in poetry.[3] Though we were together in Bosnia for only a short time, the indelible mark her presence left on me has only strengthened.

Insofar as what brought us together – in the way that only such short, but intense residential experiences can – was a desire to bear witness to violence against women, it seems appropriate that this chapter looks again at that subject, through engagement with stories of the violence encountered by women of the Hebrew Bible. I offer it as a tribute to the women Nicola and I met together and to ones we did not meet, both living and dead. We must never forget.

The subject of violence against women in the biblical text is now vast. From Phyllis Trible's ground-breaking work *Texts of Terror: Literary Feminist Readings of Biblical Narratives*, first published in 1984, to Rhiannon Graybill's overt response *Texts After Terror: Rape, Sexual Violence, and The Hebrew Bible* decades later, the ground has been well covered.[4] To name but a few: Sarah, Hagar, Bilhah, Zilpah, Dinah, the daughter of Yiftah, the nameless *pilegesh* of the Levite, Bathsheva, Tamar (King David's daughter), Abishag, Gomer, Bat Zion, Vashti, Esther – male violence against women, particularly sexual violence, is pervasive in the Hebrew Bible. In faith communities, some of these stories are better known than others; yet, even those known are rarely thought of as stories of sexual violence against women. In contrast, among feminist and womanist Bible scholars, these names are well-trodden ground for commentary. These stories encompass rape, sexual assault, coercive control, sex trafficking of minors, servants and enslaved women, public shaming of victims, murder, mutilation of corpses, child sacrifice and, though not always in obvious ways, the process of resistance. Trible's description appears more than apt.

Such texts of terror reveal that women are not only assaulted when alone with a perpetrator – in the king's bedchamber or on the doorstep when locked out of their accommodation for the night or in the fields of a new country – but also even when they are together in public, even when under the watchful eye of other men. In the biblical text, to be alive and be female is to be at risk, whenever, wherever. All biblical women must watch their step lest someone mistake their sincerity for inebriation (Hannah) or their midnight wanderings as an excuse for a beating (the female lover in the Song of Songs).

By and large these women have names or, at the very least, appellations that identify them as someone's (secondary) wife or daughter. They are a tangible individual; a person we can focus on, a face to put with a story, someone's shoes that we can imagine inhabiting. As I rediscovered in Bosnia, putting a name, an individual, into the story enables the narrative to become humanized. In their individuality we are more attentive to hearing their stories.

In contrast to the usual focus on individual women, I want to try to reclaim the stories of the many. I will focus on two different stories from two parts of the biblical text. The first story is one that we may have heard many times, but never recognized it for what it is – a story of violence against women, hidden in plain sight. The second story is less well known, insofar as it serves as a sort of coda to perhaps the most gruesome story in the Hebrew Bible. It is a story that is swept under the carpet, when it is told at all.

Exhibit A: Esther 2.12–14

וּבְהַגִּיעַ תֹּר נַעֲרָה וְנַעֲרָה לָבוֹא אֶל־הַמֶּלֶךְ אֲחַשְׁוֵרוֹשׁ מִקֵּץ הֱיוֹת לָהּ כְּדָת הַנָּשִׁים שְׁנֵים עָשָׂר חֹדֶשׁ כִּי כֵּן יִמְלְאוּ
יְמֵי מְרוּקֵיהֶן שִׁשָּׁה חֳדָשִׁים בְּשֶׁמֶן הַמֹּר וְשִׁשָּׁה חֳדָשִׁים בַּבְּשָׂמִים וּבְתַמְרוּקֵי הַנָּשִׁים:
וּבָזֶה הַנַּעֲרָה בָּאָה אֶל־הַמֶּלֶךְ אֵת כָּל־אֲשֶׁר תֹּאמַר יִנָּתֵן לָהּ לָבוֹא עִמָּהּ מִבֵּית הַנָּשִׁים עַד־בֵּית הַמֶּלֶךְ:
בָּעֶרֶב הִיא בָאָה וּבַבֹּקֶר הִיא שָׁבָה אֶל־בֵּית הַנָּשִׁים שֵׁנִי אֶל־יַד שַׁעֲשְׁגַז סְרִיס הַמֶּלֶךְ שֹׁמֵר הַפִּילַגְשִׁים לֹא־תָבוֹא
עוֹד אֶל־הַמֶּלֶךְ כִּי אִם־חָפֵץ בָּהּ הַמֶּלֶךְ וְנִקְרְאָה בְשֵׁם:

When each girl's turn came to go to King Ahasuerus at the end of the twelve months' treatment prescribed for women (for that was the period spent on beautifying them: six months with oil of myrrh and six months with perfumes and women's cosmetics, and it was after that that the girl would go to the king), whatever she asked for would be given her to take with her from the harem to the king's palace.

She would go in the evening and leave in the morning for a second harem in charge of Shaashgaz, the king's eunuch, guardian of the concubines.[5] She would not go again to the king unless the king wanted her, when she would be summoned by name.[6]

Embedded in the story of Esther becoming Queen of Persia are these few verses that describe the process by which a new queen was to be chosen. In Jewish communities, particularly when retelling the story to children, we often refer to this passage as the 'beauty pageant' section or something similar.[7] But this passage is no beauty contest – even with all of the problems that would arise were that all that was going on here. In place of the 'Miss Persia' narrative, I want to unpick what is really happening.

Esther 1 relates the story of the extensive banquet thrown by King Ahasuerus to display his wealth and power. While intoxicated, the king orders Queen Vashti to leave the banquet she is throwing for the women and attend the king's banquet, wearing her crown in order to show off her beauty (Esther 1.11).[8] Vashti resists, defying the king's order publicly to objectify her. But Vashti's fate is wrapped not only in her own personal choice, but in what it represents to the wider circle of men and male power. Vashti's permanent removal from the position of queen is as much about a personal punishment for her rebuff to a drunken king as it is about making an example to women throughout the Persian empire – if even the queen can be dispensed with for refusing her husband, imagine what fate lies in store for any other women who seek to contradict male authority. The biblical text is entirely explicit about this motivation:

> For the queen's behaviour will make all wives despise their husbands, as they reflect that King Ahasuerus himself ordered Queen Vashti to be brought before him, but she would not come. This very day the ladies of Persia and Media, who have heard of the queen's behaviour, will cite it to all Your Majesty's officials, and there will be no end of scorn and provocation! (Esther 1.17–18)

Only after the king's anger subsides (Esther 2.1), can he begin the search for a new queen. Yet his anger and power form the toxic backdrop to the process of choosing the new queen. In Esther 2.2, the king's servants propose that נְעָרוֹת בְּתוּלוֹת טוֹבוֹת, beautiful teenage girls of marriageable age (probably virgins), be gathered from across the realm and assembled in the women's house under the authority of the king's eunuch, Hegai. From there these young women would be provided with a beauty regime until a young woman could be found that would please the king and who could, therefore, become the new queen.

Before coming to the more precise description of the process in Esther 2.12–14, I want to pause and imagine more clearly what is being described in the opening of chapter 2. Across the whole of the Persian empire, which according to Esther 1.1 constituted 127 provinces spanning Ethiopia to India, any attractive, unmarried teenage girl could be sent without her consent to be prepared in some opaque fashion to see if she might please King Ahasuerus, known for his wealth, inebriation and temper. To be clear, this story describes the human trafficking of pubescent girls for the pleasure of a mercurial man, who has absolute authority over them.[9] The question of consent is never raised; indeed, against the background of the Vashti story, we must assume that female agency (and consent) is precisely what the king and his advisers are seeking to suppress.

As to the more detailed portrayal of what happened in the women's house, these teenage girls are subjected to a beauty routine lasting a year – six months marinating them in expensive oils and six months perfuming and painting them. This description is reminiscent of sheep or cattle being fattened for slaughter, but instead of fattening them up they are being shaped to match some external notions of what constituted female attractiveness. What we have here is a sort of year-long *Love Island* preamble, but with contestants who have never been given any choice in the matter.

Once her year of beautification was over, one by one each of these teenage girls was taken to the king's chamber of an evening and sum-marily escorted to a second chamber the following morning. Here she would be under the careful attentions of a new eunuch, who guarded the women in perpetuity, unless they were ever recalled by the king. The text never spells out explicitly what these girls must do during the night that they spend with the king. Often when faced with a lacuna in the narra-tive, midrashic or other later interpretations fill in the blanks, but not here. The overnight stay of these vulnerable young women in the king's chambers is glossed over as an irrelevant detail.

To be clear, Esther 2.14 relates the rape of innumerable, unnamed girls. All but Esther are then discarded and their fate never mentioned again. Are they consigned to this second women's house for the rest of their lives, waiting in case the king decides he wishes to rape them again? What happens to the ones who become pregnant? What were these women's aspirations for their lives? Who do they become under the perpetual gaze of the eunuch, Shaashgaz? Esther has a future, which our story goes on to narrate, but these women have no voice at all. They become used goods with no consideration for their personhood. These women hide in plain view, with no thought given to them. As readers, we are directed to focus on Esther, our heroine. But she is as much victim as every other one of these girls and, in ignoring their victimhood, we ignore Esther's as well.

Perhaps more crucially, in allowing ourselves to glance past the full horror of what is perpetrated, we grant the text, and whatever authority it has over us, *carte blanche* to dismiss these girls and their abuse, and in so doing create a mind-set in which such experiences are both normal and acceptable. If we cannot look face-on at the trafficking of young women for the sexual gratification of a male authority figure and name it for what it is in an ancient story, then how much harder does it become to do so when we see similar acts of violence in the world around us?[10]

Exhibit B: Judges 21.12–14, 20–23

וַיִּמְצְא֞וּ מִיּוֹשְׁבֵ֣י ׀ יָבֵ֣ישׁ גִּלְעָ֗ד אַרְבַּ֤ע מֵאוֹת֙ נַעֲרָ֣ה בְתוּלָ֔ה אֲשֶׁ֧ר לֹא־יָדְעָ֛ה אִ֖ישׁ לְמִשְׁכַּ֣ב זָכָ֑ר וַיָּבִ֣יאוּ אוֹתָ֣ם אֶל־הַֽמַּחֲנֶה֙ שִׁלֹ֔ה אֲשֶׁ֖ר בְּאֶ֥רֶץ כְּנָֽעַן׃

וַֽיִּשְׁלְחוּ֙ כָּל־הָ֣עֵדָ֔ה וַֽיְדַבְּרוּ֙ אֶל־בְּנֵ֣י בִנְיָמִ֔ן אֲשֶׁ֖ר בְּסֶ֣לַע רִמּ֑וֹן וַיִּקְרְא֥וּ לָהֶ֖ם שָׁלֽוֹם׃

יָּ֤שָׁב בִּנְיָמִן֙ בָּעֵ֣ת הַהִ֔יא וַיִּתְּנ֤וּ לָהֶם֙ הַנָּשִׁ֔ים אֲשֶׁ֣ר חִיּ֔וּ מִנְּשֵׁ֖י יָבֵ֣שׁ גִּלְעָ֑ד וְלֹֽא־מָצְא֥וּ לָהֶ֖ם כֵּֽן׃

They found among the inhabitants of Jabesh-gilead 400 maidens who had not known a man carnally; and they brought them to the camp at Shiloh, which is in the land of Canaan.

Then the whole community sent word to the Benjaminites who were at the Rock of Rimmon, and offered them terms of peace.

Thereupon the Benjaminites returned, and they gave them the girls who had been spared from the women of Jabesh-gilead. But there were not enough of them.

וַיְצַוּ֕וּ אֶת־בְּנֵ֥י בִנְיָמִ֖ן לֵאמֹ֑ר לְכ֥וּ וַאֲרַבְתֶּ֖ם בַּכְּרָמִֽים׃

וּרְאִיתֶ֗ם וְהִנֵּ֤ה אִם־יֵצְאוּ֩ בְנוֹת־שִׁילוֹ֙ לָח֣וּל בַּמְּחֹל֔וֹת וִֽיצָאתֶם֙ מִן־הַכְּרָמִ֔ים וַחֲטַפְתֶּ֥ם לָכֶ֛ם אִ֥ישׁ אִשְׁתּ֖וֹ מִבְּנ֣וֹת שִׁיל֑וֹ וַהֲלַכְתֶּ֖ם אֶ֥רֶץ בִּנְיָמִֽן׃

וְהָיָ֡ה כִּֽי־יָבֹ֣אוּ אֲבוֹתָם֩ א֨וֹ אֲחֵיהֶ֜ם לָרֹ֣ב ׀ אֵלֵ֗ינוּ וְאָמַ֤רְנוּ אֲלֵיהֶם֙ חָנּ֣וּנוּ אוֹתָ֔ם כִּ֣י לֹ֥א לָקַ֛חְנוּ אִ֥ישׁ אִשְׁתּ֖וֹ בַּמִּלְחָמָ֑ה כִּ֣י לֹ֥א אַתֶּ֛ם נְתַתֶּ֥ם לָהֶ֖ם כָּעֵ֥ת תֶּאְשָֽׁמוּ׃

וַיַּֽעֲשׂוּ־כֵן֙ בְּנֵ֣י בִנְיָמִ֔ן וַיִּשְׂא֤וּ נָשִׁים֙ לְמִסְפָּרָ֔ם מִן־הַמְּחֹלְל֖וֹת אֲשֶׁ֣ר גָּזָ֑לוּ וַיֵּלְכ֗וּ וַיָּשׁ֙וּבוּ֙ אֶל־נַ֣חֲלָתָ֔ם וַיִּבְנוּ֙ אֶת־הֶ֣עָרִ֔ים וַיֵּשְׁב֖וּ בָּהֶֽם׃

So they instructed the Benjaminites as follows: 'Go and lie in wait in the vineyards. As soon as you see the girls of Shiloh coming out to join in the dances, come out from the vineyards; let each of you seize a wife from among the girls of Shiloh, and be off for the land of Benjamin.

And if their fathers or brothers come to us to complain, we shall say to them, "Be generous to them for our sake! We could not provide any of them with a wife on account of the war, and you would have incurred guilt if you yourselves had given them [wives]."'

The Benjaminites did so. They took to wife, from the dancers whom they carried off, as many as they themselves numbered. Then they went back to their own territory, and rebuilt their towns and settled in them.

Judges 21 is both the final chapter in the book of Judges and the ending to the narrative that begins in Judges 19 with the story of the Levite's secondary wife.[11] As a result of the brutal gang rape and subsequent death of the Levite's secondary wife, a war ensues between the tribe of Benjamin and all of the other tribes.[12] By the end of chapter 20, all that is left of the tribe of Benjamin is 600 men who have fled the fighting.

Chapter 21 opens with the problem of these 600 remaining men. In 21.1 we learn that the leaders of all the other tribes have taken an oath not to marry any of their daughters to a Benjaminite. Yet in the very next verses these same men bemoan the loss of the tribe of Benjamin to the people of Israel. They find themselves at an apparently insurmountable impasse and contrive a violent plan to rectify the situation. They remember that one town, Jabesh-gilead, had not participated in the war against Benjamin and so they send troops to kill all the inhabitants of Jabesh-gilead, bar the virgin girls. Once the slaughter is complete, 400 unmarried girls remain, whom they give to the remaining Benjaminites.

Alas, they have not done their maths well, for 400 girls are some 200 short for the 600 remaining Benjaminites. So in order to find more unmarried girls, they tell the men to go to the annual festival at Shiloh. There the Benjaminites are told to lie in wait in the vineyards for the young women to come out dancing at which point they are to carry off a girl each to marry. Having done so, the men return to their lands and rebuild their communities.

While much has been written about the Levite's secondary wife and her plight, less has been written about the girls of Jabesh-gilead or Shiloh.[13] Here the biblical text presents us with two matter-of-fact stories of mass abduction, forced marriage and rape, portrayed in a neutral fashion. The text does not recount any debate around these solutions, just a casual acceptance that massacring the men, married women, and children of Jabesh-gilead, and forcing the grieving daughters into marriage (with men who were previously not seen fit as marriage partners) is a perfectly reasonable activity under the circumstances. Equally, allowing the remaining 200 Benjaminites to carry off unsuspecting young women into rape-marriage is also presented as a perfectly acceptable way of dealing with the problem that the tribal leaders had created for themselves.[14]

Might other options have existed for the tribal leaders to deal with their self-imposed situation? Earlier in the book of Judges, Yiftah also makes an ill-thought-through vow (Judges 11.30–31), for which the rabbis in their midrashic commentary castigate him, suggesting he should have annulled it.[15] Could not the tribal leaders have similarly annulled their vow (making appropriate sin offerings at the Temple, etc.), thus leaving them free to contract marriages in the proper fashion for the remaining Benjaminites? Yet the rabbinic commentary on Yiftah does not extend to these tribal leaders. Something in the stories of Judges 21 remains unseen.

In the story of Yiftah's daughter, the text relates the story of individuals – Yiftah and Yiftah's daughter. Just as in the case of the Levite's secondary wife, where the story concentrates on the Levite and his secondary wife, Judges 11 focuses the reader on another unnamed female character, allowing us to focus on her personhood – at least to a degree. In contradistinction, the mass abduction, rape and trauma inflicted on a large group of women is not problematized by the text. Indeed, the violation of this large group of undifferentiated women is presented as the solution to a problem. These women are no less possessions than Yiftah's daughter or the Levite's concubine (note the possessive fashion in which we are forced to refer to these women), but the women of Jabesh-gilead belong to the wrong men and while the women of Shiloh belong to the right men, those men are sworn not to give them in marriage to Benjaminites. The solution, therefore, is to allow their fathers and brothers to 'be generous' and allow their abduction to take place.

Unlike the book of Esther, Judges is not read liturgically within a Jewish context. These stories at the very end of the book are hardly known in Jewish communities as a result. The situation is not so much that we glance over them, or fail to see the horror in these stories, but that we simply avoid reading them altogether. If we did read them aloud in communal life, how would we fail to notice the full horror of what is described here? And that is precisely why we ought to read them together. Just as in the book of Esther, where our failure to see the victimhood of the sexually trafficked young women of Esther 2 prevents us from seeing also the traumatic experiences of Esther herself, in the case of the forced rape-marriages of Judges 21 our failure to read these stories prevents us from seeing the intergenerational trauma that could well have affected the most famous descendant of these women – King Saul.

We know from the first moment that Saul is introduced to us in 1 Samuel 9.1 that he is from the tribe of Benjamin. Although the text only names Saul's father (and his ancestors), any astute reader will know the stories of Judges 21 and can, therefore, deduce that among Saul's ancestry (mother, grandmother?) must be one of the girls captured at Jabesh-gilead or abducted from Shiloh. The intergenerational memory in Saul's family includes the experience of a recent female ancestor forced into marriage through an act of sexual violence. The biblical text never overtly refers to this part of Saul's ancestry or draws explicit links to how it may have affected him, but we as readers can.[16]

Recent scholarship has considered possible psychiatric diagnoses for Saul, ranging from mania to depression to bipolar disorder.[17] These are evidenced not only by the insecurities that Saul displays – for example, his inability to wait for Samuel (1 Samuel 13.8–14) – but more clearly by the explicit statement in 1 Samuel 16.14–15, 23 that Saul was troubled by an 'evil spirit'. Of course, many factors are at play in mental health disorders, but one significant factor can be intergenerational trauma, which can affect children both genetically and emotionally. Saul, after all, would have been raised not only in a single family, but as part of an entire community affected by gender-based violence. At some point, which could well have been the generation into which Saul was born, every single mother in Benjamin would have been the victim of gender-based violence.

Imagine a community in which every mother had either watched as their entire families were slaughtered before their eyes or had been abducted against their will before they were trafficked to a group of men known previously for their lack of hospitality and ability to gang rape a woman until she died. What would the lives of these women have been like? How would their experiences have shaped the lives of their children and their children's children? Might Saul's 'evil spirit' have been, even in part, a legacy of the experience of the women of his community?

Carrying this intergenerational trauma forwards allows us to consider another question. When rape-marriage is part of the communal memory, does that legitimate it or warn against it? If the tribe of Benjamin's very existence is dependent on violent rape-marriage, then does that make it easier for their descendants to carry on the tradition or could it make them more wary of it? Saul is not the only significant biblical character descended from the tribe of Benjamin and, hence, from the women of Jabesh-gilead and Shiloh, and their collective trauma.

Harkening back to my first example, Mordechai too is described as a Benjaminite, a descendant of Kish (Esther 2.5).[18] Might Mordechai's identity as a member of the tribe of Benjamin problematize one more aspect of the story of Esther? The biblical text implies that the fathers of eligible girls had no choice but to give them over to Ahasuerus. But it does not recall a long queue of worried fathers, encamped outside the gates of the palace waiting to learn of the fate of their daughters. Yet that is precisely what Mordechai does. Why? Does the collective memory of his Benjaminite ancestry make him more attuned to what will happen to his foster daughter, Esther? Does he accept her fate more or less willingly than others as a result? Does he have insights to grant to her that might make her more resilient for coping with the violence and ensuing trauma she will face? Or does Mordechai, like so many generations of readers, not even view what happens to Esther and the other girls as a problem but rather just a normal part of life? Does he stay because he cares for her or because he wants to make sure she stays the course? Does he care for her or the power she may gain?

But it is not only Mordechai who is a Benjaminite. Hiding in plain view is another Benjaminite, Esther. According to Esther 2.7, she is the daughter of Mordechai's uncle, who we can reasonably assume is also of the tribe of Benjamin. As a female descendant of the women of Jabesh-gilead and Shiloh, Esther's story illuminates both the ways in which women's lives are marred by sexual violence, and the inner fortitude to resist such violence. Esther is the victim of rape-marriage, in this case to King Ahasuerus. But in Esther 4.15—5.1, Esther transforms herself from victim to resistor. We know nothing of her life in the palace, but having been raped into marriage through a contest that she could have had no expectation that she would win, we can only imagine how she must have felt forced to live an unchosen life – not unlike her ancestresses before her, forced to propagate the tribe of Benjamin against their will. Yet ultimately Esther finds her voice when the existential threat to her entire people comes to rest on her ability to resist the violence of her marriage and to approach the king unbidden.

And what does Esther require to face the king? In Esther 4.16 she makes this request of Mordechai – that all the people, as well as Esther herself and her young women, fast on her behalf. Esther requires the support of community. To know that she is not alone, that others care for her fate. And that is the same lesson that Nicola and I learned in Bosnia.

Resistance is made possible when we do not feel ourselves to be alone, when we are not isolated from the support of others. We have no record of the voices of the other young women in Esther 2, only the ongoing story of Esther herself. I have often wondered about the young women to whom Esther refers (Esther 4). Do they share the experience of sexual violence or at least its threat? Are they a support to her not only in the precursor to approaching the king, but through every day that she lives as a survivor of sexual violence?

In 'Witnessing to What Remains', Slee recounts in poetry the story of Bakira Hasečić, a survivor of rape during the Bosnian War. Like Esther, Bakira was alone when she was raped, without the support of others, but her life's mission since then has been to resist the isolation of sexual violence. As Slee writes:

> For twenty-five years
> she has been amassing evidence from women's broken
> narratives to convict the men living with impunity
> in flats and streets all around. She never goes out without a camera.
> She knocks on neighbours' doors, urging them to testify.
> She will not take no for an answer.[19]

Bakira speaks as often as possible to others, to groups of foreign women like ours. In listening to Bakira, we become part of her resistance and the resistance of so many other women whose stories are so like her own.

Slee also writes of Branka Anti-Štauber, a psychologist whose work at the Snaga žene association supports women as they work through the trauma of sexual violence.[20] I drink the tea from their social enterprise as I write these words; my personal way of continuing to remember, continuing to care. These women resist daily through the simple act of mutual support of one another. Maybe the women of Jabesh-gilead and Shiloh did likewise. We have no record of their resistance, though perhaps we can imagine that in quiet corners of their homes and fields they were able to support one another, out of sight of the men who had violated them:

The sounds of women's silence runs deep.
Let us attune our ears to the sounds of women's silence,
to attend and listen to what is not said,
what is only beginning to be said.
Let this silence cry aloud in our ears,
let it resound and reverberate inside our heads,
let it deafen our whole being with its colossal roar.[21]

Let the women of Jabesh-gilead, the women of Shiloh, the women of biblical Persia, the women of Bosnia, and so, so many more – roar.

Notes

1 Nicola Slee includes a chapter entitled 'Theological Reflection *in extremis*: Remembering Srebrenica', in *Fragments for Fractured Times: What Feminist Practical Theology Brings to the Table* (London: SCM Press, 2020), 153–68.

2 I am honoured that Nicola remembers this moment much as I do, immortalizing it in her poem 'Visiting Tuzla', *Fragments for Fractured Times*, 161–2:

Meanwhile, I am gripping Deborah's hand for dear life,
to keep me upright in this factory of death.

3 Again, from 'Visiting Tuzla', Nicola says:

Slip-sliding down the steep steps
to the Jewish cemetery, snow silences
the sound of traffic. The peace is profound
in this place of the four thousand dead.
Deborah recites the mourners' kaddish
in Aramaic as the rest of us huddle round.

4 Phyllis Trible, *Texts of Terror: Literary-Feminist Readings of Biblical Narratives* (Minneapolis: Fortress Press, 1984), and Rhiannon Graybill, *Texts After Terror: Rape, Sexual Violence, and the Hebrew Bible* (New York: Oxford University Press, 2021).

5 In most standard English translations, this term is still translated as 'concubine'. According to *The Dictionary of Classical Hebrew*, however, *pilegesh* means 'secondary wife (rather than concubine)'. See David J. A. Clines, ed., *The Dictionary of Classical Hebrew* Volume VI ס–פ (Sheffield: Sheffield Phoenix Press, 2007), 681.

6 All translation from the Jewish Publication Society *Tanakh* (1985), unless otherwise noted.

7 Or at least that has happened traditionally. Through my teaching of student rabbis at Leo Baeck College, I sincerely hope that none of my students has ever described it that way again.

8 According to midrashic tradition (Esther Rabbah 3.13 and Midrash Lekach Tov to Esther 1.11.1), Ahasuerus commanded Vashti to wear nothing else except

the crown – that is, to attend his drunken, male banquet naked but for her crown, which was the source of her refusal.

9 To my shame I had not noticed this reading of the text until I read Randall C. Bailey, '"That's Why They Didn't Call the Book Hadassah!": The Interse(ct)/(x) ionality of Race/Ethnicity, Gender, and Sexuality in the Book of Esther', in *They Were All Together in One Place? Toward Minority Biblical Criticism*, eds Randall C. Bailey, Tat-siong Benny Liew and Fernando F. Segovia (Atlanta: Society of Biblical Literature, 2009), 227–50 (234). Bailey credits Nicole Duran, 'Who Wants to Marry a Persian King? Gender Games and Wars and the Book of Esther', in *Pregnant Passion: Gender, Sex, and Violence in the Bible*, ed. Cheryl Kirk-Duggan (Atlanta: Society of Biblical Literature, 2004), 71–84, for bringing this idea to his attention. See also Ericka Shawndricka Dunbar, *Trafficking Hadassah: Collective Trauma, Cultural Memory, and Identity in the Book of Esther and in the African Diaspora* (London: Routledge, 2022).

10 Gina Hens-Piazza, *Nameless, Blameless and Without Shame: Two Cannibal Mothers Before a King* (Collegeville: Liturgical Press, 2003), 20.

11 For a more comprehensive introduction to this section of Judges, see Susan Niditch, *Judges: A Commentary* (Louisville: Westminster John Knox Press, 2008), 185–212. I have translated the Hebrew term פילגש *pilegesh*, meaning here 'secondary wife'.

12 See Judges 19—20 for the complete story.

13 See Alice Bach, 'Rereading the Body Politic: Women, Violence, and Judges 21', in *Judges: A Feminist Companion to the Bible*, Second Series, ed. Athalya Brenner (Sheffield: Sheffield Academic Press, 1999), 143–59. Bach also refers to the rape of Bosnian women during the Bosnian War.

14 See Wil Gafney, 'Mother Knows Best: Messianic Surrogacy and Sexploitation in Ruth', in *Mother Goose, Mother Jones, Mommie Dearest: Biblical Mothers and Their Children*, eds Cheryl A. Kirk-Duggan and Tina Pippin (Atlanta: Society of Biblical Literature, 2004), 26–30 on rape-marriage (28–9 on Judges 21 in particular).

15 Midrash Tanchuma, Bechukotai 5.1.

16 Although interestingly, in 1 Samuel 11 Saul saves the men of Jabesh-gilead from Nahash the Ammonite. After Saul's death in 1 Samuel 31.11–13, the men of Jabesh-gilead retrieve his body and that of his sons, burying his bones and fasting for seven days.

17 See, for example, George Stein, 'The Case of King Saul: Did He Have Recurrent Unipolar Depression or Bipolar Affective Disorder?', *British Journal of Psychiatry* 198, no. 3 (2011): 212; Ephraim Nissan and Abraham Ofir Shemesh, 'King Saul's "Evil Spirit" (Ruach Ra'ah): Between Psychology, Medicine and Culture', *La Ricerca Folklorica* 62 (2010): 149–56; Louba Ben-Noun, 'What Was the Mental Disease that Afflicted King Saul?', *Clinical Case Studies* 2, no. 4 (2003): 270–82; Martijn Huisman, 'King Saul, Work-Related Stress and Depression', *Journal of Epidemiology and Community Health* 61, no. 10 (2007): 890.

18 Perhaps the same Kish that is Saul's father.

19 Slee, 'Bakira Hasečić', *Fragments for Fractured Times*, 161. Also published in 'Witnessing to What Remains, or the Power of Persisting: Power, Authority and Love in the Interim Spaces', in *Contemporary Feminist Theologies*, eds Kerrie Handasyde, Cathryn McKinney and Rebekah Pryor (London: Routledge, 2021), 21–32 (27).

20 Slee, 'Witnessing to What Remains', 33–4.
21 Nicola Slee, 'Speaking of Silence: A Reproach', *Praying Like a Woman* (London: SPCK, 2004), 29.

8

Mary the Crone

KAREN O'DONNELL

Inspired and Informed

As one whose theological education was sorely lacking in any classes in feminist theology, or any feminist approaches to reading the Bible, I discovered the world of feminist theology as a doctoral student as I began to read and engage with feminist perspectives on Christianity.[1] This had a profound impact on my doctoral studies and subsequent scholarship.[2] Of course, this is now where I situate myself most usually, as any of my students will tell you. No subject in my classroom escapes a feminist perspective and I am committed to the principle that feminist approaches to theology, as well as disability, queer, postcolonial and racial perspectives, do not need to be sidelined into some separate optional class but rather should inform all theological engagement. I have been both inspired and informed in my approach to theology and in my feminist perspective on the theological classroom by a wide range of feminist and womanist theologians. Chief among these has been the work and the person of Nicola Slee. So it is with great pleasure that I attempt work here that is both informed and inspired by Slee and her work.

This chapter particularly centres upon feminist ways of reading and responding to texts. I am inspired here by Slee's work in *The Book of Mary* and in her work outlining the patterns at work in women's faith and spiritual development.[3] I bring these pieces of research and theological imagination into dialogue with the under-examined seventh-century text *The Life of the Virgin*. This text gives a startlingly egalitarian account of the early churches and Mary's particular place of leadership and authority within them. My aim in bringing these disparate texts to bear on one another is to imagine the older Mary. That is, to imagine the 50-year-old mother who stood at the foot of the cross and her subsequent 30 years of ministry as an older woman. This Mary is strikingly absent from our traditions. But this is the menopausal Mary, the Crone Mary, the arthritic, stooped Mary retelling the stories and teachings of her son.

I want to develop this image of the older Mary as a basis for giving new liturgical space to older women in our midst. Far from being invisible women, these women are often the very lifeblood of the local church. Menopause might then be understood as a transition into wisdom and new ministries – as indeed it was for Mary.

Feminist Ways of Reading

In the preface to *The Book of Mary*, Slee writes that she 'wanted the freedom to create the kind of poetic space in which it is possible to try out different kinds of voices and forms and to come at Mary from a wide variety of angles – some of them oblique or apparently tangential'.[4] Rather than a systematic treatment of the life of Mary, Slee takes an approach grounded in poetry, demonstrating the working out of her thinking and giving her the space to take risks with the ways in which she approaches the always ambiguous and often out-of-reach person of Mary.

In this approach, Slee is demonstrating and embodying decidedly feminist principles of engaging with the text and reading with a feminist hermeneutic that is attuned to silences, absences and gaps within the material available to us. Heather Walton utilizes this technique in reading texts, often but not exclusively religious texts, and engaging in acts of re-visioning texts that are intended to re-fashion and transform women's futures.[5] Similarly, the late Grace Jantzen engages in what she calls a 'double reading' of texts in which she is focused on drawing out that which is not immediately apparent.[6] This is an effective – and long established – method for highlighting that which has been excluded, unattended or repressed within a text. It allows for a particularly fecund gap to arise between what is said and what is unsaid. This fertile space is frequently the ground for feminist theological work and lends itself particularly well to imaginative, quirky, risky and creative theological engagements.

This feminist hermeneutic of reading and creative imagining is one in which, taking my lead from Slee, I am engaged in this chapter.[7] Seeking to highlight the gaps, absences and areas of inattention, I draw on this feminist principle of reading and imagining as one that is particularly suited to engagement with both the life of the person of Mary (to which the Gospel narratives are particularly inattentive) and to the lives of older women of faith who are often similarly overlooked and paid little attention by theologians and clergy.

Slee's *Book of Mary*

The Book of Mary is a collection of poems and reflections on the life of Mary, the mother of Jesus, and the narratives surrounding that life. Slee considers, as well, the ways the stories and traditions of Mary – full of paradox and subject to various changes – can be explored and received by women today. Slee highlights the ways these feminist hermeneutics can be applied fruitfully to the person of Mary. Given that we know so little detail of her life from the canonical gospels, Mary is ripe for the kind of creative reimagining that can characterize feminist ways of engaging with texts. She notes that Mary functions as 'a kind of reflective screen upon which has been projected a culture's shifting ideals and aspirations around humanity, sanctity and deity. Specifically, Mary has functioned as a mirror for society's notions of the female, of the holy and of the divine feminine at any one time.'[8]

The themes within Mary's life are treated by Slee through the medium of poetry rather than through abstract and systematic theology, and thus Slee invites us to reimagine again the person of Mary. Mary is made decidedly human, hairy armpits, smelly farts and all. This is, of course, in marked contrast to a narrative tradition that has sought to emphasize Mary's holiness so much that she has become an unachievable model of womanhood, far out of reach of the lives of ordinary women. Slee encourages us to see Mary not just as a real woman, but as a real woman who has a life outside and beyond the scenes of nativity and crucifixion. She offers us a woman who dances, who reminisces, who grows old, who tells stories, who has friends and loves them.

A particular favourite poem of mine in this collection, especially given my emphasis in this chapter on menopause, the crone, and older age, is the poem 'Mary, in Old Age'.[9] Here Slee depicts an older Mary reminiscing on her life. She is telling her stories, and those young ones who respect her as a wise woman are listening attentively. Here, in the midst of a group listening to an old woman's stories, stirs the breath of the Holy Spirit and a second Pentecost occurs. Mary closes her eyes and lifts her hands as she says 'Let the fire come down' and she sees the heavens open.[10] This is a striking image of an elderly woman calling down the power of God on those with whom she is speaking. Here we see a woman attuned to the movements of the Spirit because she has experienced them before. I imagine the delight on her face, the spark in her eyes as she witnesses those young ones sat with her experiencing the great deluge of the Spirit poured out on them.

These are the theological accounts Slee offers in the book. She offers a creative re-visioning of a familiar, and often dull, character. She lifts

Mary out of her typical scenes and gives her a new voice in new land-scapes, allowing her to come to life and become a fully developed woman, away from traditional Mariological doctrines and towards a holistic perspective deeply rooted in feminist theology.[11]

The Life of the Virgin by Maximus the Confessor

While the New Testament is notoriously light on information and char-acterization of the person of Mary, limiting her to the beginning and end of Jesus' life, with a couple of cameos in between, there are a mul-titude of other sources from antiquity that serve to flesh out the missing parts of Mary's life. The *Protevangelium of James* is one particularly well-known text, as are the Dormition narratives which focus on Mary's assumption into heaven. However, *The Life of the Virgin* is unique in the way in which it offers a full account of the life and ministry of Mary, the mother of Jesus. This seventh-century text is purportedly written by Maximus the Confessor. It is, of course, possible that the attribution to Maximus was added to the text later in order to protect the text. Maxi-mus would make an ideal author as he was devoted to Mary throughout his life. However, Stephen Shoemaker notes that we have no real reason to suspect that Maximus was not the author of this text.[12] The text was probably originally written in Greek and now exists only in Old Georgian which would account for its long absence from scholarship in the West. Shoemaker offers the first full translation into English of this valuable text which demonstrates how Christians, by the end of antiquity, had come to remember Mary.

The text itself is a fascinating one. It is the earliest complete narrative of the whole life of Mary. Accounts of her birth and dormition were already in wide circulation by the seventh century, and of course the Gospels attend, however briefly, to some elements of her life in relation to Jesus. What makes *The Life of the Virgin* unique and so interesting is the developed account of Mary's involvement in Jesus' ministry during his lifetime, and the narratives of her leadership of the apostles and the early church after Jesus' ascension. Mary is a significant spiritual and ecclesial authority in this period. There is also evidence that this text had a liturgical function in at least some of the surviving manuscripts.[13]

In *The Life of the Virgin* the author brings to the fore the person of Mary and the many other women who followed Jesus at every oppor-tunity.[14] Indeed, the text is littered with references to the women that followed Jesus. It was this group of 'disciples' (it is clear in the text that the women are disciples in exactly the same way that the men are) that Mary leads. Mary is recognized as one who has uniquely authoritative knowledge of Jesus' teachings. She leads the apostles in their prayers and their preaching, offering guidance both on spiritual matters and on preaching.[15] Most significantly, Mary performs a parallel serving of the women at the Last Supper, alongside Jesus' serving of the men, acting as co-priest. Ally Kateusz notes of this scene:

> The author of the *Life of the Virgin* described both men and women there, as if Jesus' first-century followers had participated in a gender-parallel meal similar to that of the first-century Therapeutae Jews of Judea. The very oldest manuscript of the *Life of the Virgin*, the eleventh-century Tbilisi A-40, preserved yet one more scene of gender parity at this shared meal. During the meal, first Mary and then her son, modeled a ritual of female and male co-priesthood. According to the text, Mary was the teacher of the women and, 'for this reason', at the supper, 'she sacrificed herself as the priest and she was sacrificed, she offered and was offered'.[16]

It is significant, and disconcerting, to note that Shoemaker amends the gender of the one who does the sacrificing and offering in this text to masculine (thus making it Jesus who sacrifices and offers) because he found the concept of a text that elevated Mary so high 'rather difficult to imagine'.[17] A lack of imagination is no reason to doubt a text! This is one of the reasons, among others, that this text lends itself well to a feminist reading hermeneutic – an approach to the text grounded in imagination as it reads what is both there and not there, attending to the words, bodies, stories and experiences that fall between the lines of the text.

Feminist Reading of *The Life of the Virgin*

The Life of the Virgin offers insight into 30 years of Mary's ministry after the death of Jesus. If we assume she was about 16 when she gave birth to Jesus, Mary would have been around 50 when Jesus died. The text here then recounts her ministry among the believers for the last 30 years of her life, up to her dormition aged about 80.[18] The Mary of this text is not just the young virgin of the Annunciation, nor the young mother who loses her son during the festival. This Mary – the older woman who continues to live beyond her son's ascension into heaven – is a Mary who is paid little attention in our narratives. Perhaps, like Shoemaker, we can hardly imagine such a woman. Older women are largely invisible. Indeed, novelist Hilary Mantel has described women over 50 as 'the invisible generation'.[19] It is no surprise that Mary's life as an older woman has been largely invisible to us.

But the text itself is a feminist treat. Here we find a depiction of Mary as a woman in charge, a woman who leads not just other women but the male apostles too:

> [She] took charge of every good thing, and while she was dwelling in the land, she was herself the model and leader of all good things. Thus, after his Ascension, the holy mother of Christ was the model and leader of every good activity for men and for women through the grace and support of her glorious King and Son.[20]

She sent the disciples forth from Jerusalem. But when she herself tried to leave Jerusalem as a missionary, she was turned back by God and told to remain in the city. The text notes that 'the return of the holy Theotokos [Mary] to Jerusalem was excellent, for she was the strength, the haven, and the rampart for the believers who were there. And every need and ministry of the Christians was entrusted to the all-immaculate one.'[21] Mary leads both the men and the women, she has a position of authority in the early church, she has a wise and authoritative knowledge of Jesus' teachings, she is an experienced pray-er, she can give guidance on spiritual matters, she is a preaching expert able to give direction to those who are learning to preach, she is a comfort and inspiration to many, and the one to whom every need and ministry of the early church was entrusted. What a woman!

The equality of Mary and the other women with the male disciples is a striking feature of this text. The author of this text is clearly demonstrating (and perhaps remembering through sources no longer known to us) 'a discipleship of equals'.[22] As Kateusz notes, 'in stark contrast to theologians who emphasized a chain of male apostolic authority, the *Life of the Virgin*'s author also called women "apostle" and portrayed Mary Magdalene "as an apostle equal in rank to Peter"'.[23]

Throughout the text, we hear Mary's voice loud and clear as the author depicts both Mary's faith and her wisdom. At the burial of Jesus, Mary sings a hymn of praise, ending with the words:

> And behold, the mystery of the divine economy and your gracious for-bearance and the love of humanity has been fulfilled. Now, then, reveal your power; hasten and come to our aid. I know truly that you will arise and have mercy on your mother first of all ... But blessed will be the day when you will make me to hear your sweet voice again, when I will see your divinely beautiful face and be filled with your desirable grace.

Blessed will it be when I see you clearly, true God and Lord of the living and the dead.[24]

In stark contrast to the ignorance and lack of faith of the male disciples portrayed in the Gospels where Peter denies Christ, all but John are too afraid to be present at the crucifixion, and Thomas refuses to believe his eyes as he witnesses the risen Christ, Mary knows that Christ will rise again and she will hear him and see him once more.

We can read *The Life of the Virgin* as offering somewhat of an alternative reading of the life of the early churches to the one portrayed in the New Testament. Here we see a clearer vision of gender equality, an obvious sense of the significance of not just Mary but women in general both as followers of Jesus and as leaders in the early church. Perhaps this offers clarity on the passages in Paul's letters where he is writing to female apostles and commending their ministries. And this is a text where Mary frequently speaks. She is not silent as she is for the majority of the Gospel narratives. However, it is important to note that this text, in keeping with many other portrayals of the Virgin Mary, is one that is written by a man and the narrative is shaped towards depicting a woman so holy and immaculate that she is idealized to the point of fiction. I think one of the great gifts of this text, however, is the way it makes Mary's relationship with other women and men very clear. In the Gospel texts, Mary is depicted in the company of other women, but here her relationality and companionship are made explicit. She is a comfort and a friend to many.

Women's Faith Development

In her research on women's faith development, Slee highlights the significance of the project of lifelong faithing.[25] Faith and spiritual development are lifelong projects that do not cease when one enters middle or older age. Indeed, for many people, including many women, this period of time might be where the project of faithing really starts to get going. Mary's age as she moves into a role of leadership within the early church bears much in common with those researched by Abby Day in her book *The Religious Lives of Older Laywomen: The Last Active Anglican Generation*. Day notes that these women are the 'backbone of the church'.[26] Day is interested in women who were in their eighties and nineties within the Anglican church – Mary ministers up until about the age of 80 before her dormition. Day argues that we know surprisingly little about these women:

They attend the mainstream churches every Sunday, polish the brasses, organize fund-raisers, keep the church open on weekdays, bake cakes, and visit vulnerable people in their homes. Their often invisible labour not only populates the physical space of the church but helps ensure its continuity and enriches surrounding communities.[27]

As a member of a rural parish church that is part of a benefice of six churches, I am always astounded at the energy and commitment of the older women in my own church without whom, it is safe to say, church would simply not happen.

In her work focused on articulating some of the patterns and processes of women's faith development, Slee highlights a number of characteristics that are pertinent to our consideration of *The Life of the Virgin* and its depiction of an older Mary who occupies a significant position of leadership and authority. Most importantly, Slee argues, women's faithing and faith development is uniquely embedded in relationship.[28] This is faith that is personal and relational, developed through conversation and dynamic forms of meaning-making, which draws the other into dialogue with the self. Such faith is grounded in commitment, compassion and conviction.[29] Furthermore, the kind of faith developed by the women in Slee's study highlights concrete, narrative, visual and embodied forms of thinking over and against more systematic, abstract or analytical ways of faithing. This resonates with Day's recognition of the importance of the 'everyday' in the faith lives of the older women with whom she conducted her research.[30]

Unsurprisingly, then, *The Life of the Virgin* reveals an older woman to whom relationship is important. She is one who comforts and cares for those around her, a woman who is attentive to the needs of her fellow Christians and the ministries they engage with – both female and male. *The Life of the Virgin* depicts Mary developing her faith in God through her close relationship with her son throughout his life, even as Jesus learns his Jewish faith through his mother. She is one who teaches, even as she continues to learn throughout her lifetime. We might imagine an older Mary who delights in telling stories of the younger Jesus, in remembering his miracles and reminding the early church of his teachings. We might imagine a Mary who inhabits an embodied faith; one that makes itself known in hugs, kisses, gestures, arthritic hands, stiff knees and an insistence on the importance of food, especially for those who are poor. As she educates the disciples in how to be good preachers, we might imagine Mary emphasizing the power of the story, reminding the disciples of the way Jesus used parables to make difficult ideas more understandable to those to whom he was speaking. We might imagine Mary as one who shares both her successes and failures in this arena. Perhaps with a hearty laugh as she recounts particular flops or mis-steps.

Mary the Menopausal Crone

The Life of the Virgin pays little attention to Mary's body throughout the text, except to tell us that she slept on a stone floor for her bed.[31] For at least some portion of the time recounted in this text, Mary would have been a menopausal woman. I do not think there is any reason to imagine that Mary did not menstruate. Indeed, her ability to become pregnant with Jesus in the first place is predicated on her ability to produce an egg that provides the human DNA for the incarnation. If Mary is ovulating then she is also menstruating. And ultimately, she is also a woman who eventually ceases to menstruate by entering the menopause. Most women enter the menopause between the age of 49 and 52 – the age Mary would have been at the time of Jesus' death and resurrection.[32] It is, therefore, no stretch of the imagination to see Mary as a menopausal woman who stands at the foot of the cross, perhaps experiencing a hot flush and the low mood and anxiety that so often accompanies the progression of the menopause, compounded by the agony of watching her son die. Can we imagine Mary experiencing such a response to her body? Feeling the sweat of a hot flush pool between her breasts? Feeling her clothing stick to her armpits? Wiping the beading sweat from her brow and her top lip? Recognizing the ways in which her own body is transitioning from mother to crone even as her son is dying?

The crone has often been considered a negative term, evoking images of ugly, old, hunched women with cats, spindly fingers and often evil.[33] In her work in this area, Rosemary Radford Ruether reflects on the connection between the words 'crone' and *cronus*, meaning time. And so she draws out the 'wisdom of long life and experience'.[34] Here the crone is the wise woman, past child-bearing and raising, who has 'gathered up the fruits of their long experience into profound understanding and who serve as resources of wisdom for younger women'.[35] Given what we have read and imagined about the person of Mary in *The Life of the Virgin* it seems fitting to give her the title of 'crone' – a new name, marking a new period of (spiritual) life.

Of course, the figure of the crone is often seen, in pagan and neo-pagan contexts, in accompaniment with the Maiden and the Mother, offering a 'feminine trinity' in contrast to the more traditionally depicted Holy Trinity of Father, Son and Holy Spirit. Although occasionally the Holy Spirit is figured as female, the references to Father and Son are decidedly masculine. However, as Elizabeth Johnson notes, 'simply identifying the spirit with the stereotypical "feminine" leaves the total symbol of God fundamentally unreformed and boxes actual women into a restrictive ideal'.[36] Johnson goes on to argue that using metaphors for God and the Trinity coined from women and women's experiences would be a boon to theology. Some feminists, both inside and outside of the Christian tradition, have found great spiritual resource in this more explicitly feminine imagery.[37] This feminine trinity is frequently associated with the cycle of the moon. Thus, the new moon is associated with menarche as a girl becomes the maiden with her first period. The new moon represents the beginning of a new stage, full of potential. The waxing and full moons can be understood as a symbol of pregnancy – a time of growth and increase, as well as wholeness and fulfilment. This is the part of the lunar cycle associated with motherhood. The final part of the cycle is then the waning moon – the end of the cycle, having passed through phases of potential and new life. This is the phase of the crone. And yet this phase is not merely a slow death; it is not a giving up. Rather, this is a new beginning in and of itself as well.[38] Ruether notes:

> The monthly cycle is particularly a ritual cycle of women, since it links the lunar cycle of the moon with the monthly cycle of their bodies by which their powers of life making wax and wane. This may include a new moon celebration, as well as some way by which women mark the monthly processes of their bodies. In patriarchal culture, menstruation [and by extension menopause], the ebb time of the cycle after it peaks in ovulation, has been particularly turned into misogynist contempt for women's bodies. Thus new ways of affirming the period of bleeding and cleansing of the body from the old potency, in order to make way for the new, are particularly good for women.[39]

New ways of affirming these bodies that bleed is necessary, particularly for those 'invisible women' who, in their post-menopausal lives, are both the backbone of the Christian faith, and at ever increased danger of being sidelined and ignored.

Feminist Liturgies for Menopause

I admit to a long fascination with feminist liturgies. I have collected a number of texts that include creative and powerful prayers and actions written for all stages of women's lives including menarche, pregnancy, miscarriage, divorce and menopause to name but a few. And yet I have never experienced these liturgies! I have a vast collection of potential liturgical resources aimed at women that have never been in a spiritual community in which enacting these liturgies has been possible or desirable.

In my own work on theology and reproductive loss,[40] I discuss the significance of offering ritual markers beyond the standard pattern of birth, marriage and death that are covered by most Christian liturgical resources. Ritual markers such as liturgies can help to understand, frame and ease transitions. To women, who often articulate an embodied and concrete sense of knowing, embodied liturgical ritual can be essential to a flourishing spiritual life. Indeed, Jan Berry, in her work on women's rituals, notes that '[W]omen's ritual making is imaginative subversion, playing in the space between essentialism and determinism to create through bodily symbols and enactments a theo/alogy which speaks in and through and to the passages of their lives.'[41]

Of course, several feminist theological thinkers have offered liturgies and rituals that are focused on the experience of menopause. In her work on the theology and practices of feminist liturgical communities, Rosemary Radford Ruether offers a liturgy for croning which is for women who are past their child-bearing and child-rearing years, those who are menopausal or post-menopausal.[42] Similarly, in her *Book of Uncommon Prayer* Annie Heppenstall includes a set of prayers and actions entitled 'Waning Moon: A Blessing on the Menopause or on Becoming an Elder'.[43] Berry also touches upon the experience of menopause as one of a number of experiences that might prompt women to want to take control of their narrative of self and engage in ritual action as a mode of transformative practice that enables women to re-write themselves.[44]

I will draw on these extant liturgies, alongside the feminist reading of *The Life of the Virgin* and Slee's *The Book of Mary*, engaged with in this chapter, as I write a new feminist liturgy for croning. I reflect here Slee's own interest in feminist liturgies as well as the proposed liturgical use of the text of *The Life of the Virgin* which is historically attested.

The Liturgy of the Crone

A small group gather, at the invitation of the woman who is requesting this liturgy. It might be part of a celebration of a significant birthday or life event.

Opening Prayer	As the moon moves through its ebb and flow, we remember you, O God, who are unchanging. As the autumn leaves fall and the flowers die, we remember you, O God, who brings purpose to each season.

As the tide pulls back from the shore, we remember you, O God, who reveals treasures in all places.

May we be held in your steadfast hand, even as our world is one of change. Amen.

The Transition *A symbolic object or similar is brought before the gathered group.*	I bring this symbol of my life so far. I recognize in it my stories, my joys, my sorrows, my times of giving and my times of receiving.

All: Mother God we thank you for the life of N.

Sophia, Wisdom of God, I ask that you would be near me in this time of transition. As I move into this new phase, I pray that I would know your Wisdom at work in my life and my ministries.

The Reading *A member of the gathered group reads. This would also be a good opportunity to read a poem such as one from Slee's The Book of Mary.*	Do not fear, for I have redeemed you; I have called you by name, you are mine. When you pass through the waters, I will be with you; And through the rivers, they shall not overwhelm you When you walk through fire you shall not be burned. And the flame shall not consume you. (Isaiah 43.1b–2)

The New Name   As I pass through these waters and fires of
transition, echoing the beautiful changes of the
natural world, I accept and delight in my new
name of Crone. I commit myself to the guidance
and comfort of those younger than me, and to
the wisdom of age and experience that will be
my gift to the people of God. God, keep me
in intimate relationship with you, that I may
continue to seek to know you deeper each day.
Draw me into your likeness, that I may be like
your mother, who wept with longing to see your
face. Amen.

A member of the   Crone N., you are a wise woman indeed, may
group anoints her   you be anointed for the ministry ahead of you,
hands and head with   and may you be sister to Sophia, the Wisdom of
oil saying: God.

Closing Prayer   Our Mother who is within us
we celebrate your many names.
Your wisdom come; your will be done,
unfolding from the depths within us.
Each day you give us all that we need.
You remind us of our limits and we let go.
You support us in our power and we act with
courage.
For you are the dwelling place within us,
the empowerment around us
and the celebration among us,
now and for ever. Blessed be![45]

Conclusion

The person of Mary is a locus of profound creativity. Mary has long acted
as an imaginative cipher for the projection of cultural and societal norms
and fears. She has, in previous decades, been lifted to such great heights
that she serves as no helpful model for contemporary woman, idolized as
holy perfection, immaculate. She is similarly kept young in this imagination. Our images of Mary in art, in icons, and even in miraculous visions
is one of a young woman – often a young white woman – which plays
into our continued obsession with youth and its association with beauty

(which, of course, has strongly racialized elements to it as well). And yet, Mary is a woman who grows old. She is not a woman whose life ends when her child is no longer present in her life. She is 50 and likely menopausal when she witnesses his crucifixion, and then she goes on to lead the early church, occupying a place of significant authority in the Jerusalem church for the next 30 years. Where is this Mary in our art? Where is this Mary in our imagination? *The Life of the Virgin* gives us an opportunity to reclaim this older Mary and to draw her into the light once again, as a model for older women, and as an encouragement that the crone phase of our lives might be a period that is rich and potent. Far from being a slow death, this crone phase is a new beginning and, as the life of the older Mary demonstrates, one that can bring adventure, excitement, stability and opportunity. Inspired by this older Mary and by the poetic approach to theology that Slee engages in so well, I finish with a poem to Our Lady of hot flushes.

> Our Lady of hot flushes,
> pray for us now as we frantically flap
> at our reddened faces and pull our shirts away from
> our slick breasts.
> Pray for us as we daily remove
> our carefully chosen layers, revealing
> our sticky skin to the cooled air.
> Our Lady of hormonal transitions,
> give us cooling peace as we pray
> before the bedroom fan, turning our soft bodies to and fro
> in the gentle breeze.[46]

Notes

1 My title has been inspired and informed by Nicola Slee. See Nicola Slee, 'In Praise of God as Feisty Crone', *Fragments for Fractured Times: What Feminist Practical Theology Brings to the Table* (London: SCM Press, 2020), 255–8 and 'Christa, Crone', *Seeking the Risen Christa* (London: SPCK, 2011), 126.

2 For example, in my book *Broken Bodies: The Eucharist, Mary and the Body in Trauma Theology* (London: SCM Press, 2018) and in subsequent feminist theological scholarship I have undertaken such as 'The Voices of the Marys: Towards a Method in Feminist Trauma Theologies', in *Feminist Trauma Theologies: Body, Scripture and Church in Critical Perspective*, eds Karen O'Donnell and Katie Cross (London: SCM Press, 2020), 3–20, and 'Surviving Trauma at the Foot of the Cross', in *When Did We See You Naked? Jesus as a Victim of Sexual Abuse*, eds Jayme R. Reaves, David Tombs and Rocío Figueroa (London: SCM Press, 2021), 260–77.

3 Nicola Slee, *The Book of Mary* (London: SPCK, 2007) and her *Women's Faith Development: Patterns and Processes* (Aldershot: Ashgate, 2004).

4 Slee, *The Book of Mary*, vii.

5 Heather Walton, *Imagining Theology: Women, Writing and God* (Edinburgh: T&T Clark, 2007), 79.

6 Grace Jantzen, *Becoming Divine: Towards a Feminist Philosophy of Religion* (Manchester: Manchester University Press, 1998), 61.

7 See Slee's essay on 'Reading and Writing as Transformative Spiritual Practice', in *Fragments for Fractured Times*, 197–204.

8 Slee, *The Book of Mary*, 7.

9 Slee, *The Book of Mary*, 71.

10 Slee, *The Book of Mary*, 71.

11 These are the doctrines, as identified by the Roman Catholic Church, that Mary is the Mother of God, that she was Immaculately Conceived, that she is Perpetually Virgin, and that at the end of her life she was Assumed into heaven.

12 Stephen J. Shoemaker, *The Life of the Virgin: Maximus the Confessor* (New Haven: Yale University Press, 2012), 7.

13 Shoemaker, *The Life of the Virgin*, 161. Shoemaker includes an appendix that outlines the way in which the text is to be read across a liturgical year based on the annotations in one particular copy of the text.

14 Shoemaker, *The Life of the Virgin*, 22.

15 Shoemaker, *The Life of the Virgin*, 23.

16 Ally Kateusz, *Mary and Early Christian Women: Hidden Leadership* (New York: Palgrave Macmillan, 2019), 132.

17 Stephen J. Shoemaker, 'The Virgin Mary in the Ministry of Jesus and the Early Church According to the Earliest Life of the Virgin', *Harvard Theological Review* 98, no. 4 (2005): 441–67 (448).

18 Shoemaker, *The Life of the Virgin*, 128. There are various narratives about Mary's 'dormition' including *The Life of the Virgin*. 'Dormition' refers to the idea that instead of dying, Mary fell asleep (i.e. became dormant) and was assumed into heaven.

19 Hilary Mantel, 'Women over Fifty: The Invisible Generation: When I Was a Child, Older Women Ran the World', *The Guardian, G2* (4 August 2009): 9.

20 Shoemaker, *The Life of the Virgin*, 121.

21 Shoemaker, *The Life of the Virgin*, 125.

22 Kateusz, *Mary and Early Christian Women*, 131.

23 Kateusz, *Mary and Early Christian Women*, 131.

24 Shoemaker, *The Life of the Virgin*, 116.

25 Slee, *Women's Faith Development*, 61.

26 Abby Day, *The Religious Lives of Older Laywomen: The Last Active Anglican Generation* (Oxford: Oxford University Press, 2017), 6.

27 Day, *The Religious Lives of Older Laywomen*, 8.

28 Slee, *Women's Faith Development*, 63.

29 Slee, *Women's Faith Development*, 73.

30 Day, *The Religious Lives of Older Laywomen*, 17.

31 Shoemaker, 'The Virgin Mary in the Ministry of Jesus and the Early Church According to the Earliest Life of the Virgin', 128.

32 Traci A. Takahashi and Kay M. Johnson, 'The Menopause', *Medical Clinics of North America* 99, no. 3 (2015): 521–34 (521).

33 Rosemary Radford Ruether, *Women-Church: Theology and Practice of Feminist Liturgical Communities* (San Francisco: HarperCollins, 1985), 206.

34 Ruether, *Women-Church*, 206.

35 Ruether, *Women-Church*, 206.

36 Elizabeth A. Johnson, *She Who Is: The Mystery of God in Feminist Theological Discourse* (New York: Crossroad, 1992), 133.

37 For example, see Starhawk, *The Spiral Dance: A Rebirth of the Ancient Religion of the Goddess* (London: HarperCollins, 2011), and Melissa Raphael, *Introducing Thealogy: Discourse on the Goddess* (Sheffield: Sheffield Academic Press, 1998).

38 For powerful liturgies based on this lunar cycle, see Annie Heppenstall, *The Book of Uncommon Prayer* (Bury St Edmunds: Kevin Mayhew, 2015), 334–59.

39 Ruether, *Women-Church*, 115.

40 Karen O'Donnell, *The Dark Womb: Re-Conceiving Theology through Reproductive Loss* (London: SCM Press, 2022).

41 Jan Berry, *Ritual Making Women: Shaping Rites for Changing Lives* (London: Routledge, 2009), 224.

42 Ruether, *Women-Church*, 206.

43 Heppenstall, *The Book of Uncommon Prayer*, 352–9.

44 Berry, *Ritual Making Women*, 146–7.

45 Prayer by Miriam Therese Winter cited in Carolyn Riswold, 'Our Mother …', Patheos, 27 January 2014.

46 This is an original poem I have composed for this chapter. It is inspired by Slee's poems in *The Book of Mary*.

PART 3

The Praying Body

Christa has Bunions

Nicola Slee

Her knees aren't what they once were, either.
It hurts to kneel on the cold, ancient flagstones
where the flowers are ordered in tidy piles.
She prepares herself with a sharp intake of breath,
bending forwards to reach for an armful of lilies
and frothy gypsophila, working at the crossing
while the vicar and ministry team pray the office
in a side chapel, ahead of their meeting.
She might have joined them, though no-one asked her
and, besides, there is too much to do.
After the flowers, there is the sweeping and polishing.
Later, at home, she'll make a fruit cake for the fête.
She's been buying discounted chocolates
for the raffle for months, spreading the cost.
She'll need to check the coffee rota and remember
to tell the vicar about Hilda's daughter's lymphoma.
She'll pop round later with a cake and roses from the garden.
The vicar won't get round to visiting for weeks.

She's seen dozens of them come and go,
but throughout her long tenure at All Souls,
baking, cleaning and flower arranging have never
been rendered redundant. She eases herself up slowly,
regards her handiwork with a half-satisfied nod,
and heads on down the nave towards the kitchen.

9

Presiding Like a Woman:
Menstruating at the Altar

SHARON JAGGER

This is how we do it ... the carrying in our bodies the marks of the
  risen One
Seeing the light reflected in each other's eyes,
Seeing Her beauty mirrored in each one's softened face.[1]

When I was a teenager, at a time when women's ordination in the Church
of England seemed unlikely, I was told by my vicar that women could not
be priests because they menstruated. While the theological rationale was
never explained, the implication seemed to be that the priesthood – and its
symbolic life – requires protection from female menstrual blood. As Tina
Beattie argues (from a Catholic perspective), menstrual blood is a potent
bodily fluid 'with its powerful associations with pollution and disorder
in sacrificial religious systems'.[2] Male blood, on the other hand, is associated with sacrifice and atonement,[3] and the eucharist (or communion) is a
vital ritual in which this is symbolized. How can women preside over this
ritual if there is suspicion about the polluting powers of their biology?
In 'Presiding Like a Woman', Nicola Slee expresses a consciousness of
what women bring to the altar, not simply in the anticipation of a non-
hierarchical communal experience, but in a radical appeal to the female
body as a viable representation of the symbolic divine.[4] Elsewhere, Slee
argues that women may find it difficult to recognize their presence and
power in the church because of the absence of vital symbols and narratives that express femaleness as representative of the divine. Presiding *as*
a woman, then, involves visceral meaning-making, co-creation between
the female body and the altar. In this chapter, I explore the ways the
biological, fleshy and leaky presence of the woman priest enacting the
ritual of the eucharist is used to construct women as differently human
and, as a corresponding resistance to the menstrual taboo, the ways in
which women priests develop somatic theology to allow their bodies a
form of belonging. Based on my research with ordained women in the

Church of England,[5] I see the female body as troubled by the priesthood; equally, the woman priest's physical presence is a challenge to the symbol system within which the priesthood operates. Writing before the inclusion of women in the priesthood in the Church of England, William E. Phipps suggested there was doubt around the viability of women's corporeal presence in sacred space, arguing that the menstrual taboo needed to be eliminated before women could be fully accepted in a ritualistic role.[6] My research shows that, despite the increasing numbers of ordained women in the church, the doubt and the taboo have not been deconstructed. Feminist theory has excavated the symbolic foundations of sex and gender constructions to explain how women are pejoratively associated with the material and given powers to pollute,[7] which reproduces the gendered binary of immanence/transcendence; a woman priest who bleeds as she presides is a 'body out of place', to borrow from Sara Ahmed's exploration of situated bodies.[8] Menstruating while presiding at the altar triggers both revulsion and rebellion. The stories I have gathered from women priests show that pollution discourses attached to female biology still circulate within the church and impact on their belonging, but also that women priests are developing theological approaches to create new meanings within the eucharist that include, rather than exclude, the female body.

There is an interesting character in the *mise-en-scène* of the eucharist that is not often acknowledged as active in meaning-making: the altar itself. I am leaning on theorists who see the material world as made up of objects with biographies that possess ways of affecting us as we interact with them.[9] Sara Ahmed's discussion of the table explores how, when the table and the body coincide within a space, meaning-making becomes a two-way process.[10] In the case of the priest, the table has a biography that includes being consecrated – set aside for a special and holy purpose – and generates meaning for the bodies around it. Following Ahmed's argument, the altar is in contact with different forms of labour: bodies clean it, place cloths and objects on it, pray over it, and bless symbols upon it. These relationships with the altar vary. A woman who cleans it is not said to have powers to deconsecrate in this act (though within Ahmed's analysis she still has a phenomenological relationship with the altar). But a woman who presides over the eucharist, where the altar plays its part, can attract the belief that she has polluting powers that call into doubt the status of the table. Ahmed explains: 'what we can tell through [the table's] biography, is also what allows us to tell a larger story: a story not only of "things" changing hands but of how things come to matter by taking shape through and in the labour of others'.[11] The labour of priested women is where the story of the altar is changed.

As I will show, the meanings given to the altar are tactically employed in the rejection of women priests, a dynamic most acutely active when menstrual blood is present. To mitigate the pollution discourse, there needs to be a shift in how blood is perceived in the eucharist, but also how the altar performs its consecrated affect. If objects are shaped by work, as Ahmed suggests, then the altar is shaped by the priestly work done around and upon it and, equally, the interaction with the table is part of identity-making for the priest. The difficulty for women priests is that the space in which the altar stands has been shaped by the assumed maleness of the priested body. 'If spaces extend bodies, then we could say that spaces extend the bodies that "tend" to inhabit them' according to Ahmed.[12] Women perform the same actions as their male colleagues, in partnership with the altar and the eucharist symbols of bread and wine, yet their bodies generate different meanings that are ill-matched to the ritual. While the women priests in my research discuss the need to reconstruct the eucharistic symbols to align with the female (bleeding) body, there is also a need for the altar itself to break free from its affective powers that are drawn from the masculine paradigm.

The View from Liminal Space

My research has led me to understand the female priest in the Church of England as a 'liminal identity' operating from a position between ordination and unequivocal acceptance as priest.[13] The Church of England operates a dual structure (previously known as the 'two integrities') that allows parishes to avoid the ministry of women priests.[14] This structure holds women priests in liminality, because regardless of the ordination ritual their status as priests is structurally contested. Given this position within the structure of the church, how can the menstrual taboo be overcome? I interviewed 26 women priests who shared stories that reveal a continuous negotiation between the female body and the Christian symbol system, most dramatically at the eucharistic table.[15] Some women priests have embarked on an exploration of the differentiated meaning of male and female blood, arising from their experiences of being framed as polluting and with the wrong body for the purpose of representation at the altar. Somatic thinking – using the body to access the symbolic – was a strong theme in my research. Women priests often read their bodies theologically. Using their menstruating bodies as a point of contact with the symbols of the eucharist as they preside, ordained women attempt to create a female ontology of the priesthood, a route for some to *in persona Christi* that is at once radical within a masculine paradigm and fundamentally necessary should women priests ever be liberated from their structural and theological liminality. Establishing a relationship between menstrual blood and the eucharist symbols, therefore, is a feminist theological project. Alison Green, for example, whose writing is underpinned by an Irigarayan account of sexual difference, works to realign the symbolic with the difference that women priests bring to the altar.[16] This realignment work is also the focus of Nicola Slee's search for the feminine in christology, coalescing around the physical presence of the woman priest at the altar in ritual motion, drawing the gaze to the potential of feminine meaning-making within the eucharist itself.[17] I do not intend to rehearse these theological insights, but I will highlight some of the striking stories shared with me about menstruating at the altar to open the dialogue about how the female body is made abject through leveraging the symbolism of the eucharist. This discussion invites the question of whether female priests are required to overcome their biology (a Beauvoirian insistence) to gain parity with male priests,[18] or whether the eucharistic symbols themselves need to represent and be represented by femaleness (an Irigarayan need to reveal sexual difference, rather than mask it) which involves a fundamental shift in what is meant by body and blood in the eucharist.

Women Priests and 'Involuntary Witchcraft'

Theological reasoning for the rejection of women's ordination often focuses on their bodily difference; that is, the notion that women are unable to represent the maleness of Christ is particularly irresolvable.[19] How these theological beliefs manifest in behaviours towards women priests as they preside at the eucharist reveals an underlying fear of the female body's polluting powers. Some of the stories told to me by ordained women cluster around the overt ways they are rejected as priests presiding over the eucharist, generating for them feelings of shame and anger as they are dislocated from the symbolic. The dubiety of female belonging in the priesthood is made more acute when they bleed at the altar. Alice,[20] an anglo-catholic priest, believes that many women priests feel uncomfortable and 'wrong' when they preside while menstruating. She says her first thoughts were 'we shouldn't be doing this ... I never thought about menstruation so much since starting this process [of becoming of priest]'. Her role as priest brings into focus how her female body is problematized within the Christian symbol system. Suzanne, also an anglo-catholic priest, describes being taken aback when she was newly ordained, when her friends asked if she presided at the altar while menstruating. Becoming a priest had thrown this biological function into a previously hidden symbolic paradigm – puzzling and irritating for Suzanne, who dismissed the notion of avoiding the altar when she menstruated as ludicrous. Another priest, Polly, who identifies as middle-of-the-road theologically, articulates the notion of fear and loathing of the female – a concept explored by feminist philosopher Julia Kristeva in her discussion of how women are made abject.[21] Polly explains how she views male clergy who recoil from the female body acting out the role of the priest: 'what they're really scared about, it's primitive in these blokes, it's about you menstruating in the sanctuary'. Moreover, Polly has learned that male clergy who oppose women's ordination believe that her presence as a priest deconsecrates the altar – an example of how table and priest are made to act upon each other, as Ahmed describes (and both the woman priest and the altar are diminished in the encounter).[22]

This is an extraordinary position for women priests. They are ordained yet made abject. The church gives them authority to preside, yet they are given powers by some to pollute in the act of presiding. These discourses have material implications for women priests. One ordained woman told me she was turned down for a parish job because clergy in neighbouring parishes believe the altar's consecrated status would be compromised by a female presiding. The cost is also borne in the emotional economy when the rejection is in the public realm. Stories in my research show that congregants and male clergy sometimes openly refuse the bread and wine that is blessed by a woman priest, a potent and outward sign of the fear of the polluting powers of the female. This act of refusal must be managed on a personal level by women priests. Alice told me that 'they [some members of her congregation] won't receive communion from me. I notice it. Everyone in church comes up and they don't, and I feel it, I notice it.' Sometimes, the theological distaste is dramatic and performative. Karen, an ordained woman from a middle-of-the-road church, tells the story of a male priest physically leaving the room because a female priest blessed the bread and wine for the eucharist. It seems to me that this is a recoiling from the physical bodily presence of a woman who is acting as priest that cannot be dismissed as a symbolic gesture only – a refusal to ingest woman-blessed bread and wine is a physical reaction to a visceral fear of pollution.

These stories speak of a deep fear and loathing of the female in ritual, as though there is something communicably unholy about bread and wine handled ritualistically by a woman. This is one of the most revealing examples of what Julia Kristeva termed the 'radical evil' of the female and Mary Douglas's 'involuntary witchcraft' projected on to women.[23] Douglas's anthropological discussion about how the female body is constructed as possessing innate polluting powers explores the use of ritual to alleviate this pollution, usually cleansing rituals that purify bodily functions, and women's own involuntary negative powers. Yet, in the case of the eucharist, the ritual itself – and the symbol system that forms it – constructs the female body as having powers of pollution. Those who do not accept women as priests and see them as unable to deliver the sacraments reproduce a tautological cycle, attempting to protect the ritual from a source of pollution that the symbolic system has itself generated. Women priests are aware that this Kristevan radical evil is placed on them.

Alice, as an anglo-catholic priest, is attuned to specific approaches to the symbolism of the eucharist and is aware of the pejorative meaning her body attracts within ritual. Talking about the controversies of women at the altar, she is sarcastic. 'How powerful are we? That by our very presence we can taint. By our very presence. How powerful are we?' Alice is overtly challenging the dynamic built into the symbolic system whereby the female body, as Kristeva puts it in her discussion of abjection, has 'wily' powers.[24] Two powers, writes Kristeva, are attempting to divide out social positioning: 'One of them, the masculine, apparently victorious, confesses through its very relentlessness against the other, the feminine, that it is threatened by an asymmetrical, wily, uncontrollable power ... That other sex, the feminine, becomes synonymous with a radical evil that is to be suppressed.'[25]

The lived experience of women priests generates the sense of needing to overcome wily and evil femaleness. As Ahmed's notion of 'bodies out of place' indicates, the framing of women priests' bodies as an ill-fit with the symbolic is accompanied by the discourse of uncleanness.[26] Because the bodies of priests are perceived to be under constant surveillance (by parishioners and by God) there is an element to the priesthood that demands self-regulation of all priestly bodies, but some bodies are 'out of place' when they stray from the idealization of a priest – through pregnancy for example and as they menstruate.[27] Helping to create this ill-fit is the meaning given to the symbols of the eucharist.

The Eucharistic Symbols and the Female Body

Two approaches can be taken in exploring the way the eucharist problematizes the female body. One view is that the ritual is (mis)construed as male by the emphasis on masculine symbols, and this presents an opportunity for the woman priest to readjust symbolic meaning to align with her bodily presence (making the meaning fit the somatic reality so that female blood, for example, has a symbolic value within the eucharist). Or it may be that the eucharist is fundamentally androcentric (and that Christ, in the context of the ritual, is unable to be perceived beyond the male incarnation), in which case women's bodies are necessarily at odds with the symbols of the eucharist. To answer the question of why women's bodies are contested at the altar, some commentators argue that the eucharist is indeed deeply androcentric. According to Alison Green, the eucharist is a window into the masculinization of the priesthood and the masculinization of the detail of the ritual itself, to the extent that women's bodies destabilize the symbolism that is laid down in the Christian psyche.[28] She writes, 'the male function of sacrifice makes it psychologically just about impossible for female priests to preside at the eucharist'.[29] This is the discomfort that women priests like Karen, Polly and Alice identify as they talk about rejection at the altar when they preside.

The psychological barrier Green examines revolves round what is stored in the symbols of the eucharist. Catherine Bell's work on ritual helps us to understand the eucharist as a key site for women's other-ing.[30] She critiques anthropologist Clifford Geertz's identification of two elements that synchronize in ritual: ethos (moods and motivations) and worldview (religious belief). The eucharistic symbolic objects (and the accompanying imagery and language) have within them patterns and codes that reveal ethos and worldview, modelling a version of what is played out in social reality. If the ethos and worldview built into the eucharistic ritual are androcentric, the female priest is problematized. Rituals can be either fluid and open to absorb changes in the social world, or they can be closed and static, at odds with the changing social world. In the two-way process, rituals can also attempt to keep the social world in the same state of stasis. Susan Shooter suggests the eucharist is a closed symbolic system and that the changes required to recalibrate the ethos and worldview are outside the theological framework in which the ritual stands.[31] In other words, it remains symbolically masculine, even when attempts are made to introduce feminine meaning that allows the female body to represent and be represented. This does not bode well for women priests who bleed female blood that is constructed as polluting. What is stored in the symbolic and ritualistic is important in how a woman priest occupies the presiding role, since these signs either reveal dispositions in the real world, or they reflect back into it.[32] If the eucharist, and the wider symbolic system in Christianity, is unable to store anything but that which is produced by an androcentric worldview, women and their bodies are subjugated both symbolically and in the real world, since the two are reflected in each other. So, while I have argued that abjection is generated within the priesthood itself, it is rooted in social attitudes. Taking this argument a step further, women priests experience abjection on behalf of all women.

Menstruating at the Altar

The discussion above explores the context in which menstrual blood has a relationship to the altar. A question is raised by Slee that underscores the importance of this enquiry. If the premise of the eucharist is the body and blood of Christ as redemption, she asks, 'what does that have to say to the life-giving blood of women and the bodies of women who bear life, through agony, into the world?'[33] It is this gendered understanding of blood that generates the fundamental othering of female bodies. Because of the meaning some theological positions give to femaleness, the altar is drawn in as active confirmation of the disruptive presence of women priests. Menstruation magnifies this troubled relationship with the eucharistic table. Green sees this problematizing of the female body presiding at the eucharist as derived from the pivotal concept of sacrifice within the Christian symbol system: this is male sacrifice, the spilling of male blood.[34] Female blood is framed in opposing terms. During our interview, Alice described how she is aware of the symbolic implications of gendered blood but is committed to downplaying the association with the maleness of Jesus and his blood sacrifice: 'I don't think on the cross Jesus was busy bleeding men's blood. I don't think there was any "this is man's blood. None of you dirty women, this is clean man blood."' This is not masking the duality that exists between the symbolic values of male and female blood but is a challenge to it. Alice is challenging how male and female blood are made to symbolize purity and pollution, respectively. Challenging the masculinity of the symbol of the blood sacrifice becomes a fundamental question about the meaning inherent within the ritual of the eucharist. Can female blood find a way into the symbolism of the ritual and free women priests from the abjection they experience?

The argument reaches back to the establishment of a masculinized Jewish, and then Christian, monotheism that is based on a blood covenant with the male and culminating for Christians with Jesus' blood covenant.[35] This long history is important to acknowledge. Nancy Jay explores the anthropology of ritual and concludes that sacrificial activity is an almost exclusively male practice designed to mitigate female pollution manifested in the reproductive functions of the body.[36] In this light, the eucharist can be understood as the maintenance of this male dominance through the ritualization of male sacrifice – the cosmic and enduring Father/Son continuation. By putting this together with theories of how feminine divinities were overrun by the masculinized God, particularly the monotheism of the Abrahamic faiths, it is possible to build a broad and slowly evolving picture of female exclusion from the sacred.[37] But psychoanalytical discussions also point to the male anxiety about women, also articulated through masculine blood sacrifice.[38] The male monopoly of the ritual enacting male blood sacrifice (and I see this as one motivation for the continued resistance to women's ordination) means that men own the re-enactment of a male death, as conduits for the sacramental, and reproduce the underlying anxiety of female pollution.[39] For Green, there is a lingering fear and resentment of embodied women focused on the eucharistic ritual: 'Is sacrifice solely the prerogative of men, an act so intimately associated with the male psyche and with male-dominated society that women neither have place in it, nor should desire to, since it perpetuates the male remedy for having been born of woman and upholds the patriarchal social structure?'[40]

The eucharist, then, can be seen as a male ritual re-enacting male sacrifice to cleanse the original sin passed down from Eve through women – Eve's creation being the first mythical act of female bodily subjugation to the male.[41] The male blood sacrifice seated within atonement theology is, according to Shooter, part of a set of discourses that produces violence against the bodies of women. 'The intimate violence of the cross preached down the centuries has … wrought damage on the bodies of women and children in the private sphere.'[42] So, while there are controversies about representation and femininity, the fundamental symbolism runs deeper, touching on primal male fear of the female. The difference between the male and female bodily presence is most acute in the framing of male blood as heroic and sacrificial and female blood as polluting.

We have, in part, inherited the menstrual taboo from ancient Hebrew purity laws and there is evidence of restrictions on menstruants in the Christian church from the third century.[43] Returning to the work of Douglas, whose anthropological study of the concept of purity gives us a sense of the ubiquity of purifying rituals, impurity is that which departs from the symbolic order. The symbolic order woven into the Christian story is most profoundly manifested at the altar – and Ahmed's discussion about the active table brings this to life.[44] A conundrum is created as women priests, whose bodies are the source of earthy sexuality made manifest through menstruation, are now performing the ritual intended to cleanse and uphold the symbolic order. As Kristeva explores in her essay on abjection, the purity laws of the Hebrew Bible are linked to access to the holy parts of the Temple and this systemic purity is extended to the church's most important ritual.[45] That the symbols of atonement offered by Christ do not purify the woman's body, especially as she menstruates, is suggestive of the alienation that women experience in relation to their place in the salvific order.

The accrual of meaning around the female priest's body that makes it so different from that of the male priest, especially in the biological process of menstruation, is something Melinda, an anglo-catholic priest, suggests is used against the woman priest. Moreover, the discourse of the female body as polluting is not, in her experience, hidden or unconscious, but part of an active understanding of the female body at the altar; women's bodies in the priesthood become public property. Melinda is aware that where menstruation is perceived to spoil the sacraments, it requires disclosure of when female blood is flowing. She explains:

This came up in a conversation with the bishop recently, but there is this symbolism to do with menstruation and blood and the sanctuary. If you ask people who are men who object to women priests, that is still a real sort of stumbling point which is fascinating. This woman priest ... went to do cover somewhere where they'd never had a woman before and just before the service she went into the vestry and found the church warden going through her handbag. She said, 'what do you think you're doing?' or something like that, and he said, 'well, I was just checking to see if you were carrying tampons, because if you're menstruating, I won't be able to take communion from you'. It's quite a good story, isn't it?

Melinda knows this story is potent, it is a 'good' story because it encapsulates the fear, loathing and abjection that menstruation causes, not simply in everyday circumstances, but specifically in the context of the eucharist. It also highlights the entitlement to knowledge of the woman priest's body so pollution can be avoided. The 'stumbling point' of menstruation may be at the core of some of the theological objections to women's priesthood (as I was led to believe in my youth), even if this is no longer an overt part of the argument. Yet women priests are the ones who must continue to negotiate the lived experience of recoiling from their bodies and manage the discourses of pollution and shame that menstruation attracts. The anxiety of the church warden in Melinda's story is a result of the incurable nature of the pollution of the menstruating female body. Again, the eucharist, rather than perceived as a ritual of cleansing, is seen as vulnerable to, and therefore becoming a carrier of, female pollution.

The recoiling from women priests and their habit of menstruating while presiding offers an opportunity to challenge masculine anxiety around female bodily functions. Given the understanding that male blood sacrifice is deeply separated from female bleeding, menstruation may be a useful subversion of the masculine symbolic system. Alice has a rebellious thought as she talks about menstruating at the altar: 'I don't go around saying "right, oh look at the diary, I'm going to wear my white alb and no pants". Although sometimes, sometimes, when I get on one, what if?' Alice's story is a fantasy of menstrual rebellion at the altar, of staining the white alb, and is a deliberate invoking of the pollution taboo with the purpose of deconstructing it and re-valuing blood in the symbolic – female life-affirming blood balancing male sacrificial blood. Breanne Fahs, writing about resistance to the menstrual taboo, sees significance in the menstrual stain, which she explores as a confrontation with death through abjection, and a disruption of the narrative of women as shades (felt as lack/absence).[46] The menstrual stain is a chance to reveal a more powerful, violent female presence, and for Kristeva this is at the crux of female abjection. 'It thus becomes a fascinating semantic crossroads, the propitious place for abjection where death and femininity, murder and procreation, cessation of life and vitality, all come together.'[47] The symbolic death the menstrual stain represents disrupts the male blood sacrifice played out on the altar. In asking 'what if?' Alice is provoking a symbolic usurpation of the dominance of male blood. The menstrual stain on the alb is the answer to the male blood sacrifice on purely female terms, which simultaneously challenges the abjection that women priests experience. The notion of menstrual blood having symbolic currency dovetails with Slee's exploration of how birthing fluids are mapped on to the sacrificed body of Jesus – for Slee, the blood and water that we are told poured from the wounds ties the female reproductive body into the Christian symbol system.[48] Similarly, Alice is seeking to leverage the meaning of a cycle of life and death that is played out through bodies that bleed.

Alice's fantasy free-bleed could symbolically close the circle of male blood sacrifice as a sign for death and female vital blood as a sign for life. Her vision of bleeding through on to her alb forces menstrual blood (her violent presence) into the symbolic either to be purified, or to affect meaning. However, the rehabilitation of female bleeding is not an easy task. Fahs sums up Kristeva's discussion thus:

> Kristeva ultimately suggests that theorizing about something as abject as menstrual blood and menstrual stains can only lead to terror itself; short of uprooting the patriarchal (and psychoanalytic) claims about women's bodily fluids as an inherent signifier of horror and death, we are left only with partial language, traces, shadows, hauntings, slight possibilities, hints, and suggestions at the margin.[49]

Women's bodies are a direct challenge to the symbolism at the altar, yet this challenge is forced to the edges. There are also implications for how a post-menopausal woman is framed and how trans men and women might be differently articulated bodily with the symbolic.[50] Are these bodies less or more polluting?[51] Even if there is no *a priori* pollution perceived in menstruation, the eucharist, and the altar on which it is performed, creates a boundary that defines and projects polluting power on to the female, maintaining the female as different and other. So female bodily functions are part of the narrative that supports the male as transcendent and the female as immanent. Alice tries to find a parallel pollutant from the male body but, as she says, 'there isn't anything comparable. Male priest ejaculate. Wet dreams?' Alice is searching for an equivalent involuntary leakiness in male biology (that hints at regulations concerning emissions in Leviticus 15 that apply to both men and women) that might impact on their relationship with the altar. However, the conclusion is that bodily pollution at the altar is a profoundly female problem, and that male sexuality and emissions are not conceived as symbolic or material pollution *per se* for a priest. Teresa Berger does make a case for the anxiety around male nocturnal emissions in relation to liturgy and ritual and argues that, historically at least, both male and female body fluids were seen as problematic in the liturgical context.[52] The point for Alice is that such anxieties are gendered because menstruation is constructed as a reason not to receive bread and wine from a woman at the altar. Menstruation and the blood that disrupts the boundary of the material body and the social body is made the sign of sexual difference – and this becomes the element that is so threatening. Kristeva identifies the source of such ideas of pollutions as the fundamental fragility of the symbolic system.[53] This is an important idea, since female priests need to make their bodies fit the symbolic system, but it poses a dilemma. Is it a choice between preserving the symbolic system in its frailty and remaining outside it, or changing the symbolic to make the female belong as subject, risking damage to what is already fragile? In other words, if menstrual blood had parity with male blood in the symbol system, would the eucharist lose its ritual significance and become unrecognizable as the Lord's Supper? Is it better, then, for menstruating priests to simply manage their abjection?

Returning to the question of whether female blood can find a place in the symbolic, some interviewees in my research do attempt to turn abjection on its head when they reassess the symbolic meaning attached to their bodies. Menstruation and the female body bring something symbolically significant to the ritual that bolsters its meaning rather than polluting it. Melinda sees this potential for a symbolic rebellion as she weaves together the blood sacrifice that is male and the female blood of menstruation as another form of suffering.[54] More profoundly still, Melinda suggests there may be a viable theology that develops eucharistic symbolism derived from female bleeding:

> And there is something strange for me as well, or something meaningful to me celebrating mass while I'm menstruating. I've never talked about this to anybody else. But there's something about the whole kind of sense of sacrifice, suffering, blood that sort of links together. I think I noticed as a layperson at mass that there is something quite powerful and female about that. There's probably feminist theology on this, mass as some sort of menstruation envy.

It is possible, then, for women priests to imagine how their bodies are symbolically in harmony with the ritual of the eucharist outside the masculine paradigm that defines the female body as problematic. Melinda's statement also invites us to imagine that if men bled in a monthly cycle of fertility, there would be a symbolic celebration of such blood in ritual. Shame is not associated with masculine signs. Melinda sees the eucharistic ritual potentially as a sublimation of male envy of fertility in women, and this taps into the exploration of how myth and art have become ways of imagining the male ability to procreate.[55] This envy may contribute to the fear and sense of danger that is generated by women's bodies at the altar. If there is power attached to the symbols of fertility and fecundity, then treating such signs as polluting diminishes the source of power. As Jay argues, nullifying female power enables the continuation of 'the power of sacrifice as a ritual instrument for establishing and maintaining an enduring male-dominated social order'.[56] Weaving menstruation into the symbolic is therefore subversive and potentially liberating for women priests. Melinda is retrieving the symbolic power by disrupting the symbol of male blood through reference to her menstrual blood. The rebellion against the menstrual taboo in ritual that both Melinda and Alice discuss may open the symbolic realm to possibilities of meanings that go beyond the androcentric male heroic blood sacrifice. The deconstruction of the heroic male christology is part of Slee's quest to (re)reveal the Christa, whereby the focus is shifted to community rather than hierarchy.[57] The importance of this project cannot be overstated. Eliminating the taboo, as Phipps argues,[58] is required to ensure women priests are not made abject and involves a radical overhaul of how menstrual blood relates to the eucharist and the altar.

Conclusion

My research suggests that women priests remain aware of the doubt their bodies create when they preside at the altar as priests. The stories they tell about how they feel about menstruating and how they have experienced the taboo still at work indicate that women priests carry a projected suspicion about their priestly status. Women are still viewed as somatically disconnected from the divine in multiple ways. For theologians such as Green, an Irigarayan search for the feminine in the divine offers a way of mapping the female body on to the eucharistic symbols. The blood that originates from the uterus (either materially or symbolically) can be semiotically (and semantically) about life-giving essence and about the maternal qualities of God. In light of my research, I am left with concerns that the bleeding female body not only remains hierarchically compromised, but that the menstrual taboo, leveraging theological discourse, serves to undermine the subjectivity of women priests. Yet resistance takes place, and some women priests are plotting a far more radical path because their liminality forces them to do so. The contradictions with which women priests contend on an everyday basis are most visible when their bodies are constructed as a destructive element within the eucharist. They are ordained as priests, yet they are vulnerable to being perceived as possessing involuntary powers of pollution. To menstruate and preside at the eucharist is made into a subversive act because of the ways women are alienated from the Christian symbol system. I also wonder how the menstruating priest can hope to have her blood made representative of something divine while she remains in structural liminality in the Church of England. In her liturgical poem 'Confession for Good Friday', Slee's response to the abhorring of women's menstrual blood is a plea: 'Christa, forgive us.'[59] The appeal is to a female cosmic Christ who shares in the harm done to women's subjectivity by making female blood a source of pollution and, by their bodily presence, deconsecrating powers. While the meaning-making at the symbolic level underpins social processes and should therefore be scrutinized and challenged, I want to end by drawing attention once again to how the Church of England's structural arrangements endlessly reproduce notions of women as differently human with the ability to pollute, spoil and deconsecrate. If theological interpretations based on the abjection of the immanent female are protected, given parity and legitimized by the church, then I am unsure how female blood can find its way on to the altar.

Notes

1 Nicola Slee, 'Presiding Like a Woman', in *Presiding Like a Woman: Feminist Gesture for Christian Assembly*, eds Nicola Slee and Stephen Burns (London: SPCK, 2010), 8.

2 Tina Beattie, *God's Mother, Eve's Advocate* (London: Continuum, 2002), 195.

3 Breanne Fahs, *Out for Blood: Essays on Menstruation and Resistance* (Albany: State University of New York, 2016); Alison Green, 'Priest, Blood, Sacrifice: Re-Membering the Maternal Divine', *Feminist Theology* 18, no. 1 (2009): 11–28.

4 Slee, 'Presiding Like a Woman', 26.

5 Sharon Jagger, 'The Dialectic of Belonging: Resistances and Subversions of Women Priests in the Church of England' (University of York, 2019).

6 William E. Phipps, 'The Menstrual Taboo in the Judeo-Christian Tradition', *Journal of Religion and Health* 19, no. 4 (1980): 298–303.

7 For example, Mary Douglas, *Purity and Danger: An Analysis of Concepts of Pollution and Taboo* (London: Routledge, 2002); Julia Kristeva, *Powers of Horror: An Essay on Abjection* (New York: Columbia University Press, 1982).

8 Sara Ahmed, 'Embodying Strangers', in *Body Matters: Feminism, Textuality, Corporeality*, eds Anne Horner and Anne Keane (Manchester: Manchester University Press), 85–96.

9 For example, Bruno Latour, *Reassembling the Social: An Introduction to Actor Network Theory* (Oxford: Oxford University Press, 2005); Karen Barad, 'What Flashes Up: Theological-Political-Scientific Fragments', in *Entangled Worlds: Religion, Science, and New Materialisms*, eds Catherine Keller and Mary Jane Rubenstein (New York: Fordham University Press, 2017), 21–88.

10 Sara Ahmed, 'Orientations Matter', in *New Materialisms: Ontology, Agency and Politics*, eds Diana Coole and Samantha Frost (Durham: Duke University Press, 2010), 234–57.

11 Ahmed, 'Orientations Matter', 243.

12 Ahmed, 'Orientations Matter', 250.

13 Victor Turner, *The Ritual Process: Structure and Anti-Structure* (London: Transaction Publishers, 2008).

14 For an explanation of this structure, see Monica Furlong, ed., *Act of Synod – Act of Folly?* (London: SCM Press, 1998).

15 The make-up of the cohort of interviewees was significant: more than half were anglo-catholic. These women were more likely to be confronted with objections about their sex that revolved around ontology rather than authority. Eucharistic doctrines, such as *in persona Christi*, were also more likely to require some negotiation. I argue that the 'candle' continuum (how priests identify from conservative evangelical through to anglo-catholic) has a significant impact on women priests' bodily experience at the altar, and how and why they experience rejection when they preside.

16 Alison Green, *A Theology of Women's Priesthood* (London: SPCK, 2009). Luce Irigaray, a feminist philosopher, has argued that sexual difference is masked in a Western cultural context and that 'feminine' with a masculine paradigm is a mirror to the male, with woman being framed as 'other of the same'. Revealing sexual difference, Irigaray argues, ultimately means women being able to represent,

and be represented by, the feminine divine. See Luce Irigaray, 'Divine Women', in *French Feminists on Religion: A Reader*, eds Morny Joy, Kathleen O'Grady and Judith Poxon (London: Routledge, 2002), 40–8.

17 Nicola Slee, *Seeking the Risen Christa* (London: SPCK, 2011), 42.

18 Simone de Beauvoir, in *The Second Sex* (London: Jonathan Cape, 2009), famously expounds the need to move beyond biological difference to achieve equality between the sexes.

19 For example, see Jonathan Baker, ed., *Consecrated Women? A Contribution to the Women Bishops Debate* (Norwich: Canterbury Press, 2004).

20 Pseudonyms are used throughout.

21 Julia Kristeva, *Powers of Horror: An Essay on Abjection* (New York: Columbia University Press, 1982).

22 Ahmed, 'Orientations Matter', 254.

23 Kristeva, *Powers of Horror*, 70; Douglas, *Purity and Danger*, 6–7.

24 Kristeva, *Powers of Horror*, 70.

25 Kristeva, *Powers of Horror*, 70.

26 Ahmed, 'Embodying Strangers', 86.

27 Nigel Peyton and Caroline Gatrell, *Managing Clergy Lives: Obedience, Sacrifice, Intimacy* (London: Bloomsbury, 2013).

28 Alison Green, 'Being and Becoming: How the Woman Presider Enriches Our Sacred Symbols', in *Presiding Like a Woman*, eds Slee and Burns, 102–11.

29 Green, 'Being and Becoming', 106.

30 Catherine Bell, *Ritual Theory and Practice* (New York: Oxford University Press, 1992), 26.

31 Susan Shooter, 'How Feminine Participation in the Divine Might Renew the Church and its Leadership', *Feminist Theology* 22, no. 2 (2014): 173–85.

32 Bell, *Ritual Theory and Practice*, 26.

33 Slee, *Seeking the Risen Christa*, 68.

34 Green, *A Theology of Women's Priesthood*, 145.

35 Gerda Lerner, *The Creation of Patriarchy* (New York: Oxford University Press, 1986); Leonie Archer, '"In Thy Blood Live": Gender and Ritual in the Judaeo-Christian Tradition', in *Through the Devil's Gateway: Women, Religion and Taboo*, ed. Alison Joseph (London: SPCK, 1990), 22–49.

36 Nancy Jay, 'Sacrifice as Remedy for Having Been Born of Woman', in *Women, Gender, Religion: A Reader*, ed. Elizabeth Castelli (New York: Palgrave Macmillan, 2001), 174–94.

37 Lerner, *The Creation of Patriarchy*; Joan Engelsman, *The Feminine Dimension of the Divine: A Study of Sophia and Feminine Images in Religion*, 2nd edn (Wilmette: Chiron Publications, 1994).

38 Green, *A Theology of Women's Priesthood*, 149.

39 Jay, 'Sacrifice as Remedy for Having Been Born of Woman', 174.

40 Green, *A Theology of Women's Priesthood*, 150.

41 Lisa Isherwood and Elizabeth Stuart, *Introducing Body Theology* (Sheffield: Sheffield Academic Press, 1998).

42 Shooter, 'How Feminine Participation in the Divine Might Renew the Church and its Leadership', 177.

43 Phipps, 'The Menstrual Taboo in the Judeo-Christian Tradition', 300.

44 Ahmed, 'Orientations Matter'.

45 Kristeva, *Powers of Horror*, 102.

46 Fahs, *Out for Blood*, 38.

47 Kristeva, *Powers of Horror*, 96.

48 Slee, *Seeking the Risen Christa*, 19.

49 Fahs, *Out for Blood*, 39.

50 Interestingly, while there is a taboo that makes menstruation a pollutant, it is used to draw boundaries around the category of woman, as reflected in controversies around how trans women who do not menstruate are placed in liminality.

51 See Sarah Frank, 'Queering Menstruation: Trans and Non-Binary Identity and Body Politics', *Sociological Inquiry* 90, no. 2 (2020): 371–404.

52 Teresa Berger, *Gender Differences and the Making of Liturgical History: Lifting a Veil on Liturgy's Past* (Farnham: Ashgate, 2011), 98.

53 Kristeva, *Powers of Horror*, 26.

54 Following Melinda's train of thought, one might also be drawn to the notion of a type of salvific process in how female anger is nearer to the surface during menses. At the same time, and without wishing to universalize this type of experience, I argue we need to resist the cultural habit of diminishing female anger by using menstruation as a masking device.

55 Rosi Braidotti, 'Mothers, Monsters and Machines', in *Writing on the Body: Female Embodiment and Feminist Theory*, eds Karen Conboy, Nadia Medina and Sarah Stanbury (New York: Columbia University Press, 1997), 59–79.

56 Jay, 'Sacrifice as Remedy for Having Been Born of Woman', 190.

57 Slee, *Seeking the Risen Christa*, 17.

58 Phipps, 'The Menstrual Taboo in the Judeo-Christian Tradition', 302.

59 Slee, 'Confession for Good Friday', *Seeking the Risen Christa*, 77.

balm yard musings –
decolonizing worship

MICHAEL N. JAGESSAR

makabuka and a decolonial imagination

My excursions and incursions into liturgy and worship are as an insider-outsider.[1] Although a minister, I am no scholar of liturgy nor an expert in any theological discipline. My premise, though, is simple. It is in and through worship and liturgy that we find the primary space where minds and hearts are catechized. Hence, worship needs to be subject to critical epistemic work in order to expose the reach of coloniality, Whiteness and heteronormative euro-centric beliefs and teachings.[2] As an ill-disciplined learner and critical voice, my incursions have been in collaboration with or through invitations from Stephen Burns.[3] My transgression of boundaries liturgical, theological and otherwise is situated in my journey as a minister, first in a Lutheran tradition (Guyana), and then moving across the ecumenical family in the Caribbean, ending up as an 'ambi-*veil*-ent' in a united and uniting tradition (UK).

Teaching across various spaces of formation for ministry I have been struck by the liturgical creativity and boundary-pushing passion of students, but also by how this often gets tamed or lost following ordination. Alongside this observation about formation, I also note how the most radical sermon can sometimes be located within worship steeped in coloniality of words, images and rituals – from prayers to hymn singing to benedictions. What is it about our liturgy that makes some seem to genuflect to inherited traditions that continue to lock us into suffocating predictability? Do we presume the Spirit's partnership in such acts? My questions do not diminish all the good that may be found in outward-facing generosity and inclusivity in liturgical theology and practice. But good intentions are not always matched by the lived worship experienced for many in our worshipping communities: what may be imagined as 'inclusive' may be less than we presume.

One popular view across liturgical theology and practice – and by practitioners of all ecclesial stripes – is the mantra that at the heart of liturgy lies people's work and public service.[4] Variously put, theorized and contended, the idea is captured in liturgy as 'work of the people'. Though contentious – and notwithstanding the ways scholars and our various traditions describe and locate liturgy as 'work of the people' – one may still wish to ask: is it a gathered group performing or participating in a liturgical rite, act or *ordo* already determined for them by an ecclesial tradition, a group of experts, or by the presider? Can imagination and spirit not do more work among and in the people gathered for worship in spite of or outside of a crafted liturgy? How about liturgy as 'makabuka', which in Taino (an Arawak people and among the early inhabitants of the Caribbean) means a state of 'carefree',[5] perhaps spaces where Spirit runs riot on colonial hegemonic tendencies?

In what follows, I contend that liturgy needs a radical decolonial frame to reflect its claim to be people's work. What are some of key decolonial moves and radical flipping needed in our current liturgical theology and worship practice?[6] Can a poetics of the imagination be a possible way for liturgy to break out of the ways it is locked in colonial frameworks, perpetuating an euro-centric view of what it means to be human in its theological and philosophical underpinnings?

The inability to see what is happening in our world and work towards an alternative reality that gives agency to freedom is evidence that we do not live in a postcolonial world. Coloniality 'is constitutive of modernity' and its reach means that 'there is no modernity without coloniality'.[7] Through successive and cumulative stages from salvation to democracy, ecclesial communities continue to be part of this. Thus, the plea for 'dreaming' that Nicola Slee makes in her *Fragments for Fractured Times* can still be colonial.[8] Decolonial work has to interrogate the geopolitics of knowing, being and assumptions that continue to hold dreams in captivity. This is a challenge before all of us. While feminist theology may not always have grasped a post/decolonial agenda, neither has Black theological discourse in the UK. Discerning the intersections, learning from one another, and recognizing the urgent need to scrutinize the reach of coloniality in our producing and reproducing of knowledge is urgent. Decolonizing worship is work in progress.

I have written previously on various themes of decolonizing Christian worship.[9] While the initial writings arose during my time at the Queen's Foundation for Ecumenical Theological Education in Birmingham, I continue to reflect on specific aspects relating to liturgy and worship as a minister of the United Reformed Church and researcher at large. I mention this briefly to locate myself, and especially the perspectives that shape my decolonial moves and the ensuing contribution in this chapter.

I reside in the UK, though it is not the space/place from *where* I write, think and do. I write, think and do from where I *dwell*. This is the place called Caribbean which has been configured by the European colonial matrix of power and the ongoing legacies.

hearts and minds suspended

Performer-poet Bhanu Kapil invites us to imagine 'a heart suspended'.[10] Kapil uses her poetry to interrogate coloniality's reach in good intentions of generosity and inclusivity, often unmatched in the lived experience of minorities. Coloniality and its legacies continue to crucify many. What new heart will decoloniality engender? Consider the coronavirus pandemic as an example. Arundhati Roy sees it as a portal or 'a gateway between one world and the next'.[11] She notes, 'we can choose to walk through it, dragging the carcasses of our prejudice and hatred, our avarice, our data banks and dead ideas, our dead rivers and smoky skies behind us. Or we can walk through lightly, with little luggage, ready to imagine another world and ready to fight for it.'[12]

Decolonizing worship calls for a different kind of heart, mindful of the reach of our inherited traditions on us. Our liturgical inheritance has not been left untouched by imperial history. What carcasses and deadly ideas are we dragging across the portal? Decolonizing worship asks us to acknowledge, question and interrogate the assumptions around the reservoir of inherited knowledge and ongoing knowledge production in theology and liturgy. Where are spaces for multiple versions of meaning-making of self, relationships, community, world and more? As it stands, the dominant house of liturgical enunciations is constructed around a particular group, culture and framework, with the rest then obligated to aspire and reach for standards set by that house. Within the house there are voices, allies and colleagues in solidarity with decolonial moves. But are we really up for the consequences of thinking, doing and dwelling 'decolonial'? Have we considered the critical demand of a decolonial habit, that of a radical change of the terms of engagement with deposits and current practices, including our own?

Such will be moves beyond 'tinkering with rituals', tolerating 'festival celebrations of ethnicity', singing 'world church music' in our appropriating versions, translating traditional texts in multiple languages, donning multicoloured costumes, reading and quoting world church voices. Our hermeneutics of *suspicion* must include hermeneutics of *suspension* (our colonized mind and heart) in order to expose the theological assumptions that continue to frame our practices. Richard Fenn observed how liturgy has a history of social control and, in spite of good intentions of renewal, 'the liturgy itself has remained under the ownership and control of the clergy' with little agency and empowerment for laity.[13] Decolonial questions around worship, though, are larger than permission given to laity. The decolonial gaze is concerned with epistemic underpinnings around worship and would question Slee's observation around 'givenness' when she speaks of the reforming breath of Spirit 'calling new truths out of the givenness of scripture and tradition'.[14] Decolonial thinking will be alert to ways in which the house of the enunciation all too easily remains that of White, Western, colonial gatekeepers.[15]

As an example, consider assumptions around 'time'. How much liturgy operates within a colonial framework of time, though worship has the potential to break out towards what might be unthinkable?[16] Coloniality steals time, framing it as linear, extractive and transactive. It organizes time around commodification and production, emptying life of meaning. Coloniality deployed 'time' as the basis in the construction of 'the imaginary of the modern/colonial world and an instrument for both controlling knowledge and advancing a vision of society based on progress and development'.[17] Even globalization (in which world church music, etc., are implicated) is a cover for global coloniality as an invention of global capitalism and a linear understanding of time cut from the same imperial cloth. This has been named as *chrono-politics*, 'a specific aspect of theo- and ego-politics of knowledge' and 'a civilizational principle that serves to ostracize all who do not conform to the modern conventions of time'.[18] The colonization of knowing and being still operate within a 'system of ideas built around the colonization of time'.[19] Our liturgical inheritance and practices (Advent, Easter, Harvest etc.) are implicated. The commodification of time is linked to what it means to be human, a key decolonial question. What view of the human does our worship communicate?[20]

hybrid floating rib

In 2021, the National Gallery of The Bahamas carried an exhibition entitled 'Floating Rib'.[21] Various Black women artists in the Bahamas and of the Bahamian diaspora explored negotiating roots, bodies and belonging, displacement, homecomings and goings, Black body politics and nationalism. I was struck by the artists' multiverse vision and fluidity in their imagery of 'floating rib'. This imagery resonates with Ernesto Laclau's 'floating signifiers', advocating a multiplicity of meanings in conversation.[22] The idea of 'floating' can be found across the works of

Caribbean writers, poets, musicians and artists.[23] 'Floating' points to a central task of decolonizing worship: that of de-provincializing liturgy/worship from 'Western' fixed moorings around universality by giving agency to a multiplicity of voices and sources both within and beyond borders.[24] Can it be that the world of Christian worship is locked into a colonial sense of singularity? Be it original sin and its binary tendencies or ideas of a Galilean Jewish rabbi crucified for our sins that only ecclesial institutions (not even all of them) seem able to mediate our release from: is it possible that our resulting liturgical productions remain fixed to colonial moorings? Can worship reflect a more open and spacious understanding of what it means to be human given the baggage of original sin, and the church's complicity in the commodifying and death-dealing dehumanizing of certain kinds of bodies? While it is a commonplace Christian view that we are all created in God's image and likeness, the lived reality of current worship practices can easily suggest otherwise: grandiose presiding styles, ill-chosen language for 'content' (for example, ideas about what and how 'sins' are named), the aesthetics of space, what is considered beautiful (or even acceptable), how progress and growth are depicted and ritualized, and the symbols deployed all might mean that worship continues to represent one hegemonic understanding and definition of human supposed to represent all of humanity. The rest are subtly deselected and viewed as lacking full humanity.

Caribbean philosopher Sylvia Wynter argues for exorcising the curse of European enchantment with the pervasive 'Man1' running through the colonial project into modernity and beyond.[25] Wynter calls for a (re)humanizing impulse to release and recuse our dead rituals,[26] deploying 'being human as a verb' and speaking of human as praxis.[27] Wynter pushes rehumanizing around the hybridity of our humanness. The idea of humans-as-hybrid disrupts anthropological classifications of human groups as 'naturally selected' and 'naturally dysselected'.[28] Thinking intentionally of human as hybrid challenges many ways of thinking.[29] There are insights here for worship that are of help in challenging closed-order models of knowing what it means to be human. More hybrid thinking is needed about all of this. Liturgical productions need to be able to include those who have been left out by a system of knowing and being that continues to question and grade their humanity. Liturgical theorizing and liturgical renewal commissions have much to learn in terms of tracking colonial process, epistemic manoeuvres, inbuilt ideological hegemonies, and the ensuing codes of human/non-human distinction. The decolonial insistence is to delink from this system of knowledge and instead practise floating epistemic disobedience.[30]

epistemic disobedience

Decolonizing worship has to contend with the fact that so much liturgical theology and so many worship practices are grounded in Whiteness.[31] Most liturgical productions and knowledge (inherited and current) – as well as how they make their way into print via publishers – are framed by White hegemony. From liturgical commissions to academic writings, from peer reviews and referencing to publishing, again and again the operative framework is 'Whiteness'. Far too much discourse around liturgy favours and buttresses Whiteness in the construction of knowledge. My haunting is how I can advocate decolonizing worship of its imperial tendencies while I continue to inhabit and be part of colonizing spaces and structures. While worship may be an act of treason against empires and its avatars, epistemic disobedience to its own colonizing frames and tendencies is costly.

Consider the imagery of 'table', a central and important symbol in Christian liturgical theology and practice. Nicola Slee, among many others, has articulated 'table theology' as a 'key concern in feminist theology and liturgy'.[32] Many associated with this book will be familiar with the nicely designed round table in the chapel at Queen's. With Stephen Burns and Nicola Slee, I was a key advocate of removing the old square table with sharp corners and replacing this with a new round one with no corners that allowed for multiple liturgical poetics. Yet I could never figure out why I still felt uncomfortable with the 'table' imagery though I also deploy it often. Was my view 'evolving', 'complexifying', or was there something I was unaware of working overtime in my head and imagination?

It was only at my parents' funerals a few years ago that I realized why I was uneasy. In my family home in Guyana there is a large table my father made from special purple-heart wood. That table stood at home for years (and is still there) and was only used to rest things on. It was never a space to sit around, eat, have conversations and discuss family matters. Such discussions happened seated on the floor or on benches in the yard. The table symbolized 'arrival' or 'progression' to the standard imitated from the home of White sugar plantation managers. 'Table' remains a foreign, internalized and uncomfortable space for many people who are outside 'table' cultures. This is not to suggest that spaces outside of 'table' cultures are necessarily any better at being inclusive. The question for our purpose is how aware are we, and when we use the image of the table and craft lines of liturgy around that imagery, how can we be conscious of the historical baggage and assumptions (theological, socio-economic, political and cultural) to do with the table? What are we actually communicating via our rites and their words?

Another consideration for epistemic disobedience is to do with the bodies of knowledge that are remembered and recalled. Puerto Rican artist Víctor Vázquez's recent exhibition invites us to reflect on historical memory, especially the relationship between memory, language and word, with the view that 'reality/memory' is constantly invented and re-invented as power tends to generate constructions that would legit-imize the power structures.[33] For all the theological ink and blood spilled over eucharist, I am not sure that we have fully investigated the content of our remembering around the 'eucharistic table' as a narrative construc-tion within hegemonic Western colonial categories of knowing and being. Kwok Pui-lan has been signalling 'epistemic disobedience' although she has not named it as Sylvia Wynter and Walter Mignolo do.[34] Writing on the need to subject 'tradition' to critical interrogation Kwok observes how 'tradition defines the memory of the Christian community' but also that this has been compromised as '[w]omen have been shut out from the collective memory of the church: they have been excluded from the discussions of biblical canon, the debates on the creeds, the deliberation on church pronouncements, and the formulation of church'.[35]

Epistemic disobedience – or insurrection – interrogates Whiteness as a system not just about ethnicity or geographical location. It is then that we begin to see how our liturgy upholds coloniality, privileging particular behaviours, which becomes hegemonic through the practice of worship and in church. Diversifying the *geography* and *language* of our hymnody is commendable. The other critical part is the *epistemology*, especially if we are singing hegemonic melodies of Whiteness.[36] A cursory look at what passes for Black or gospel music on the BBC programme *Songs of Praise*, and what is sung in Black churches in the UK or in churches in the Caribbean or Africa, would reveal the reach of Whiteness and its under-lying epistemic corruptions. It may be the global music some wish to advance, but it is certainly not decolonial if the theology and theological assumptions of the songs continue to raise up the 'god' produced out of colonial Whiteness. Global church and global music may just be a re-boot of the constructed colonial imperial gaze, with 'interest convergence' of the status quo safely in place.

The disobedience in unravelling and rethinking dominant worldviews has a larger goal: de-linking from the knowledge systems we take for granted and into which we get co-opted.[37] This practice can open 'a parallel road to knowing, sensing, believing and living'.[38] Marcella Althaus-Reid's deploying of 'indecent' is radical epistemic disobedience in 'the unmasking of ideologies' through 'provocative and heavily con-tested transgressive discourse'.[39] 'Decent' is the colonial agenda of a heteronormative order with a regulatory and idolatrous function. Our theo-liturgical imagination would benefit from this delinking of the colonial geopolitics of knowing and being towards constructions of alternative options. What from our liturgical tradition(s) do we hold as unquestionable truths and find currently calcified in our practices because of commitment to our belief systems, the *ordo* self-replicating systemic beliefs at the core of our traditions, in order to protect them from challenge and change?[40] Liturgical theology has much more work to do on how differences are constructed in ways that perpetuate hierarchical orderings and binaries. If the 'liturgy after the liturgy', for instance, is to help create global decolonial futures, then on whose version of nature and environment will our liturgical chants draw, especially since the dominant enunciators and ideas on nature and environment continue to marginalize those of indigenous practices?[41]

disruptive dancing from full stops to 'parenthesis'

In an essay on 'Measuring up the Universe' Stuart Clark observes that since the universe is much larger than humans can see, and that dark matter outweighs normal matter, then our view of cosmology needs rethinking.[42] It means our describing of the universe has to be provisional; for before us is a multiverse (not universe), a landscape of universes with multiple physical laws. One is reminded of how Copernicus' proposed new astronomy, supported by Galileo, breached what was then the hegemonic and theologically absolute Scholastic order of knowledge. It was a direct challenge to the premise that the earth did not move, which was central then to Christian theology of salvation and the ordering of things. If the earth moved, then the church's views of salvation needed to be changed to include this knowledge/awareness.[43]

Decolonizing worship is interested in interrogating any Christian myth of universality that has mapped and colonized minds. Notions of universal truth and knowledge cover up the colonial matrix of power and the contexts within which racial, binary and hierarchical thinking allow for construction of imperial knowledge. Liturgy needs to move from a universal view to a pluri-versal or multiple perspectives. Theological and doctrinal 'full-stops' in worship and in worship's work of catechizing minds must give way to parenthesis and commas. Decolonizing worship 'is about truth in parenthesis'.[44] There is no hegemony in truth; truth is shaped by a variety of trajectories and understandings.[45] Decolonial worship is against any colonial imperial design purporting one truth. The legacies of imperial worship are scoured across hymns, eucharistic and other prayers, other parts of the *ordo*, and rituals that continue to

perpetuate uniformity, oneness, binary and excluding views, and hierarchical ceremonies that privilege one particular culture over others. The
work of decolonizing worship involves learning to 'dance' in the face of
bearers and gatekeepers of tradition(s) who are themselves unable to join
in because of their own liturgical anxiety. But such 'dancing' might also
be like a kind of low-intensity guerrilla warfare![46] I can imagine that Slee
would identify with this sentiment given her own work of 'troubling' and
'subverting' so much of ecclesial hegemonic deposits.

decolonial liturgical 'work': towards 'breathing' spaces

In her essay 'The Crucified Christa: A Re-Evaluation', Slee suggests that
'*neither* the image of a naked female body on the cross *nor* the reclaimed
sexual body of the male Jesus on the cross, however potent and liberating
these may be, can do all the work required for a "turning of the symbols"
and a renewed religious imaginary'.[47] Such reimaging goes some way to
shifting the conversation.

The conversation also needs to be about the reach of coloniality in liturgy – which is thoroughly pervasive: inherited traditions (the collections
if we deploy an archival term), the site of the work of the people (worship spaces) and our ongoing liturgical knowledge outputs all need to be
brought into shifting conversation. However much we push boundaries
and wrestle with the overarching theological framework of knowing and
being it is a struggle to shake off the control of the colonial matrix, shaped
as it is by Whiteness. The epistemic disobedience and delinking required
is not about disengaging with what we are all part of. It is about *changing*
the terms or rules of engagement to counter underlying logics of entrap-
ment. It means focusing on the knower, the knowing and subsequent
knowledge production. Important questions are: How do we acquire
knowledge? Who are the producers? Who perpetuates it? Who controls
knowing and being? How is the knowing and knowledge produced and
reproduced? The tasks involved include locating, naming, understanding
and being aware of how coloniality in worship has worked and continues to sustain hegemonic and exclusive notions and practices. We
are all implicated. Where in our worship will fresh and new *con*spiring
(breathing together) happen? How will ecclesial spaces, worship and
the liturgy after the liturgy help create empowering 'breathing spaces'
to redress deficits, inequities, and affirm truths and multiplicity fostering
life, flourishing communities and open spaces?[48]

When church is called out for its colonial complicity, 'humility' is
sometimes suggested as a Christian virtue in how we respond, mindful of

the 'cloud of witnesses' who all had good intentions. Decolonial liturgical 'work' of creating breathing spaces will require a whole load of humility from ecclesial gatekeepers, given nasty penchants towards arrogance and exceptionalism. Those engaged in decolonial work will constantly need to be wary of 'interest convergence' where coloniality (Whiteness as one example) somehow continues to benefit from the process.

Speaking about his book *The Good Ancestor*, Roman Krznaric contends that humankind has colonized the future as if no one is and will be there.[49] Arguing for a radical shift from the biblical aspiration of 'good Samaritan' to becoming 'a good ancestor', Krznaric asks what we are handing over or leaving as legacies to future generations. Identifying robbing of future generations as a colonial habit, Krznaric sees the need to decolonize politics and suggests that the archaic House of Lords should be renamed and reoriented as House of the Future. What would a liturgical house of the future look like? What legacies is Christian worship leaving for future generations? Can our liturgy avoid colonizing God and the future so that all can freely breathe again? Will the largely male gerontocracy, minding the liturgical traditions of our ecclesial communities, be able to imagine a new and different liturgical present and future?

Notes

1 I am deploying the terms 'liturgy' and 'worship' interchangeably.

2 Among others, Nicola Slee's work would largely fall in the latter category, not about coloniality. See Nicola Slee, *Fragments for Fractured Times: What Feminist Practical Theology Brings to the Table* (London: SCM Press, 2020), 31, 57.

3 Stephen Burns, Nicola Slee and Michael N. Jagessar, eds, *The Edge of God: New Liturgical Texts and Contexts in Conversation* (London: Epworth Press, 2008); Michael N. Jagessar and Stephen Burns, *Christian Worship: Postcolonial Perspectives* (Sheffield: Equinox, 2011).

4 See Stephen Burns, *SCM Studyguide: Liturgy*, 2nd edn (London: SCM Press, 2018), 5–14.

5 'Carefree' is used in the sense of 'freedom' without restrictions. French: *insouciant*.

6 See Becca Whitla, *Liberation, (De)Coloniality, and Liturgical Practices: Flipping the Song Bird* (New York: Palgrave Macmillan, 2020). Whitla's brilliant deploying of the metaphor of 'flipping' serves as both a necessary method and habit in the decolonizing journey.

7 Walter Mignolo, *The Darker Side of Western Modernity: Global Futures, Decolonial Options* (Durham: Duke University Press, 2011), 3. This idea has been articulated earlier by Caribbean philosopher Sylvia Wynter in various essays in the 1970s through to the 1980s. See David Scott, 'The Re-enchantment of Humanism: An Interview with Sylvia Wynter', *Small Axe* 8 (2000): 119–207.

8 Slee, *Fragments for Fractured Times*, 222.

9 For example, Michael N. Jagessar, 'Table Habits, Liturgical *Peleu*, and

Displacing Conversation: A Postcolonial Excursion', in *Postcolonial Practice of Ministry: Leadership, Liturgy and Interfaith Engagement*, eds Kwok Pui-lan and Stephen Burns (Lanham: Lexington, 2016), 77–90; Michael N. Jagessar, 'beyond words, gestures and spaces: evoking and imagining liturgical contra*dictions*', in *Liturgy with a Difference: Beyond Inclusion in Christian Assembly*, eds Stephen Burns and Bryan Cones (London: SCM Press, 2019), 126–36.

10 Bhanu Kapil, *How to Wash a Heart* (Liverpool: Liverpool University Press, 2020), 22.

11 Arundhati Roy, 'The Pandemic is a Portal', *Financial Times* (3 April 2020). See also Slee, *Fragments for Fractured Times*, 101.

12 Roy, 'The Pandemic is a Portal'.

13 Richard K. Fenn, 'Diversity and Power: Cracking the Code', in Brian K. Blount and Leonora Tubbs Tisdale, eds, *Making Room at the Table: An Invitation to Multicultural Worship* (Louisville: Westminster John Knox Press, 2000), 63–77 (66, 74).

14 Slee, *Fragments for Fractured Times*, 3.

15 See Mignolo, *The Darker Side of Western Modernity*, 118–48.

16 This connection I make after listening to an online event where Dionne Brand spoke on 'A Short Entry on Time: Capitalism, Time, Blackness and Writing' (3 March 2021).

17 Mignolo, *The Darker Side of Western Modernity*, 161.

18 Mignolo, *The Darker Side of Western Modernity*, 177–9, quoting Daniel Innerarity Grau.

19 Mignolo, *The Darker Side of Western Modernity*, 178.

20 See Andrew Prevot, 'Mystical Bodies of Christ: Human, Crucified, and Beloved', in *Beyond the Doctrine of Man: Decolonial Visions of the Human*, eds Joseph Drexler-Dreis and Kristien Justaert (New York: Fordham University Press, 2020), 134–60 (139).

21 See National Gallery of The Bahamas.

22 See Nicolas Panotto, 'Per-verting the Foundations: Epistemological and Methodological Challenges to the "Corporeality" of Latin American Liberation Theologies', in *Indecent Theologians: Marcella Althaus-Reid and the Next Generation of Postcolonial Activists*, ed. Nicolas Panotto (Alameda: Borderless Press, 2016), 105–32 (116).

23 See the work of Cuban artist Flora Fong and her piece titled 'Habitat' which depicts the floating and spreading roots of mangroves.

24 This is the epistemic trick to which Mignolo refers in *The Darker Side of Western Modernity*, 201.

25 Wynter deploys Man1 to call into question the 'Western' concept of the human and the epistemologies anchoring it. Western epistemology built itself on the concept of the White male (Man1) as the ideal human. She notes this as the European Renaissance invention of the idea of Man1 which is at the heart of racism and its legacies (against Man2, the other part of the invention). See Katherine McKittrick, ed., *Sylvia Wynter: On Being Human as Praxis* (Durham: Duke University Press, 2015), 46–7; *Beyond the Doctrine of Man*, eds Drexler-Dreis and Justaert, which takes its departure from Wynter's work.

26 See McKittrick, ed., *Sylvia Wynter*. See also Mayra Rivera, 'Where Life Itself Lives', in *Beyond the Doctrine of Man*, 19–35. Rivera engages with this aspect of the work of Wynter in her essay.

27 McKittrick, ed., *Sylvia Wynter*, 16–17.

28 McKittrick, ed., *Sylvia Wynter*, 16–17.

29 McKittrick, ed., *Sylvia Wynter*, 17.

30 Decolonizing worship is not about geography but about epistemology as all the above is found and reproduced by colonials, the colonized and those not even colonized.

31 See Sarah Travis, *Decolonizing Preaching: The Pulpit as Postcolonial Space* (Eugene: Cascade Books, 2014). Travis, while writing about preaching, underscores challenges and pitfalls. With April Hathcock, I interpret Whiteness as not only 'racial and ethnic categorizations but a complete system of exclusion based on hegemony'. Whiteness refers 'not only to the socio-cultural differential of power and privilege that results from categories of race and ethnicity; it also stands as a marker for the privilege and power that acts to reinforce itself through hegemonic cultural practice that excludes all who are different'. See April Hathcock, 'White Librarianship in Blackface: Diversity Initiatives in LIS', *In the Library with the Lead Pipe* (7 October 2015).

32 Slee, *Fragments for Fractured Times*, 10.

33 The exhibition was titled 'Ciudad sobre ruinas: Memoria y la metafísica de la presencia y el yo' ('City over Ruins: Memory and the Metaphysics of Presence and the Self') at the Delta de Picó Gallery, located at Liga de Arte in Old San Juan, Puerto Rico.

34 See McKittrick, ed., *Sylvia Wynter*; Scott, 'The Re-enchantment of Humanism', 119–207; and Mignolo, *The Darker Side of Western Modernity*.

35 Kwok Pui-lan, *Postcolonial Imagination and Feminist Theology* (Louisville: Westminster John Knox Press, 2005), 66.

36 See Michael N. Jagessar and Stephen Burns, 'Hymns Old and New: Towards a Postcolonial Gaze', in *The Edge of God*, eds, Burns, Slee and Jagessar, 50–66.

37 See Kwok, *Postcolonial Imagination and Feminist Theology*, 67.

38 Mignolo, *The Darker Side of Western Modernity*, 161.

39 Marcella Althaus-Reid, 'From Liberation Theology to Indecent Theology: The Trouble with Normality in Theology', in *Latin American Liberation Theology: The Next Generation*, ed. Ivan Petrella (Maryknoll: Orbis Books, 2005), 20–38 (25).

40 Walter Mignolo, 'Sylvia Wynter: What Does it Mean to be Human?', in *Sylvia Wynter: On Being Human as Praxis*, ed. Katherine McKittrick (Durham: Duke University Press, 2015), 106–23 (107–8).

41 Mignolo, *The Darker Side of Western Modernity*, 10–11.

42 Stuart Clark, 'Measuring up the Universe', *New Scientist* (2 January 2021), 32–8.

43 McKittrick, ed., *Sylvia Wynter*, 14. The observation about the view of salvation was made by Cardinal Bellarmine at Galileo's trial.

44 Mignolo, *The Darker Side of Western Modernity*, 44.

45 Mignolo, *The Darker Side of Western Modernity*, 44.

46 See Michel-Rolph Trouillot, *Silencing the Past: Power and the Production of History* (Boston: Beacon Press, 1995).

47 Slee, *Fragments for Fractured Times*, 251.

48 Slee argued for 'Reclaiming Liturgical Spaces' in *Fragments for Fractured Times*, 60–78. 'Breathing Spaces', though, is more than engendering or reclaiming a variety of liturgical spaces. Broadened, inclusive and expansive spaces can still be spaces that regulate, allocate, suffocate and relegate.

49 Roman Krznaric, *The Good Ancestor: How to Think Long Term in a Short-Term World* (London: WH Allen, 2020).

II

Praying Like a White, Straight Man: Reading Nicola Slee 'Between the Lines'

AL BARRETT

Praying (in) the Fragments

[T]he piecing together of fragments and the poetic process of making them into something much more than the sum of the parts is not only human work; it is the work of God.[1]

For Nicola Slee, praying is entangled – together with poetry and study – in the art of 'bringing as much disciplined attention of which one is capable to one's own life in all its myriad commitments and distractions, to the complex, changing life of the world in which one is set, to the lives of others with whom one is connected both far and near, living and dead, and to God present in each of these'.[2] Such 'disciplined attention' is not focused on some already-existing, coherent whole, but instead necessarily involves a 'gathering', 'excavation', 'bringing into the light' and 'piecing together' of diverse, particular *fragments* – refusing to 'fix' or 'impose an artificial unity', but a 'to-ing and fro-ing', 'search[ing] for connections', seeking 'a whole that is always ahead of us, never fully envisaged or realized'.[3]

'[W]e always and only work in the fragments'.[4] These are not Slee's words, but those of a fellow theological educator, Willie James Jennings. From their different contexts, and writing as White woman and Black man, Slee and Jennings each bring pieces, different but overlapping, that together describe the multi-faceted nature of this 'fragment work'. Fragments, first, are an inevitability of our *being creatures* who can only apprehend with our senses – in bites, in touches, in smells, in sounds, and in focused but shifting sight'. '[T]he world is always too much for us to hold all at once,' says Jennings. And the same is true of our faith: 'the creaturely pieces of memories and ideas and practices that we work with to attune our senses to the presence of God', and with which 'God works

... moving in the spaces between them to form communion with us'.[5] We pray with, and in, the fragments of our creatureliness.

But second, between Slee and Jennings we are reminded that we live also with a *tragic* kind of fragmentation, a 'mangling' (to use Jennings's visceral term) of both our capacity and our desire to pay 'constant full attention to one another'.[6] Here we can name two of the most powerful, pervasive sources of that 'mangling'. One we will name 'hetero-patriarchy', with its dualisms of 'male/female', 'mind/body', 'God/world' and so on, dividing both our concepts and creaturely flesh itself into isolated, hard-bound-aried bodies and rigid hierarchies.[7] Another we can trace back to the beginnings of Western colonialism and the invention of 'Whiteness', which identifies 'not first ... a people' but '*a way of organizing life*', 'defined by possession, control, and mastery', through reductionism (turning the whole world into 'a vast number of things'), categorization (collapsing peoples 'into Blackness, or Whiteness', for example), and commodification (rendering things and people 'both knowable and saleable at the same time').[8] Taken together – because their histories and workings are inseparable – these describe a *structure* that continues to dominate our world: the 'master's house' (as Audre Lorde famously named it).[9]

Within this structure, one very particular and abstracted fragment of human experience – that of an idealized White, affluent, Western, non-disabled, self-sufficient, heterosexual male – has declared itself normative for *all* experience of life, simultaneously marking as 'other', marginal-izing, and carving up into isolated fragments, all other experiences that deviate from this norm (including, of course, the lives and existence of *non*-human 'others'). And most specifically, the master's house conscripts all those humans gendered 'male' into the 'gender project' of 'masculin-ity'. Characterized by both 'internal repression and external domination', invulnerable heroism and aggressive expansiveness, the performance and reproduction of masculinity demands homogeny and hegemony, denying diversity and silencing dissent, 'a control that aims for sameness and a sameness that imagines control'.[10] Whatever 'praying like a White, straight man' might look like, it must surely involve an unlearning of, and ongoing resistance to, this second kind of fragmentation.

There is, however, a third kind of fragment, through which we might catch glimpses of hope even within the suffocating oppressiveness of the master's house. There is, as Leonard Cohen sang, 'a crack in every-thing. That's how the light gets in.'[11] These cracks in the structures of the master's house, shards of light and air – 'experiences, stories, memories, relationships, dreams, prayers – all those pieces, light and dark, rough and smooth, jagged and torn' – open to the possibilities of 'another place'.[12] Such a place might be discovered, within or beyond the house's crumbling ruins, in common ground where the glorious diversity of creature-kin is caught up in what Jennings names as 'the erotic power of God to gather together': 'an uncontrollable reconciliation, one that aims to re-create us, reforming us as those who enact gathering and who gesture communion with our very existence'.[13] Prayer, then, is an insistent peering through such cracks, yearning for such an 'other place', and allowing ourselves to be caught up in this erotic power of God. And it is to this labour of love that the prayers, poetry and theology of Nicola Slee invite us: a labour through which 'something new is birthed and enacted ... that we did not and could not know before or outside [it]'.[14] Alongside other feminist theologians, Slee has been engaged in crafting a body of liturgy, research, theory, wisdom, relationship and practice that can be inhabited in ways that women can call 'home', and within which women can root themselves and grow and flourish.

But to what kind of journey does such work call *me*, as a White, straight, non-disabled, middle-class *man*?[15] That is the question at the heart of this chapter. And my answer to it, modest and tentative, is to begin in the fragments. To acknowledge my own 'fragment-ness', refusing to speak (for) any kind of 'whole'. To acknowledge my own entanglement in the structures of the master's house, and yet to *seek out the cracks*. To acknowledge (as my friend and co-author Ruth Harley has taught me) that *not* habitually needing to 'pray between the lines' (to struggle to find and maintain one's own space within the liturgies of the master's house) is a reliable indicator of privilege.[16] And, therefore, to attempt to read – and pray – 'between the lines' of writers (feminist, Black, and queer, particularly) who describe 'other places', beyond the master's house, in ways that might just be the beginnings of a journey of 'leaving home': of dismantling, re-location and reorientation.

'Leaving' and 'Building': Taking the Master's House with Us

Leaving home is, of itself, no particular threat to the stability of the master's house. For a man, in fact, leaving home is an essential step for the master's house's ongoing endurance, reproduction (handed down from father to son) and extension. Hetero-patriarchy's dualisms include dividing the world between 'private', domestic (feminine) spaces and the (masculine) 'public' sphere: men *become men* in their adventures – often risky and heroic – from the former into the latter, whether it's the hunter in the woods, the CEO in the corporate board room, or the 'explorer, missionary, merchant, or soldier' engaging in the quintessentially masculine project of 'empire-building', penetrating and conquering 'dark', mysterious and 'virgin' lands and peoples in the cause of knowledge, conversion or profit.[17] We men take the master's house with us on our journeys, and re-build it wherever we go, dragging all life into its structures.

While the 'public/private' dividing wall keeps many of White hetero-patriarchy's 'others' firmly in their places, for the privileged men (by no means all) it is a boundary that can be freely crossed, in ways that simply reinforce the power of the divide. Intertwined with Christianity's long collusion with empire-building, male-dominated patterns of praying that might have translated into subversive relational and political practices – such as self-examination, confession and self-negation (acknowledging the typically male sin of the over-inflated ego) – have all too often been 'spiritualized' and 'privatized', safely confined within an inner sanctum, not only insulated from the domestic labour expected of women, but also 'keep[ing] God (and women) safely out of politics and the public realm', as Grace Jantzen has observed:

> [This] allows mysticism to flourish as a secret inner life, while those who nurture such an inner life can generally be counted on to prop up rather than to challenge the status quo of their work places, their gender roles, and the political systems by which they are governed, since their anxieties and angers will be allayed in the privacy of their own hearts' search for peace and tranquility.[18]

Another 'men's movement' began to emerge in the 1970s – in the USA and UK especially – again calling men to leave home: this time from the 'soft', 'receptive' and 'feminized' forms of masculinity that were, supposedly, prevailing in Western society. Robert Bly's influential 1990 book *Iron John* summoned men to venture into the forest – both metaphorical and literal – on a journey guided by myths, archetypes and initiation rituals, to (re)connect with 'the Wild Man' that, in Bly's 'mythopoetic' anthropology, lies in the depths of the male psyche: a figure of 'the deep masculine', associated with spontaneity, exuberance and risk-taking, instinct and emotion, embodiedness, 'nature' and 'the nourishing dark'.[19] Although Bly and his fellow 'wild men' at least acknowledged some elements of men's 'internal repression', they nevertheless clung closely to hetero-patriarchy's foundational 'masculine-feminine' binary, and evaded the foundational feminist insight that 'the personal is the political'.[20] 'The forest' was simply colonized as another privatized, men-only space. This masculine withdrawal for 'inner personal work', combined with 'the absence of acute socio-political analyses to call men's roles in structural oppression to account', allowed little space for 'deep encounters with otherized human and other-than-human others', instrumentalized nature as merely 'a "backdrop" for the theatre of men's healing from their inner wounds', and left the misogynist, heteronormative and racist structures of the master's house firmly intact, if not in fact strengthened.[21]

As Seth Mirsky has put it, the 'spiritualizing' of masculinity (whether through the ancient 'men's movements' of Christianity or its postmodern, forest-bound incarnation) 'absolves it of its destructive, yet always-contested, history and attempts an impossible escape from the gritty field on which gendered power struggles take place'.[22] 'The logic of masculinity is demanding – protect and maintain what you are intrinsically, or you could lose it, mutate, become something else.'[23] It is in the possibility of such a 'something else', beyond the master's house, that we, with Mirsky, might discern glimmers of hope.[24]

Being Shown the Door

How, then, might we men embark on a journey of leaving the master's house, without simply taking it with us, and reproducing its structures of repression and domination, wherever we go?

Within a Christian horizon, this could be framed as a question of faith development, something to which Slee has given much attention over the years.[25] But while there has been much written *generically* about faith development (without attending either to gender or to the relationship between faith and the structures of White hetero-patriarchy), and Slee's work has listened to the particular faith lives of *women* (and mostly Western, White, middle-class women at that), it seems that there has been very little written specifically on *men's* journeys of anti-patriarchal (and anti-racist) faith development. In the remainder of this chapter, therefore, I will seek further to read 'between the lines' of Slee's rich and multi-faceted body of work – alongside a handful of male writers who, in various ways, seek to query and queer what Jennings calls 'White, self-sufficient masculinity' in an attempt to trace out at least some of the possible contours of such a journey.[26]

'Orientation': At Home in a Divided World[27]

In Slee's research into women's 'faithing', she describes women's experience of a *'divided* self', originating in adolescence, when 'society's gendered expectations' present women with a 'terrible choice': '(a) either to stop or hide one's own voice in order to become, or be thought of, as a "nice girl", and so become alienated from oneself; or (b) to refuse to be silent and take the risk, perceived and real in this society, of becoming alienated socially and politically, of being ostracized as, for example, "brash", "loud", "aggressive", "outspoken", "bossy"'.[28] Where for young women this enforced 'choice' leads inexorably to an 'alienation' of one kind or another, for young (and particularly White, straight) men the equivalent developmental stage conversely sees them orienting and embedding themselves – finding their place, making themselves 'at home' – within the master's house. What is embedded, for men just as for women, is a *divided* self, repressing internal and external voices that are not deemed appropriately 'masculine'. Superficially, however, this looks like men *finding* their own confident voices in the world – even if those voices are so often merely echoes of what Mark Pryce calls '*the* Voice' of hetero-patriarchy: 'incontrovertible, unaccountable, impenetrable'.[29]

'Disorientation': Shaken out of Obliviousness

Within the master's house, we men (and most particularly affluent, White, straight men) are brainwashed to believe that we are 'free'. The world is ours and revolves around us; we can move wherever we want and be whoever we want to be. And yet this fiction depends on a certain 'obliviousness', understood (as Mary McClintock Fulkerson defines it) as a 'power-related willingness not-to-see'.[30] For Nicola's female research participants, 'awakening' from alienation happened through *remaining in* an experience of 'impasse ... marginalization and muteness', often for many years.[31] For (affluent, White, straight) men, conversely, the beginnings of change are much more likely to come only if something happens to us (from 'outside') that stops us in our tracks, de-centres us, breaks us open. We might describe this as 'being *shaken*' out of our individual and collective dishonesties, through encounters, often unintended and unsought, with impenetrable otherness and our own creaturely limits.[32] We encounter 'other worlds' of reality, agency and voice that interrupt, enlarge, question and challenge our limited worldview that we previously imagined was universal.

It is significant that, in Slee's research, women's 'awakenings' happened much more often at the levels of emotion and bodily experience than through 'analysis, strategy or logic'.[33] Verbal and analytical modes of thinking are too adept at deflecting or absorbing challenges. We men, especially, are well trained in pushing back, contradicting, explaining away and silencing our 'others'.[34] Instead, we would do well to pay attention to con-texts of friction and resistance: to the material vibrancy of 'obstacles' and the revelatory opportunities offered by 'dead ends', as Bayo Akomolafe highlights, for example;[35] and to the invitations to solidarity and 'coalition' that emerge not from opportunities for us (well-meaning, White, straight) men to 'help' our 'others', but, as Black theorist Fred Moten puts it sharply: 'out of your recognition that it's fucked up for you, in the same way that we've already recognized that it's fucked up for us. I don't need your help. I just need you to recognize that this shit is killing you, too, however much more softly, you stupid motherfucker, you know?'[36]

* * *

Encountering Christa

Would it be blasphemous to imagine those words on the lips of Jesus? They are perhaps not too far from his denunciations of the hypocrisy of the religious leaders in Matthew 23 ('Woe to you ...!') – with whom those of us who are both Christian and located in positions of structural privilege (White, straight, male, for example) might acknowledge some affinity. And this should caution us against any straightforward identifi-cations with Jesus as a man, whether it be via James Nelson's suggestion that we 'can find clues in him toward a richer and more authentic mascu-linity', Rosemary Radford Ruether's description of Jesus' life and death as 'the kenosis of patriarchy', or Ruth Harley's and my work highlight-ing the ways in which Jesus repeatedly opens himself to be changed by the 'interruptions' of his 'others'.[37] In our work, in fact, we try to hold those observations in tension with Jennifer Harvey's warning – to White Christians especially – that 'identifying with the divine is about the last thing that a white person whose life is embedded in white-supremacist structures [or indeed a man whose life is embedded in patriarchal struc-tures] should be doing'.[38] Whereas we look instead to Zacchaeus (following Harvey), and to the Roman centurion at the foot of the cross, to find our role models for 'betraying the systems' of the master's house, Nicola Slee's work opens up another possibility: *what if Christ were female?*

Widening Horizons

> When she comes to us, will we know her?
> Will her face be turned towards us
> or looking away, beyond our stifled horizons?[39]

Throughout Slee's writing, but especially in *Seeking the Risen Christa*, she seeks out 'a bodily God', and more particularly a 'body of Christ', which 'take[s]/change[s] shape in a multiplicity of sexed, gendered, ethnic and disabled forms'.[40] She locates her work alongside Robert Beckford's explorations of Black masculinity,[41] and Marcella Althaus-Reid's 'bi/Christ',[42] in seeking christological images that 'destabilize hetero-normativity as well as a variety of other power dynamics, by performing gender, ethnicity and sexuality in a range of queer ways, rendering prayer and liturgy queer not merely at its margins but at its centre'.[43] In contrast to hetero-patriarchy's obsession with male-female coupling, penetrative sex, and 'the family' – which all serve the structures of the master's house as means of control – Slee's Christa opens up the possibility of 'so many kinds of awesome love'.[44] Here Slee draws and builds on Audre Lorde's broader conception of the 'erotic' as 'the nurturer ... of all our deepest knowledge', 'the essential bridge between the spiritual and the political', 'the ground of ... joy' and 'the energy to pursue ... change within our world'.[45] Christa, risen, ascended, refuses to be 'confined and contained', 'burst[s] the bounds' of hetero-patriarchy, is always on the move, calls us to an 'ongoing dynamic of finding and losing, arriving and departing', on the way to the 'wide space' of her 'kin-dom'.[46]

Christa says, 'No'

What do you know of me?
Do not assume you can get under my skin ...
Do not think you know me
I am black and I am beautiful and I am a stranger to you.[47]

It might be tempting for a male reader to misidentify Christa's expansiveness as akin to our own experiences of phallic penetration.[48] In our attempts to read 'between the lines', we might mistake the inherent ambiguity of the poet's 'I'[49] as an invitation to insert ourselves into spaces – whether as active participant, or unseen voyeur – where we are not, in fact, written in: naked under the shower with Christa, for example.[50] But it turns out that there are in fact limits to the freedom of us men to move through and occupy spaces. Christa is indeed the 'tree of life' where '[t]here is room for all in your girth',[51] and her hospitality is indeed abundant. But sometimes the table where '[l]arge baskets of bread / and platters of fish / are piled high', where the talk is of 'Rome resisted' and 'paradise imagined', is a 'table of women' (and/or other 'others'), a male-free space.[52] Male-dominated spaces are often those 'places Christa has left', centring herself and her attention elsewhere, where there is space 'to breathe or sing'.[53] Christa is always a subject with agency, eluding the objectification of the male gaze. Many of her 'comings' – in places, in bodies – we will often not notice (because the masculinities we inhabit have trained us to be oblivious of them),[54] and the Christa who can 'talk to me [the woman pray-er] of a woman's salvation / in wounds I can recognize and touch' is speaking a body-language that male readers will hear as profoundly 'other', alien even.[55] Like the disbelieving male disciples of Luke 24.9–11, we men will know the risen Christa only by receiving the testimony of women. Outside of a proximate, 'I-Thou' (and not 'I-It') relationship with those who bear her image, she is, like Slee's 'Black Madonna', an inaccessible stranger to us.

Praying like a White, straight man, then, means learning to hear Christa's 'No', her *noli me tangere* ('do not touch me', John 20.17) which challenges our disordered desires that are 'rooted in control',[56] and which sets out for us limits, boundaries, where we should not or cannot be, when we need to stop or let go. Sam Keen may well be right that '[e]motionally speaking, men are stutterers who often use sexual language to express [our] forbidden desires for communion',[57] but to this condition Slee speaks of the need to discover 'the landscape of the gap', the 'impasse', the 'abyss' – and the 'unlearning' of the *via negativa*, along which 'we are only able to stutter [or hear spoken to us] "not this, not that"'.[58] This place – of 'stuckness', or waiting, or both – repeatedly surfaces in Slee's writing, often cast as a 'Holy Saturday' space, in which Christa is ... what? Dead, to be sure, is one answer. But Slee's poetry offers others too. Is Christa 'underground'? 'Resting'? 'Gathering her power'?[59] ... 'The gap' is an empty space ... but it is also a space pregnant with 'the salvation that cannot be hastened'.[60]

* * *

Into the Woods – and Back?

Come into the woods.
I will not come where
the way is not clear, where
there are no maps, where
the path bends out of sight.
No guide to follow.
Still she calls: *Come into the woods* ...[61]

'Alienation': At Home No Longer?

Prior to our interruptive encounter with Christa, we noted that an experience of profound 'alienation' – 'a sense of being stuck, the inability to grow and move forward' – was a common starting point for women's journeys of faith.[62] For men, I suggested, our default position of 'at-home-ness' within the hetero-patriarchal master's house means that 'alienation' is something we need to be 'shaken' into: through obstacles, crises and encounters with irreducible otherness. The expansiveness and otherness of Christa, her many 'Yeses' and her 'Nos', have fleshed out for us that 'shaking' as divine activity.

But where do we go from here? Traversing 'the gap' – between the master's house and the wide / wild space beyond – is anything but a herculean act of individual will-power, or a 'step by step' linear process, or even a journey where we are ever straightforwardly locatable as 'here' or 'there'. In this final section, then, following closely Slee's work on women's 'faithing', I will suggest some possible patterns and themes, more metaphorical than literal, that might just prove resourceful – that is, translatable into tactics, practices, ways of relating, responding and praying – for men's journeys through 'the gap'.

Slee's recent book Sabbath turns out to be a valuable additional companion for the journey from here. Interweaving the personal, the prayerful and the political, Slee focuses not directly on the master's house of White hetero-patriarchy, but on an overlapping regime, 'the relentless rule of the market and the machine', with its dedication to 'productivity, consumption and the drive to succeed'.[63] In an observation that could apply to either regime, Slee observes: 'We find ourselves caught in sys-temic cycles, locked into forms of structural injustice, which operate in spite of the good intentions of individuals, which are self-perpetuating and self-generating.'[64]

In this poem, the poet finds her feet 'place[d] ... on the shady path into the woods' while she is 'still counting the reasons / for not going'.[65] The journey 'into the woods' of Sabbath-time, then, is partly invitation, command, inexorable pull from 'beyond' – and partly the beginnings of opening ourselves to what Sue Monk Kidd describes as 'a sacred dis-integration'. 'Attachment to the patriarchal world, which we've struggled to unname and unhinge, begins to dissolve and die away, and we are immersed in feelings that go along with dyings.'[66]

'Feeling', 'Failing', 'Refusing': Becoming 'Defective Members'?

Where Monk Kidd describes, in the midst of the crumbling, 'something new and large and mysterious ris[ing] up within us', we men should approach with caution.[67] Our complicity in the ongoing erection of the master's house means we are prone to embrace enthusiastically the rising of the apparently 'new' when it is in fact the latest, re-clad version of the same old structures. Having been 'shaken' into 'impasse', what is first required of us is that we learn to *stay* there, to embrace what, on the Sabbath journey, Slee describes as the 'invitation to cessation', a 'necessary ... not-doing', 'an intentional embrace of "uselessness"'.[68] But what might at times feel like 'rest' or a 'breathing space' (as Nicola suggests of Sabbath-time), for men might often be accompanied by intense feelings of anger, guilt and shame, as we recognize our own complicity in (and benefit from) the structures, lies and deformations that the master's house has wrought, and frustration as we realize there is no easy escape route.

bell hooks is far from a lone voice in arguing that 'many men seeking to be whole must first name the intensity of their rage and the pain it masks',[69] but male rage has too often been acted out in violent and self-destructive expressions. Might it be conceivable, following the recent and suggestive 'affect theology' of Karen Bray, for us men to find ways of channelling such negative emotions such that they become 'wilful blockages' against the 'flows' of White hetero-patriarchy itself – and that this too might be a form of prayer? Bray suggests an 'apophatic' dimension to such resistance: 'to *feel* rather than to *flow*' is to 'know that [we] desire to not take part in what is on offer, but [still] leave open what might come from "coming apart" in the face of such a desire'.[70] A range of possibilities open up, for what feminist theologians Miriam Therese Winter, Adair Lummis and Alison Stokes have named 'defecting in place',[71] including a 'moody protest' of *'unwilling obedience'* (Bray),[72] but also stubborn forms of *non*-participation: a wilful embracing of *failure*; of becoming 'gender traitors' or, we might say, 'defective members' in the master's house.[73]

Embracing failure is, for Slee, one aspect of the invitation to Sabbath: 'failing to live up to the exacting demands of the Master, whoever the Master may be'.[74] Similarly, for queer theorist Jack/Judith Halberstam, consciously embracing 'failure' might be understood as both a refusal and an opening. It is a refusal of 'mastery', 'success' and 'productivity', and of 'the pressure to measure up to patriarchal ideals'. But it also opens up the possibility of 'escap[ing] the punishing norms that discipline behavior and manage human development' into a space governed not by the Darwinist mantra, "may the best man win", but by the "neo-anarchistic credo" of the film *Little Miss Sunshine*: "No one gets left behind!"'[75] There are shards of hope in the wilful embrace of failure.[76] Mark Pryce reads the Gospels of Jesus as offering 'memories of failure ... stories of flesh as narratives of grace', which might 'encourage men to cease in their attempts to be the faultless, omniscient, omnicompetent Voice'.[77] And Slee herself links failure to the organic process of 'composting', an *'un*doing' of human endeavour that works in parallel with 'the resurrection of the wild'.[78]

'Dismantling': 'Tearing Shit Down' and/or Leaving It Behind?

A tension has been emerging here, that we now need to spell out clearly. How is it possible both to be *leaving behind* the master's house, and yet also to be engaged in its *dismantling*? As Willie Jennings reminds us, 'building', both physical and institutional, is part of creaturely life, at best imaging the building of the Creator. However, 'sometimes we must abandon what has been built in order to enter God's building work, and sometimes we must tear down what we have built in order to follow God in building toward life, and sometimes God can take what we have built toward death and turn it toward life'.[79]

Jennings invites us to engage in careful processes of discernment as to which of these is required in any particular context, while holding before us the wider horizon that 'we exist inside a revolution', and that all of our 'building up' happens 'inside the Spirit's crumbling' of the 'world orders' (White hetero-patriarchy being foremost among them) that have 'claim[ed] sovereignty' over us.[80] In Fred Moten's more direct and activist language, we need to recognize that 'what it is that is supposed to be repaired is irreparable. It can't be repaired. The only thing we can do is tear this shit down completely and build something new.'[81] However, Jennings's and Moten's talk of 'building' here does not quite reckon with what Slee has called 'the gap'.[82] The gap, for us (White, straight) men particularly, is between our longing for freedom from the master's house, and our ongoing entanglement in it – including its obsessions both with building, and with directing building operations. As Jack Halberstam frames it (as they read 'between the lines' of Moten and Harney's book *The Undercommons*), 'the gap' (or Moten's term, 'the break') involves gaps of *perception*, *imagination* and *desiring*:

[W]e want to take apart, dismantle, tear down the structure that, right now, limits our ability to find each other, to see beyond it and to access the places that we know lie outside its walls. We cannot say what new structures will replace the ones we live with yet, because once we have torn shit down, we will inevitably see more and see differently and feel a new sense of wanting and being and becoming. What we want after 'the break' will be different from what we think we want before the break.[83]

'Reorientation': 'Fugitive' Communion-seekers?

Those whose bodies have been 'marked' as 'other' within the master's house (whether via the brandings of 'gender', 'sexuality' or 'race', socio-economic 'class', physical or mental 'disability'), in having to read 'between the lines' to find their place, have often glimpsed light through cracks in the crumbling structures. Those who have begun to make 'the break' from the master's house, dwelling in and traversing 'the gap', have also already been engaged in a radically different kind of creaturely building work to that of the master's house from which they are becoming disentangled. They point us, far beyond the White hetero-patriarchal structures that tear and divide, to forms of what Jennings calls *'sharing'* and *'communion'*;[84] Moten and Harney name *'social life'* and *'the undercommons'*;[85] Slee (building on the work of Rita Nakashima Brock and Ada María Izasi-Díaz) identifies as *'Christa/Community'* and/or *'the kindom of God'*;[86] and Halberstam *'no church in the wild'* (after the 2012 song by rappers Jay-Z and Kanye West).[87] 'In the wild': beyond the rigid, oppressive walls of respectability characteristic of the church that is often barely distinguishable from 'the master's house'; and yet, a building and relating *otherwise* that might – with an ironic, playful anti-echo of a deep desiring – be labelled *'no-church'*.

This wild space of communion is, on one level, rooted in *departure*. Moten describes a 'fugitivity' that comes out of the history of slavery, 'an ongoing refusal' that is also 'a desire for the outside', a 'being together in homelessness'.[88] But it is also, as Halberstam underlines, 'not simply the left over space that limns real and regulated zones of polite society; rather, it is a wild place that continuously produces its own unregulated wildness'.[89] For Slee, it is ultimately only in *Christa*'s wildness, her departure from our attempts to contain her, her being 'lost, loosed, let loose ... to rise, ascend, disperse, and be refound', that we are truly able 'to embrace the body of God', in and among our creature-kin – in 'the power of our primal interrelatedness', as Nakashima Brock puts it – 'wherever we turn and travel and touch'.[90]

What is remarkable – especially for us (White, straight) men – is that, from the wild space across 'the gap', there comes an invitation even to *us*. As we begin to 'give up male centrality', self-assertion, space-filling, and 'all forms of controlling and abusive behaviour'; as we begin to acknowledge our insufficiencies and our limits; as we begin to 'learn new skills' of listening attentively and receiving willingly that will help us 'to negotiate the intricate, demanding transition[s] which lie ahead',[91] so we begin also to discover ways towards becoming guests – not hosts – who are welcomed at 'the table of Christa', at which:

The women do not serve
but are served
The children are not silent
but chatter
The menfolk do not dominate
but co-operate
The animals are not shussed away
but are welcomed.[92]

Around such tables – or indeed, as Slee suggests following poet Marge
Piercy, 'sitting on the floor, "on stones and mats and blankets"' – we
might discover new kinds of 'earthy, respectful, collaborative' conversational space 'in which women and men can listen and talk to each other
in more mutual and cooperative ways'.[93] Men in such spaces need continually to develop and deepen our practices of 'de-centring' and radical
receptivity but, as Mark Pryce reminds us, we also need to learn, in conversation, to 'speak for [our]selves about [our]selves' (that is, speaking
out of our particularity, rather than assuming the position of normativity
or universality for our experience), seeking to 'confront [our] feelings
and behaviour[s]' and histories and the many ways in which splinters
of the master's house are still stuck within us.[94] We need to face both
our *own* fears – of intimacy, vulnerability and failure, of difference and
de-centredness, of anger and grief – *and* the fears and scars of those who
have been shouted down and silenced, punished and abused by the house
of White hetero-patriarchy and its masters. This is 'hard dialogue', and
'real talk', 'not afraid to confront difference, conflict and difficult conceptual work'.[95] And yet this kind of deepening conversation-conversion is
also, for Nicola, part of what constitutes 'Sabbath space': it both needs,
and at the same time continues to build and nurture, 'communities [of
women and men] where there is a fundamental commitment to mutual
care and connection'.[96]

'Return': Back to Work?

Each spiralling of the Sabbath rhythm, as Slee traces it, ends with the
(re)discovery of our 'vocation' and a 'return to the daily'.[97] 'One cannot
remain perpetually' in the 'wilds' of the woods, she reminds us: 'there is
no escaping the return'.[98] The challenge of returning, she suggests, is 'how
to survive in this environment without capitulating to the culture, how
to maintain a vision of a different way to live and work' and, ultimately,
to live and work – and to yearn and pray and fail – *towards* that vision.[99]

For those of us who are White, straight men, we cannot definitively escape from the master's house while even some of its structures remain standing – and while any of our creature-kin remain trapped within it. Embracing 'fugitivity' from White hetero-patriarchy is inseparable from return journeys to continue the work of *dismantling* it. In Harney and Moten's terms, the 'with and for' of communion in the wilds cannot be disentangled from the ongoing 'within and against' of work within the institutions of world and church.[100] Traversing 'the gap' is an unavoidably two-way, back-and-forth journeying, and with Slee we should rightly be suspicious of any form of praying that promises a premature 'integration' of the fragments of life and faith, papering over the 'radical fissures and contradictions in personal and ecclesial identities'. Learning to inhabit 'a posture of tension, contradiction and disequilibrium' can be, she reminds us, potentially both 'prophetic' and 'enlivening', acknowledging 'human identity as a constantly changing and shifting eschatological process of embodied becoming'.[101]

Willie Jennings helpfully suggests – especially for those of us whose perceiving, imagining, desiring and building are still in intensive need of schooling – a kind of embodied learning (and praying) that he describes as 'sensing communion and building toward that sensing'.[102] Jennings's phrase echoes the work of trauma theologian Shelly Rambo, who calls us to the work of '*sensing* ... forms of life that are less discernible, more inchoate and tenuous, than visible and secure',[103] life that is 'not miraculously new but instead is a mixed and tenuous process of remaining', that bubbles up even as the powerful 'undertow' forces (of persons, institutions and structures) continue to exert their downward pull.[104] 'Sensing', as Rambo describes it, 'is a movement to reorient oneself in relationship to what is not immediately familiar', relying on an 'interplay of the senses', as we 'attempt to move toward life without knowing its shape'.[105] Here is the work of praying – both individually and collectively – in 'the gap': on the one hand, drawing strength, courage and wisdom to join in resisting the 'undertow' and dismantling the structures that give it power; on the other, sensing, attending to and moving tentatively towards a very different kind of life.

'Standing Together': A Coda

In the Uniting Reformed Church in Southern Africa, a coming-together of denominations historically divided down racial lines, their recent liturgies for communion have inserted, before the confession of sin, an 'affirmation of dignity', intended 'to prevent Christian worship from strengthening or perpetuating the negative self-images produced by racism or sexism'.[106] I conclude with it here, a 'last word' of prayer towards which I know I am continually being drawn:

I stand tall and dignified in the presence of God
and among my fellow human beings.
I accept myself as a precious and unique person,
created through Christ to be the image of the living God.
Together with animals, trees and rivers
we are one living community,
belonging to the earth, our common home.
Guided by the Spirit, we discover who we are, as a family:
Motho ke motho ka batho.[107]

Notes

1 Nicola Slee, *Fragments for Fractured Times: What Feminist Practical Theology Brings to the Table* (London: SCM Press, 2020), 6.

2 Slee, *Fragments for Fractured Times*, 40, referring to Simone Weil, *Waiting on God* (Glasgow: Collins Fount, 1977).

3 Slee, *Fragments for Fractured Times*, 4–6, 13, 47.

4 Willie James Jennings, *After Whiteness: An Education in Belonging* (Grand Rapids: William B. Eerdmans, 2020), 16.

5 Jennings, *After Whiteness*, 34.

6 Jennings, *After Whiteness*, 51; see also Slee, *Fragments for Fractured Times*, 4.

7 Slee, *Fragments for Fractured Times*, 52.

8 Jennings, *After Whiteness*, 6, 8–9, 35, 40–1. See also Willie James Jennings, *The Christian Imagination: Theology and the Origins of Race* (New Haven: Yale University Press, 2010).

9 Audre Lorde, 'The Master's Tools Will Never Dismantle the Master's House', in *Sister Outsider: Essays and Speeches* (Berkeley: Crossing Press, 1984), 110–14.

10 This paragraph draws insights from many places, including Mark Pryce, *Finding a Voice: Men, Women and the Community of the Church* (London: SCM Press, 1996), 15, 21, 76–8; Jennings, *After Whiteness*, 6–7; Martin Hultman and Paul M. Pulé, *Ecological Masculinities: Theoretical Foundations and Practical Guidance* (London: Routledge, 2019).

11 Leonard Cohen, 'Anthem', *The Future* (Columbia Records, 1992).

12 Jan Richardson, *What the Light Shines Through: A Retreat for Women's Christmas 2020*; quoted in Slee, *Fragments for Fractured Times*, 6.

13 Jennings, *After Whiteness*, 152.

14 Slee, *Fragments for Fractured Times*, 36.

15 When engaging with Slee's work here, the space of difference between us is primarily focused on our gendered sexualities (i.e. between lesbian woman and straight man). While we have some other significant identity markers and structural privileges (e.g. race, class) in common, I seek both to acknowledge the further dimensions of my own particularity and locatedness (e.g. as non-disabled and

middle class), and also to augment substantially Slee's brief reflections on her own Whiteness. On this, see Nicola Slee, 'Witnessing to What Remains, or the Power of Persisting: Power, Authority and Love in the Interim Spaces', in *Contemporary Feminist Theologies: Power, Authority, Love*, eds Kerrie Handasyde, Cathryn McKinney and Rebekah Pryor (London: Routledge, 2021), 21–32 (22).

16 Ruth Harley in Al Barrett and Ruth Harley, *Being Interrupted: Reimagining the Church's Mission from the Outside, In* (London: SCM Press, 2020), 23; see also Marjorie Procter-Smith, *Praying With Our Eyes Open: Engendering Feminist Liturgical Prayer* (Nashville: Abingdon Press, 1995), 31.

17 Stephen Whitehead, *Men and Masculinities: Critical Concepts in Sociology* (London: Routledge, 2006), 114, 119–23; Jennings, *After Whiteness*, 143.

18 Grace M. Jantzen, *Power, Gender, and Christian Mysticism* (Cambridge: Cambridge University Press, 1995), 346.

19 Robert Bly, *Iron John* (London: Ebury Publishing, 2013), 2–6.

20 Carol Hanisch, 'The Personal is Political', in *Notes from the Second Year: Women's Liberation – Major Writings of the Radical Feminists*, eds Shulamith Fireston and Anne Koedt (New York: Radical Women, 1970), 76–7.

21 Hultman and Pulé, *Ecological Masculinities*, 83–4; see also Pryce, *Finding a Voice*, 88–90.

22 Seth Mirsky, 'Three Arguments for the Elimination of Masculinity', in *Men's Bodies, Men's Gods: Male Identities in a (Post-)Christian Culture*, ed. Björn Krondorfer (New York: New York University Press, 1996), 27–40 (36).

23 Patrick D. Hopkins, 'Gender Treachery: Homophobia, Masculinity, and Threatened Identities', in *Rethinking Masculinity: Philosophical Explorations in Light of Feminism*, eds Larry May and Robert A. Strikwerda (Lanham: Rowman and Littlefield, 1992), 111–31 (124), quoted in Mirsky, 'Three Arguments', 36.

24 Mirsky, 'Three Arguments', 36. See also Joseph Gelfer, *Numen, Old Men: Contemporary Masculine Spiritualities and the Problem of Patriarchy* (London: Routledge, 2009).

25 Nicola Slee, *Women's Faith Development: Patterns and Processes* (Aldershot: Ashgate, 2004).

26 Jennings, *After Whiteness*, 8.

27 My subtitles here draw both on Slee's work in *Women's Faith Development* and on the threefold structure that Walter Brueggemann identifies in the Psalms. See Slee, *Fragments for Fractured Times*, 32–3, and Walter Brueggemann, *Praying the Psalms: Engaging Scripture and the Life of the Spirit* (Eugene: Cascade Books, 2007).

28 Slee, *Women's Faith Development*, 81–4, 85, quoting Maria Harris, 'Women Teaching Girls: The Power and the Danger', *Religious Education* 88, no. 1 (1993): 52–66 (56). Slee notes that this moment of choice may be experienced less intensely for some Black girls, drawing on the work of Beverly Jean Smith and others who highlight the valuing of female voice, speaking out of, on behalf of, and with the solidarity and support of, the wider community. See Beverly Jean Smith, 'Raising a Resister', in *Women, Girls and Psychotherapy: Reframing Resistance*, eds Carol Gilligan, Annie G. Rogers and Deborah L. Tolman (New York: Harrington Park, 1991), 137–48.

29 Pryce, *Finding a Voice*, 35.

30 Mary McClintock Fulkerson, *Places of Redemption: Theology for a Worldly Church* (Oxford: Oxford University Press, 2007), 17.

31 Slee, *Women's Faith Development*, 107.

32 For an exploration of 'shakenness', see Graham Adams, *Christ and the Other: In Dialogue with Hick and Newbigin* (London: Routledge, 2017), 5; on creaturely limitedness, see Amy Plantinga Pauw, *Church in Ordinary Time: A Wisdom Ecclesiology* (Grand Rapids: William B. Eerdmans, 2017), 153–4.

33 Slee, *Women's Faith Development*, 86.

34 Pryce, *Finding a Voice*, 15. Similar dynamics are at work in Whiteness, as described by Reni Eddo-Lodge, *Why I'm No Longer Talking to White People About Race* (London: Bloomsbury, 2017), and Robin DiAngelo, *White Fragility: Why It's So Hard for White People to Talk About Racism* (Boston: Beacon Press, 2018).

35 Bayo Akomolafe, *These Wilds Beyond Our Fences: Letters to My Daughter on Humanity's Search for Home* (Berkeley: North Atlantic Books, 2017), 102–3.

36 Fred Moten and Stefano Harney, *The Undercommons: Fugitive Planning and Black Study* (Wivenhoe: Minor Compositions, 2013), 140–1.

37 James B. Nelson, *The Intimate Connection: Male Sexuality, Masculine Spirituality* (Philadelphia: Westminster John Knox Press, 1988), 108; Rosemary Radford Ruether, *Sexism and God-Talk: Toward a Feminist Theology* (Boston: Beacon Press, 1993), 137; see also Pryce, *Finding a Voice*, 102–3, 108–9; Barrett and Harley, *Being Interrupted*.

38 Jennifer Harvey, 'What Would Zacchaeus Do?: The Case for Disidentifying with Jesus', in *Christology and Whiteness: What Would Jesus Do?*, ed. George Yancy (London: Routledge, 2012), 84–100 (84), quoted in Barrett and Harley, *Being Interrupted*, 79.

39 Nicola Slee, 'Questions in Search of the Risen Christa', *Seeking the Risen Christa* (London: SPCK, 2011), 1.

40 Slee, *Fragments for Fractured Times*, 57.

41 Robert Beckford, 'Does Jesus have a Penis? Black Male Sexual Representation and Christology', *Theology and Sexuality* 5 (1996): 10–21.

42 Marcella Althaus-Reid, *Indecent Theology: Theological Perversions in Sex, Gender and Politics* (London: Routledge, 2000), 116.

43 Slee, *Fragments for Fractured Times*, 57; Slee, *Seeking the Risen Christa*, 20.

44 Slee, *Praying Like a Woman*, 103.

45 Slee, *Fragments for Fractured Times*, 51, quoting Audre Lorde, 'Uses of the Erotic: The Erotic as Power', in *Sexuality and the Sacred: Sources for Theological Reflection*, eds James B. Nelson and Sandra P. Longfellow (London: Mowbray, 1994), 75–9.

46 Slee, *Seeking the Risen Christa*, 135–6. The term 'kindom' was coined by Ada María Isasi-Díaz in her book *Mujerista Theology* (Maryknoll: Orbis Books, 2005).

47 Nicola Slee, 'Black Madonna', *The Book of Mary* (London: SPCK, 2009), 113.

48 I have explored this temptation further, particularly in reference to the erotic ecclesiology of Graham Ward, in Al Barrett, *Interrupting the Church's Flow: A Radically Receptive Political Theology in the Urban Margins* (London: SCM Press, 2020).

49 Slee, *Fragments for Fractured Times*, 139.

50 Slee, *Seeking the Risen Christa*, 48.

51 Slee, 'Tree of Life', *Seeking the Risen Christa*, 93.

52 Slee, 'The Table of Women', *Seeking the Risen Christa*, 52.

53 Slee, 'Places Christa has Left', *Seeking the Risen Christa*, 118.

54 Slee, 'Come as a Girl', *Seeking the Risen Christa*, 33.

55 Slee, 'Sick Christa', *Seeking the Risen Christa*, 91.

56 Jennings, *After Whiteness*, 149.

57 Sam Keen, *Fire in the Belly: On Being a Man* (New York: Bantam Books, 1991), 78.

58 Slee, *Fragments for Fractured Times*, 101–2.

59 Slee, 'Christa, Returning', *Seeking the Risen Christa*, 119.

60 Slee, 'The Christa of Holy Saturday', *Seeking the Risen Christa*, 97.

61 Nicola Slee, 'Into the Woods', *Sabbath: The Hidden Heartbeat of Our Lives* (London: Darton, Longman and Todd, 2019), 148.

62 Slee, *Women's Faith Development*, 81–2.

63 Slee, *Sabbath*, 30–1.

64 Slee, *Sabbath*, 32.

65 Slee, 'Into the Woods', 148.

66 Sue Monk Kidd, *The Dance of the Dissident Daughter: A Woman's Journey from Christian Tradition to the Sacred Feminine* (New York: HarperCollins, 1996), 88, quoted in Slee, *Women's Faith Development*, 112.

67 Monk Kidd, *The Dance of the Dissident Daughter*, 88.

68 Slee, *Sabbath*, 18, 90.

69 bell hooks, *The Will to Change: Men, Masculinity and Love* (New York: Washington Square Press, 2004), 160.

70 Karen Bray, *Grave Attending: A Political Theology for the Unredeemed* (New York: Fordham University Press, 2019), 146, 150.

71 Miriam Therese Winter, Adair Lummis and Alison Stokes, *Defecting in Place: Women Claiming Responsibility for Their Own Spiritual Lives* (New York: Crossroad, 1994), quoted in Procter-Smith, *Praying with Our Eyes Open*, 31.

72 Bray, *Grave Attending*, 145–50.

73 Hultman and Pulé, *Ecological Masculinities*, 203–4; see also Barrett and Harley, *Being Interrupted*, 83, 173.

74 Slee, *Sabbath*, 30–3.

75 Judith Halberstam, *The Queer Art of Failure* (Durham: Duke University Press, 2011), 2–5, 11.

76 See Marika Rose, *A Theology of Failure: Žižek against Christian Innocence* (New York: Fordham University Press, 2019).

77 Pryce, *Finding a Voice*, 37–9.

78 Slee, *Sabbath*, 158–63; see also Barrett and Harley, *Being Interrupted*, 204–8.

79 Jennings, *After Whiteness*, 77.

80 Jennings, *After Whiteness*, 124.

81 Moten and Harney, *The Undercommons*, 151.

82 Slee, *Fragments for Fractured Times*, 96.

83 Jack Halberstam, 'The Wild Beyond: With and For the Undercommons', in Moten and Harney, *The Undercommons*, 5–12 (6).

84 Jennings, *After Whiteness*, 129, 133.

85 Moten and Harney, *The Undercommons*, 120.

86 Rita Nakashima Brock, *Journeys by Heart: A Christology of Erotic Power* (New York: Crossroad, 1996), and Ada María Isasi-Díaz, *Mujerista Theology: A Theology for the 21st Century* (New York: Orbis Books, 1996). Both are discussed in Slee, *Seeking the Risen Christa*, 9–10, 135; see also Jennings, *Whiteness*, 11, 147.

87 Halberstam, 'The Wild Beyond', 11.

88 Fred Moten, *Stolen Life (consent not to be a single being)* (Durham: Duke University Press, 2018), 131, quoted in Emma Dabiri, *What White People Can Do Next: From Allyship to Coalition* (London: Penguin Books, 2021), 64.

89 Halberstam, 'The Wild Beyond', 7, 11.

90 Slee, *Seeking the Risen Christa*, 135; see also Jennnings, *After Whiteness*, 149; quoting Brock, *Journeys by Heart*, 26.

91 Kathleen Carlin, 'The Men's Movement of Choice', in *Women Respond to the Men's Movement*, ed. Kay Leigh Hagan (San Francisco: Pandora, 1992), 119–25 (123–4).

92 Slee, 'At the Table of Christa', *Seeking the Risen Christa*, 56. See also Slee, 'Joseph', *The Book of Mary*, 47, of whom Slee writes: 'I like the kind of man you were content to be'.

93 Slee, *Women's Faith Development*, 174–5, quoting Marge Piercy, 'Councils', in *Circles on the Water* (New York: Alfred A. Knopf, 1982).

94 Pryce, *Finding a Voice*, 121. I am grateful to Ruth Harley for the observation that the metaphorical language of 'traversing the gap' still leaves us with a dishonest binary: in our lived reality, 'the master's house' and 'the wilds' coexist within the same space. In our co-written work, Ruth and I have been drawn to Mary Daly's description of 'Moments': 'windows' that allow us to jump from the ('male-centred and mono-dimensional') 'Foreground' into the 'Background', 'the Realm of Wild Reality'. See Mary Daly, *Outercourse: The Be-dazzling Voyage* (London: The Women's Press, 1993), 1–6; Barrett and Harley, *Being Interrupted*, 194–6.

95 Slee, *Women's Faith Development*, 175, referencing the work of Carol Lakey Hess, *Caretakers of Our Common House: Women's Development in Communities of Faith* (Nashville: Abingdon Press, 1997), 184.

96 Slee, *Women's Faith Development*, 175. See also Slee, *Sabbath*, 129–49; Moten and Harney, *The Undercommons*, 116; Dabiri, *What White People Can Do Next*, 145–6.

97 Slee, *Sabbath*, 19–20.

98 Slee, *Sabbath*, 177–8.

99 Slee, *Sabbath*, 179. The idea of 'failing towards' comes from Gillian Rose, *The Broken Middle: Out of Our Ancient Society* (Oxford: Blackwell, 1992), 88, a reflexive spiralling that involves, she suggests, 'to know, to misknow and yet to grow' (310).

100 Moten and Harney, *The Undercommons*, 120, 148.

101 Slee, *Fragments for Fractured Times*, 49; see also Halberstam, 'The Wild Beyond', 11.

102 Jennings, *After Whiteness*, 146.

103 Shelly Rambo, *Spirit and Trauma: A Theology of Remaining* (Philadelphia: Westminster John Knox Press, 2010), 162.

104 Rambo, *Spirit and Trauma*, 160–1.

105 Rambo, *Spirit and Trauma*, 162. See also Slee, 'Witnessing to What Remains', 24; Barrett and Harley, *Being Interrupted*, 201.

106 Uniting Reformed Church in Southern Africa, Northern Synod, *Worship Book* (unpublished draft, 2015), 27.

107 Uniting Reformed Church in Southern Africa, *Worship Book*, 27–8. The final line is in Setswana: 'a person is a person because of other people'. See also Ashley Cocksworth, *Prayer: A Guide for the Perplexed* (London: Bloomsbury, 2018), 200–1, and Slee, *Fragments for Fractured Times*, 108–18 on a spirituality of 'standing'.

PART 4

Moving Theology

Beaford Church

Nicola Slee

Week after week they gather and make
their simple offering. Kathleen,
twice widowed, leads the prayers, reads the sermon
the vicar has written, and smiles nervously.
Or teacher Greg in his smart black coat
bringing his motherless sons, insists
on the King James Version and speaks to us
in Shakespeare's tongue. Afterwards over coffee,
Truda in her nineties tells of the love
of art and architecture nurtured in this village.
Every day, Rob opens and closes the church
so that I can shelter from the hail and rain
and sit in the porch or venture further in
to gaze at the reredos the mice are eating.
Once in the pub, close to tears, he told me
how he's battled depression all winter, and yet
I've never met him without being blessed
by human warmth. Others keep the churchyard
in good order, clearing the leaves
for the snowdrops to lift perfect heads, and daffodils
to thrust their spikes up into light.
I love to walk among its dead,
read the headstones, sit on mossy tombs
and watch and listen to the rooks overhead.

None of them know of liturgy or lectionary,
have little use for theology. They go on
being the ordinary, everyday saints
in this unremarkable English village,
a plot of holiness hidden from view.
Their faces shine as the sun, washed clean
by rain and age and tears. The years
have gathered them in, and me with them.

12

Transformative, Christian Religious Education and Praxis Forms of Learning

ANTHONY G. REDDIE

My association and connection with Nicola Slee goes back to the mid-1990s when we were both doctoral students with the famed Professor John M. Hull. Without realizing it, I wonder if John Hull knew that within the parameters of his monthly postgraduate research seminar, he was inadvertently pioneering a mode of alternative scholarship, in which practical theology was being combined with liberative forms of theological reflection. Nicola and I were both pursuing doctoral studies looking at the nexus of practical theology and, in her case, feminist theology and, in mine, Black theology. Our respective doctoral work was undertaken in the School of Education at the University of Birmingham and not the then School of Historical Studies in which the Theology Department was located. So, in both our respective works, pedagogy and learning have been to the forefront of our theological forms of educational inquiry.

It was through the interdisciplinary mode of scholarship that emerged from my initial doctoral studies[1] that I developed a form of intellectual inquiry that brings together Black theology and Christian education for the express purpose of conscientization of ordinary people. I have remained committed to a participative approach to the task of doing theology.[2] This approach is one that seeks to engage with ordinary people and sees their presence as integral both to the method of and any resultant 'God-talk'.[3] It is an approach to the task of doing theology that attempts to improve on current practice in terms of how the theological implications of the Christian faith are lived out in particular contexts and to what ends. In this respect, my work falls within the broader arena of practical theology in terms of the desire to reflect upon practice and to interrogate the relationship between the theory and practice of faith, with particular reference to the historic praxis of the church.[4]

At the time of writing, what separates my work from many – if not all – practical theologians in the UK is my close attention to the questions posed by Black experience, 'race', racism, White hegemony and its resultant practice of White ethnocentrism. I will return to the challenges of engaging with White hegemony in the brief final section of this chapter.

My scholarship has always existed at the nexus of Black theology and Christian education.[5] In terms of the latter, my work has been concerned with using the frameworks of radical, liberative education as a conduit for undertaking Black theological-focused work. The purpose of this scholarship is the conscientization and Christian formation of ordinary lay people and those training for public, authorized, Christian ministry. My participative approach to undertaking Black theological scholarship is one that seeks to use models of experiential learning, such as exercises and games, role-play and drama as an interactive means of engaging with adult learners, in order that they can be impacted by, learn from and contribute to the development of new knowledge concerning the theory and practice of Black theology.

Christian Education as the Practice of Freedom

The development of my work as a practical theologian comes from within the more specific discipline of Christian education. The term 'Christian Education' can be defined and understood in a variety of ways. Jeff Astley, Leslie Francis and Colin Crowder provide a helpful starting point for a definition and a rationale for Christian education. The authors describe Christian education as:

> The phrase ... often used quite generally to refer to those processes by which people learn to become Christian and to be more Christian, through learning Christian beliefs, attitudes, values, emotions and dispositions to engage in Christian actions and to be open to Christian experiences.[6]

In using Christian education as a means of exploring anti-racist discipleship, I am concerned with providing an accessible framework for the radical reinterpretation of the Christian faith for the transformation of ordinary people.

Paulo Freire's groundbreaking work in devising appropriate pedagogies for teaching marginalized and oppressed peoples is legendary.[7] Freire developed a philosophy of education that challenged poor and oppressed people to reflect upon their individual and corporate experiences and begin to ask critical questions about the nature of their existence. The radical nature of this critical approach to the task of teaching and learning brought Freire to the attention of the military government in Brazil in 1964. He was subsequently imprisoned and then exiled. In exile, he began to refine further his educational philosophy and method.

He came to international attention with the publication of his first book, *Pedagogy of the Oppressed*,[8] which laid the foundations for a seismic shift in the whole conception of how poor, oppressed and marginalized people might be educated. The importance of Paulo Freire cannot be overstated. In developing a rigorous and critical approach to the task of educating those who are poor and oppressed, Freire created an essential template by which religious educators and practical theologians might re-conceptualize their task. One of Freire's central concepts was that of 'conscientization'. This is a process where poor and oppressed people become politically aware of the circumstances in which they live and the ways in which their humanity is infringed upon and blighted by the often dehumanizing contexts that surround them.[9] Allen J. Moore commenting on this aspect of Freire's work says:

> Conscientization in Freire's work is apparently both an individual experience and a shared experience of a people who are acting together in history. A way of life is not determined from thinking about the world but is formed from the shared praxis. In this critical approach to the world, basic attitudes, values, and beliefs are formed and a people are humanized or liberated. Conscientization, therefore, leads to a life lived with consciousness of history, a life lived that denounces and transforms this history in order to form a new way of life for those who are oppressed.[10]

Freire's approach to education has opened up new vistas for religious educators, along with pastoral and practical theologians. Freire's work, with its emphasis on human transformation and self-actualization, has become the template by which various models of critical pedagogy, be they liberation theologies, liberative models of psychology or transformative education, have sought to develop differing perspectives on the task of socio-cultural and political development.[11] In my scholarship, I have attempted to combine the radical intent of transformative education arising from the Freirerian tradition with Black liberation theology in order to develop a more participative and interactive mode of theo-pedagogical engagement that moves intellectual discourse beyond mere theorizing into more praxis-based forms of practice.

Transformative Christian Education in the Black Experience

Since the late 1960s, Black religious educators have sought to provide an alternative means of understanding the Christian faith. This counter proposition has refuted notions of entitlement and privilege and the constructs that are predicated on White normality. These models of Christian socialization and formation seek to affirm Black experience and embodiment, focusing on Black identities and the existential quest for self-determination. What has underpinned these radical counter-assertive models of Christian-inspired teaching and learning is the prophetic stance of Black liberation theology, the model of theological articulation that underpins this work.

Black Theology

When speaking of Black theology, I am referring to a specific self-named enterprise of reinterpreting the meaning of God as revealed in Christ, in light of existential Black experience. The point of departure in Black theology is the existential and ontological reality of Blackness and the Black experience – namely, how does it feel to be a Black body in the world and what is the theological meaning of this experience? Where is God in the midst of the existential crisis as Black bodies seek to feel and to be whole in a world where authentic being is often denied them?[12]

Black theology is a theology of liberation and is not just theology undertaken by Black people. From earliest iterations, Black theology was conceived as a form of liberation theology.[13] Like all forms of liberation theology, Black theology focuses its concerns on ortho-praxis rather than orthodoxy. The commitment to the former as opposed to the latter is partly a result of a form of existential pragmatism, in which the practical challenges of resisting racism and trying to fight for Black self-determination has taken precedence over historical arguments on what constitutes correct understandings of God.[14] Traditionally, Black theology's interest in, say, doctrine has been rooted in the extent to which particular teachings about God in Christ lend themselves to praxiological struggle, or whether they promote passivity or – even worse – utter indifference.[15]

The additional reason Black theology has eschewed a concern for orthodoxy results from the historical realization that there has been little evidence within White Euro-American Christianity that authorized teaching – 'correct' teaching – has any substantive relationship with ethical, non-racist behaviour.[16]

Black theology, therefore, has often adopted a deontological *modus operandi* that has critiqued White Christianity for its collusion with slavery, racism and colonialism while challenging Black Christianity to critical forms of resistance to White hegemony, promoting Black self-determination and radical agency as its ethical riposte.

Black Christian Education

Arguably, the single most important voice in the development of this tradition has been the late great Grant S. Shockley.[17] Shockley was one of the early pioneers of Black, liberative approaches to Christian education and the socialization and Christian formation of African Americans. His work, which began in the 1960s and extended into the early 1990s, was one of the first substantive attempts to reorient the very conceptualization of Christian socialization and formation. Shockley outlined a five-stage implementation programme for a liberative model of Christian education for Black people. In the ongoing development of this work, Shockley asserts: 'The center of education for liberation occurs when persons are able to utilize their capacities of self-transcendence to evaluate reality, and as subjects, of naming the world instead of being named by it.'[18]

An important and indeed necessary riposte to the bounded and restricted parameters set out by Western Christianity has been the fusing of Black theology and Christian education in the Black experience. Inspired by Shockley, my earliest pastoral and scholarly work was an attempt to combine Black theology and Christian education, in order to create a radical model of Christian learning that was predicated on liberative, pedagogical principles.[19] Shockley argues that the process of learning about and being nurtured into the Christian faith for predominantly Diasporan Black people should be concerned primarily with their holistic development, linking existential concerns with a liberative, biblical hermeneutic.[20]

Shockley, taking his cue from Black theology, argues that the formational process, by which Black people learn to become Christians and the ideological framing of this pedagogical task, is one that should eschew the abstractions of doctrinal purity. Rather, the emphasis must be on inculcating life skills, enabling Black people to navigate the perilous terrain created by White hegemony.[21] Shockley is clear that for many, if not most, Black people in the USA (and in the UK also, in terms of Black people of African and Caribbean descent) our experience has been one of responding to the existential travails that have marked our troubled existence.

Shockley's determination was that all models of Christian-inspired teaching and learning should be contextual, liberative and relevant to the needs and realities of Black people. In arguing for the essential link between transformative models of pedagogy and Black theology, Shockley writes:

Black Theology has been instructive at the point of letting us know that any Religious education programme that might be constructed, must grow out of and centre around the experiences, relationships and situational dilemmas that Black people face in their day to day struggle to survive, develop, and progress in an often hostile, uncaring majority-dominated society.[22]

In the context of this work, I believe a constant engagement with the seminal scholarship of Grant Shockley remains imperative, as he charts the essential building blocks for this modality of socialization and formation into the Christian faith. In effect, Shockley offers alternative constructs by which we might define the very nature and intent of Christianity.[23]

The development of Christian education for Black people that is focused on personal development and social transformation has had to respond to the wider context of socio-political ferment, marginalization and oppression. Its birth and subsequent development was as a direct consequence of racism and colonial subjugation. Delores H. Carpenter argues that the Christian education of Black people in the USA has been a struggle against the historic forces of oppression. This Christian education struggle is linked to the fight for relevance and affirmation, and the parlous nature of this enterprise within an overall context of poverty and marginalization.[24]

In reconfiguring the nature and intent of Christianity post-Donald Trump and Brexit, I am indebted to the inspirational work of Olivia Pearl Stokes who, along with Grant Shockley, is one of the pioneers of this transformative movement in liberative education. Stokes argues that the social tumult of the 1960s was the impetus that gave rise to the development of liberationist modes of Christian learning and socialization.[25] Stokes argues: 'Thus education in the Black Church, with insights from Black theology, must become a part of that indispensable structure for survival and transformation that ameliorates these societal ills Christian faith is committed to remedy.'[26] Stokes's genius lay in her appreciation that religious education needed to be aligned to liberation theology – particularly Black theology of liberation – in order that the necessary enactment of liberative praxis is released within Black churches. At the time when the temptation was to see Christian religious education in purely pietistic terms, with emphasis placed on the inculcation of Christian doctrine and behavioural virtues, Stokes's brilliance was to re-envisage the very form and intent of religious pedagogy. Stokes believed that the significance of Christian religious education lay in its ability to conscientize Black people, helping them, like the emerging Black liberation theology, to see the gospel as indispensable to and consistent with their social condition.[27]

It can be argued that Olivia Pearl Stokes remains the unheralded architect of a liberative model of religious pedagogy that sowed the seeds for what was to emerge as the liberationist approaches to Black Christian socialization and formation, alongside Shockley.[28]

Given the present epoch of rising White nationalism in the USA and across Europe, not forgetting Britain's challenge of dealing with Brexit, we need alternative constructs for conceiving the normative posture and archetypal exemplars for what constitutes Christianity.

Participative Approaches to Black Theological Pedagogy

My own approach to linking transformative religious education and Black liberation theology has given rise to an interactive and participative mode of scholarly engagement. The roots of my approach to undertaking theological work was grounded in my formative development as a community educator working with poor, working-class Black communities in Birmingham, in the West Midlands region of the UK. The significant factor in my intellectual and scholarly development has been the idiosyncratic journey I have taken in order to achieve this seemingly respectable nomenclature of an academic.

My initial development as a scholar arose from an interdisciplinary research project, during the course of which I gained the confidence to devise improvisational techniques and approaches to theological reflection that intersect with the lived realities and subjectivities of predominantly ordinary Black people.[29] This formative Black theological work was one that was conscious of the cultures, identities, historical and contemporary experiences and expressions of Christian faith within the socio-political and economic realities of inner-city life in the UK. I have developed a form of scholarship that I have named 'participative Black theology'. Participative Black theology is the creative nexus between 'traditional' Black theology and Christian education. This approach to critical pedagogy has been refined over the years and has developed into an interdisciplinary mode of practical, Black theological reflection.

At the heart of my participative Black theology is the use of exercises and games that seek to enable participants to reflect critically on self, and through the enaction of a central activity they are enabled to explore aspects of the theory and practice of Black theology in dialogue with others. In order to provide the grounding for the interactive, embodied, pedagogical engagement that lies at the heart of participative Black theology I have created a number of experiential exercises in which adult participants can explore the dynamics of encounter within a safe learning environment. The thrust for this work has emerged from previous pieces of research.[30] In this approach to Black theology, I have used drama as a means of utilizing a creative and artistic methodology for engaging with ordinary people. This approach has resonance with Slee's scholarship and her use of poetry as a means of exploring feminist theological work. In both cases, our respective scholarship explores the interface between artistic expression, creative writing and liberative theological reflection.

My work as a participative Black theologian seeks to develop models of Black theological reflection and learning that encapsulate the central tenets of Black theology within a liberative pedagogical framework. My development as a scholar has been concerned with attempting to combine Christian education with Black theology in order to provide an accessible framework for the radical reinterpretation of the Christian faith for the transformation of ordinary people.

At the heart of participative Black theology is the notion of 'performative action'. Performative action requires that we creatively engage with the 'other' in a socio-constructed space – often in a workshop setting – in which all participants promise to engage with the 'other' in a fashion that affirms mutuality, cooperation and a shared commitment to the production of new knowledge.[31] The production of new knowledge is not simply for the purposes of passing exams or writing term papers. Rather, the desire is to create new forms of knowing for the expressed purpose of changing behaviour and developing better praxis in terms of Christian discipleship.

This process of performative action often operates within informal workshop settings, in which I seek to create a safe space that affords predominantly ordinary lay people opportunities to reflect critically on self and their engagement with others as Christian disciples within contexts and cultures that inform their experience as human beings. In this pedagogical approach to Black participative theology I have used a variety of exercises and activities for enabling participants to explore their feelings and emotions in a safe space. The exercises allow them to adopt imaginary roles and to 'park' their sometimes 'extreme' feelings within a comparatively safe 'rest area' where they can notionally ascribe responsibility for their anger, frustration or sense of tension to the fictional persona of the character they have adopted in the exercise.

The use of a participative approach to Black theology, linked with Christian education, for the purposes of encouraging adult learners to engage in anti-racial models of Christian discipleship, is one that uses Martin Luther King Jr's notion of the 'Beloved Community' as its central heuristic.[32] The use of exercises and drama represents an invitation for adult learners to reflect within the hospitable and safe space of the workshop. In this context, they can explore and commit themselves to working for and becoming a part of the collective spiritual and psychological journey of the Christian church, moving towards the 'promised land' of racial justice – what in effect I would describe as the 'Reign of God' or 'God's gracious economy'.[33] In the various exercises, participants, by means of conversation and interaction, have the opportunity to reflect on their action within the context of a central activity, and to assess their agency and responses to it for its truthfulness to God's gracious activity in Jesus Christ, when juxtaposed with the historical and contemporary experience of racism and oppression.[34]

The participative element of the work challenges learners to decide how they will inhabit particular spaces and places in order to assess in what ways they are playing out learnt pathologies that are often informed by the specious binaries of 'them' and 'us'.[35] What would happen, for example, if participants were enabled to take on the persona of the 'other' in order to live out their realities and experiences within a participative exercise? To what extent would these experiences change their subjective self and their concomitant consciousness?

The journey towards the beloved community is one in which the process is as important as the destination that is reached. In the context of performative action, one is constantly challenging participants to question their assumptions on what is deemed to be 'normative' and that which is termed as 'aberrant' or 'transgressive'. The *modus operandi* of this approach to undertaking participative Black theology is for the purpose of offering participants new models of being Christian in a context where White nationalism and racism is on the rise. The purpose of this approach to undertaking Black theology lies in the belief that internalized change (spiritual and psychological) can be a conduit for externally, verified changes in behaviour and practice. Both of these modes provide the subjective, experiential basis for liberation, at an individual, interpersonal, communal and – ultimately – systemic level.

The use of participative exercises creates a scholarly connectivity between, on the one hand, teaching and learning that conscientizes students in the classroom and, on the other hand, the creation of new knowledge within the wider purview of practical theological exploration. This model of liberative, pedagogical work is predicated on a participative teaching and learning process. The natural corollary of this pedagogical approach is a model of liberative theological reflection that is undertaken by means of participative exercises through which new theories and concepts for Christian praxis are enacted.

In these participative workshops, I have often used a particular experiential exercise as a way of enabling White students, for example, to reflect on the powerful but hidden normative strength of Whiteness.[36] The exercises often work as a form of liberative pedagogy that explores theological anthropology among people engaged in various forms of Christian ministry. Here, I would like to describe briefly a particular exercise I have developed in order to demonstrate the pedagogical approach to participative Black theology.

The exercise begins with each participant receiving a piece of paper on which is printed a series of four concentric circles. The participants look at the innermost circle and are asked to put down one term (or at most two) that defines them. This term is central to how they see themselves at that moment. It may be factual (male, female, man, woman) or it may be a characteristic (kind or loving), or a relational term (mother, uncle, child of God) or generic (human being), or something else. I try not to say too much, for fear of suggesting what the participants might name. The term is located in the innermost circle as it is most central (or most important) to how that individual understands themselves as a human being.

The exercise continues with successive movements out from the central circle, with the participants invited to put down further terms that define them. When different terms have been placed in all the circles, I ask participants to share what they have listed. Is there anything immediate to note about where particular terms have been placed? The exercise is a practical, experiential-participative form of pedagogy for exploring the theological subjectivity of Christian disciples.

The exercise combines participative, experiential pedagogy and Black liberation theology in order to challenge participants to reflect critically on what it means to claim that we are created in the image of God. African American Black theologian Dwight Hopkins has shown that being a Black human being is a concept that is both complex and often illusory.[37] Black and Womanist theologians have repeatedly argued that one cannot take as axiomatic any sense of what it means to be a Black human being that has not in itself been both a bold, critical act of self-assertion and a determined act of will.[38] When asking participants to reflect on the terms they have used in the exercise, I have often found it illuminating to ask what is *not* stated by those terms. I have used this exercise on myself on many occasions, most usually when carrying it out with others in a workshop setting. I have a golden rule of never asking anyone to do something I am not prepared to do myself, and I therefore ensure that I also complete the exercise.

The exercise enables me to undertake the task of conscientizing students in forms of theological reflection that engage with issues of race, identity, power and context in Christian ministry and discipleship. This method is a form of participative, liberative pedagogy that enables students to explore theological anthropology as a form of social inquiry. This and other exercises have been used to enable students to reflect critically on their experience in learning about and being immersed into participative Black theology, but also seeks to provide them with opportunities to undertake their own research projects. So, for example, I have encouraged students to use this participative piece of work to undertake their own forms of qualitative research, particularly into contextual theological anthropology in practical theology. As a practical theologian, I am eager that all participants in the workshops become anti-racist Christians committed to living out a radical and liberative faith that means standing alongside others in solidarity against injustice. In particular, I want White participants to become Christian activists who will resist the toxic tentacles of racism.

The bulk of my participative Black theology work has occurred outside of the formal academy, as there are few places in which Black theology is taught outside of the Queen's Foundation for Ecumenical Theological Education. Conversely, in such work as 'Presiding in the Classroom', Slee has written extensively on the liturgical dimensions of her scholarship as a feminist practical theologian.[39] Our respective scholarship, whether within classroom or workshop settings, incorporates a major commitment to inclusivity, safe space and radical transformative models of teaching and learning.

This work is very much a part of the broader tradition of utilizing transformative, Christian religious education, coupled with Black theology, as a means of challenging the ubiquity of Whiteness, as an epistemological and a theological problem. In his latest text, *After Whiteness*, Willie James Jennings critiques the phenomenon of Whiteness, arguing how the conflation of European mastery, White male, colonial power and the internalization of notions of White superiority becomes the means by which epistemology is developed.[40] Jennings illustrates how Whiteness became conjoined with patriarchy and colonialism to unleash an ethic of mastery, self-sufficiency and control, as the defining elements for what constitutes notions of development and progress. Jennings's work, which is aimed primarily at theological education, distils the means by which the production of knowledge and pedagogical insights on the craft of ministry has been informed by coloniality and Whiteness. Jennings is clear that this analysis is not about White people per se. Rather, it is the epistemological underpinning of a set of theo-cultural constructs, systems and practices that govern how theology and education operate in the West and which inform our ways of being and our praxis.[41]

In my long history within theological education the underlying theme that has informed the teaching and learning of Christian theology and ministry has been one of Whiteness. It has always been the proverbial elephant in the room, but rarely seen or acknowledged, no matter how loudly it trumpeted its presence and no matter the amount of waste matter it produced. If we look at the subterranean constructs of British theological education there is no attempt to locate the ethnic and cultural positionality of the authors, as if there is no relationship between the formative identity of the creator of knowledge and the construction of that knowledge itself. As I have indicated in a previous work, this form of generic universalism is where theological ideas are developed with little in the way of contextual specificity and reflexivity is identified in the work.[42] This ongoing mode of scholarship that I have developed seeks to create a radical form of theo-pedagogical praxis that makes Whiteness a visible entity in the means by which we conceive of Christian formation.

Conclusion

In the final analysis, this overarching approach to liberative pedagogy is one that recognizes the significance of personal, subjective and affective learning as a conduit for a transformative, anti-racist practice of Christian discipleship. It utilizes a critical nexus of liberative pedagogy and participative Black theological reflection via performative forms of action, in order to raise the critical consciousness of learners and so bring about new forms of embodied, liberationist-inspired models of Christian praxis. The learning that emerges from these creative and critical encounters enables participants to reflect on their own embodied subjectivity in order to be cognisant of self and thus engage in a more informed manner with the 'Other'. It is my contention that the subjective and experiential basis of this approach to anti-racist Christian discipleship lies at the heart of the God who makes Godself known in personal encounters with all people, through the humanity of Jesus, in the power of the Holy Spirit. Given our present epoch of rising White nationalism in the USA and across Europe, not forgetting Britain's challenge of dealing with Brexit, we need alternative constructs for conceiving the normative posture and archetypal exemplars for what constitutes Christianity. It is my belief that this model of religious education can be the conduit for alternative modes of Christian formation.

This approach to Christian formation is not predicated on an axiomatic understanding of Christian discipleship that is reflected in the concealed and tacit notions of White normativity, in which Whiteness comes to represent the embodied ideal for notions of belonging. Conversely, trans-formative models of Christian education in the Black experience are forms of liberative, faith-based pedagogy whose focus is on marginalized Black bodies in which the crucified Christ is revealed. This work draws on the radical tradition of Christian education pioneered by African Americans since the late 1960s, which has been augmented by my own developing work in participative Black theology. This work is commit-ted to radical subjective change in the Christian discipleship of ordinary people, in the belief that authentic, socio-political transformation begins from the bottom up. It is a form of socio-political theo-pedagogy that has informed my life for the past 20 or so years, and to which – I imagine – I will continue to devote my energies in the years to come.

In offering this chapter as a part of this book, I do so believing that my scholarship is connected with Nicola Slee's by means of our joint commitment to liberative praxis that reflects on the dynamics of lived religious experience. Slee's work with feminist practical theology, like my own scholarship, has contained an important dimension of seeking to hear the voices of those who are often unheard and marginalized. In the context of her research into women's faith development, I have often seen echoes with my work as it pertains to those whom I have termed 'the voiceless'. In this regard, our respective approaches to practical liberative models of theological reflection incorporate an encounter with real bodies as opposed to merely theorizing about them. Both Nicola and I have remained committed to working with people and seeking to utilize the import of lived religious experience as a substantive point of departure for theological reflection. In adopting practical theological models of reflection and pedagogy, we have attempted to move beyond the more traditional modes of liberative theologies that are often content to theorize on the lives of ordinary people of faith, as opposed to talking and engag-ing with them. We both believe that the insights of ordinary people are worth hearing, and their accounts of God, faith and spirituality remain important source material for the liberation theologian seeking to make a difference. Authentic liberative praxis is achieved when we take the time to centre on the lived experiences of ordinary people, not solely as idols and icons on whom we can reflect, but as co-creators of knowledge alongside that of scholars and academics.[43] As members of the British & Irish Association for Practical Theology and having served together on the executive committee and as trustees, I trust that our respective works will continue to walk in parallel, as we each seek to engage in scholarship that is committed to liberative praxis.

Notes

1 I was a doctoral student in the School of Education, studying with Professor John M. Hull, in the University of Birmingham, between September 1995 and June 2000. My thesis was entitled 'The Christian Education of African Caribbean Children in Britain: Creating a New Paradigm by Developing Better Praxis' (University of Birmingham, 2000).

2 Please note the important semantic difference between my notion of *articulating* theology and the *doing* of theology. The latter, for me, represents a more engaged dynamic in which ideas and talk about God are undertaken through an active or participative framework in which ordinary people are actively involved in the process of theological exploration and articulation. This commitment can be seen in three of my later books. See Anthony G. Reddie, *Acting in Solidarity: Reflections in Critical Christianity* (London: Darton, Longman and Todd, 2005), *Dramatizing Theologies: A Participative Approach to Black God Talk* (London: Routledge, 2006) and *Black Theology in Transatlantic Dialogue* (New York: Palgrave Macmillan, 2006). The more 'traditional' mode of articulating theology, as witnessed in the works of many systematic and constructive theologians, does not *necessarily* contain any component to engage with people in the development of one's theological ideas or concerns.

3 In using this term, I am referring to what one might describe as 'non-professional' theologians or people who have not received any formal training in the study of theology or in theological reflection. In the context of Christianity and the church, ordinary people are lay, from predominantly poorer socio-economic backgrounds, and have experienced comparatively little success or achievement within the context of formal education. Jeff Astley has undertaken some important work in defining his understanding of the nature, intent and methodological points of departure in terms of what he describes as 'ordinary theology' undertaken by presumably 'ordinary people'. See Jeff Astley, *Ordinary Theology: Looking, Listening and Learning in Theology* (Aldershot: Ashgate, 2002).

4 See Paul Ballard and John Pritchard, *Practical Theology in Action: Christian Thinking in the Service of Church and Society* (London: SPCK, 2000); see also Duncan B. Forrester, *Truthful Action: Explorations in Practical Theology* (Edinburgh: T&T Clark, 2000).

5 Portions of this chapter have been previously published in Anthony G. Reddie, 'Teaching and Researching Practical Theology: A Liberative Participative Approach to Pedagogy and Qualitative Research', in *Qualitative Research in Theological Education: Pedagogy in Practice*, eds Mary Clark Moschella and Susan Willhuack (London: SCM Press, 2018), 118–32, and 'Participative Black Theology as a Pedagogy of Praxis', in *Black Practical Theology*, eds Dale P. Andrews and Robert L. Smith (Waco: Baylor University Press, 2015), 59–72.

6 Jeff Astley, Leslie J. Francis and Colin Crowder, eds, *Theological Perspectives on Christian Formation* (Grand Rapids: William B. Eerdmans, 1996), x.

7 See Paulo Freire, *Pedagogy of the Oppressed* (New York: Herder and Herder, 1999); see also Paulo Freire, *Education for Critical Consciousness* (New York: Continuum, 1990), and *A Pedagogy of Hope: Relieving Pedagogy of the Oppressed* (New York: Continuum, 1999).

8 Freire, *Pedagogy of the Oppressed*.

9 Paulo Freire, *Education for Critical Consciousness* (New York: Continuum, 1990), 18–20.

10 Allen J. Moore, *Religious Education as Social Transformation* (Birmingham: Religious Education Press, 1989), 27.

11 For an excellent distillation and application of Paulo Freire's ideas that move from theological reflection to community forms of transformative education, see Anne Hope, Sally Timmel and Chris Hodzi, *Teaching for Transformation: A Handbook for Community Workers* – Books 1–3 (Gweru: Mambo Press, 1994), and *Teaching for Transformation: A Handbook for Community Workers* – Book 4 (London: Intermediate Technology Publications, 1999).

12 See Delroy Hall, 'The Middle Passage as Existential Crucifixion', *Black Theology: An International Journal* 7, no. 1 (2009): 45–63.

13 James H. Cone, who is acknowledged as the founder of the systematic articulation of Black theology, has argued convincingly that the discipline and its accompanying practice is committed to human liberation. See James H. Cone, *A Black Theology of Liberation* (Maryknoll: Orbis Books, 1990).

14 See Gayraud S. Wilmore, *Pragmatic Spirituality: The Christian Faith through an Africentric Lens* (New York: New York University Press, 2004).

15 James Cone asserts that most White theology that has emerged from White Christianity has led to indifference to the existence of racism and the suffering that this has exerted on Black people. See James H. Cone, 'Theology's Great Sin: Silence in the Face of White Supremacy', *Black Theology: An International Journal* 2, no. 2 (2002): 139–52.

16 See Anthony G. Reddie, 'Not Just Seeing, but Really Seeing: A Practical Black Liberationist Spirituality for Re-interpreting Reality', *Black Theology: An International Journal* 7, no. 3 (2009): 339–65.

17 For the best scholarly appraisal of Shockley's life, see Charles R. Foster and Fred Smith, *Black Religious Experience: Conversations on Double Consciousness and the Work of Grant Shockley* (Nashville: Abingdon Press, 2004).

18 Grant S. Shockley, 'Christian Education and the Black Religious Experience', in *Ethnicity in the Education of the Church*, ed. Charles R. Foster (Nashville: Scarritt, 1987), 31.

19 See Anthony G. Reddie, *Growing into Hope: Christian Education in Multi-Ethnic Churches* – 2 Volumes (Peterborough: Methodist Publishing House, 1998); see also Anthony G. Reddie, *Nobodies to Somebodies: A Practical Theology for Education and Liberation* (Peterborough: Epworth Press, 2003).

20 Grant S. Shockley, 'Black Pastoral Leadership in Religious Education', in *The Pastor as Religious Educator*, ed. Robert L. Browning (Birmingham: Religious Education Press, 1987), 195–7.

21 Grant S. Shockley, 'Black Theology and Religious Education', in *Theologies of Religious Education*, ed. Randolph Crump Miller (Birmingham: Religious Education Press, 1995), 315–32.

22 Shockley, 'Black Theology and Religious Education', 315–21.

23 Shockley, 'Christian Education and the Black Religious Experience', 31–5.

24 Delores H. Carpenter, 'A Response to Brian Tippen', *Religious Education* 88, no. 4 (1993): 622–6.

25 Olivia Pearl Stokes, 'Education in the Black Church: Design for Change', *Religious Education* 69, no. 4 (1974): 433–45 (438).

26 Stokes, 'Education in the Black Church', 438.

27 Stokes, 'Education in the Black Church', 433–45.

28 See Kenneth H. Hill, *Religious in the African American Tradition: A Comprehensive Introduction* (St Louis: Chalice Press, 2007), 83–4.

29 An example of this eclectic and participative practical methodology within the context of my preaching ministry can be found in Anthony G. Reddie, 'An Interactive Odyssey', in *Pulpit Journeys*, ed. Geoffrey Stevenson (London: Darton, Longman and Todd, 2006), 149–65.

30 See Reddie, *Acting in Solidarity* and Reddie, *Dramatizing Theologies*.

31 See Jose Irizarry, 'The Religious Educator as Cultural Spec-Actor: Researching Self in Intercultural Pedagogy', *Religious Education* 98, no. 3 (2003): 365–8; see also Clark C. Apt, *Serious Games* (New York: Viking Press, 1970).

32 See Lewis V. Baldwin, *Toward the Beloved Community: Martin Luther King, Jr., and South Africa* (Cleveland: The Pilgrim Press, 1995).

33 I am very much indebted to my friend and colleague Michael N. Jagessar for the latter term or phrase for naming the eschatological hope of God's justice and equity for all persons that constitutes our futuristic hope within the Christian faith. See Michael N. Jagessar, *Full Life for All: The Work and Theology of Philip A. Potter – A Historical Survey and Systematic Analysis of Major Themes* (Zoetermeer: Boekencentrum, 1997).

34 See Dale P. Andrews, 'African American Practical Theology', in *Opening the Field of Practical Theology: An Introduction*, eds Kathleen A. Cahalan and Gordon S. Mikoski (New York: Rowman and Littlefield, 2014), 11–29.

35 African American Womanist theologian Kelly Brown Douglas demonstrates the extent to which binary notions of 'in groups' and 'out groups' within Christian communities can be traced back to the notion of a 'Closed Monotheism' within Judaeo-Christian theologies of the Hebrew Bible and the New Testament. See Kelly Brown Douglas, *What's Faith Got To Do With It?: Black Bodies/Christian Souls* (Maryknoll: Orbis Books, 2005).

36 Anthony G. Reddie, *Is God Colour Blind? Reflections on Black Theology for Christian Faith and Ministry* (London: SPCK, 2009), 37–52.

37 Dwight N. Hopkins, *Being Human: Race, Culture and Religion* (Minneapolis: Fortress Press, 2005), 1–52.

38 Emile M. Townes, *Womanist Ethics and the Cultural Production of Evil* (New York: Palgrave Macmillan, 2006).

39 See Nicola Slee, *Fragments for Fractured Times: What Feminist Practical Theology Brings to the Table* (London: SCM Press, 2020), 171–81.

40 See Willie Jennings, *After Whiteness: An Education in Belonging* (Grand Rapids: William B. Eerdmans, 2020).

41 Jennings, *After Whiteness*, 23–156.

42 See Reddie, *Nobodies to Somebodies*, 68–70 and 142–6.

43 The idolization of the poor is a central argument of Tim Noble in his excellent, constructive critique of liberation theology. See Tim Noble, *The Poor in Liberation Theology: Pathway to God or Ideological Construct?* (London: Routledge, 2013).

13

Beyond Words: 'The Voyage Out'

ALISON WOOLLEY

One blizzarding, mid-January morning, after trudging uphill past the site of a large but now almost obliterated monastery-hospital, I lay on top of a deep fall of snow in the shelter of a small pine wood. On my slow walk there I'd intentionally taken time to let the lens of a camera awaken my being to images that, in their depiction of eerily whited-out landscapes and icicles formed around whisps of wire-snagged wool, were contemplative in their nature: a perceiving that needed me to be open to the confluence of my visual field and the deeper aware-ness of the eyes of the heart if it was to yield more salient impressions than everyday snaps. Only when I surrendered my eyelids to the sting of accumulated snow slumping from over-burdened branches above did I finally register the muffled soundscape that attends any snow-fall. Each heartbeat thrummed its ceaseless pulse, a counter-rhythm to the steady waves of out-breaths that slackened in the deep echo-chamber of the encircling pines. As time deformed in the softening of silence, the snowdrift's paradoxical insulation repelled any chill. Sleep beckoned, seductively.

All else was
quiet

and still.
So
still

until, without warning, a rush of awareness of the cold and some thing that I wouldn't let into view propelled me to my feet, reflexively brushing off the handfuls of snow that were my covering. Involun-tary laughter ruptured the now dis-eased peace amongst the trees, warding further away what I had refused to look in the eye. Heedless of the obliterated path, I was grateful for the sounds of snapping as I trampled across the blanketed undergrowth, out of the woods and back along the line of the old Roman Dere Street. Only then could I name what I had glimpsed: fear. Incomprehensibly, I puzzled over its source until, passing the still intact burial aisle at the monastery, well-known words surfaced, bidden by their association with the shrouding silence of the blizzard in which I walked: 'I may be some time'.[1]

Exploring the Shores of Silence

From the moment infants begin to understand speech, language becomes an increasingly dominant component of our lives. Once we have also learned to read, humans are forever attentive to text. Since the technological advances of the late twentieth century the amount of word-laden content that most of us must sift each day has grown significantly and information overload is familiar. In today's Western world it is rare to have extended periods of time away from language in its various forms, even though the pleasures of silence have, however questionably, been referred to as 'one of the most democratic of experiences – available to everyone in a noisy world; young or old, rich or poor, religious or secular'.[2] As a result of this unfamiliarity, many people are fearful of sustained silence for, no longer 'padded' by conversation and perceiving silence as 'absence', its sudden exposure of their 'naked condition in front of the universe' is unbearable.[3] Sarah Maitland offers this explanation for such fears. Our capacity for language and the 'rational' thought that emerges from it distinguish us from the rest of creation. Humanity therefore lives in an unconscious state of 'Great Chthonic Terror' that our words and thoughts will be overwhelmed by the darkness of the eternal silence of the infinite cosmos and we will cease to exist. We 'must' do 'everything we can to allay the terror ... that silence will gobble up' our words, overwhelm their meaning, and reinstate the void in which we do not feature. So we deny the realities contained in silence and attempt to take away its power by banishing it from our lives, saying that silence needs to be broken, otherwise our 'language will break down and the lights will go out'.[4]

One of Nicola Slee's most recent books, *Sabbath: The Hidden Heart-beat of Our Lives*,[5] extends to readers a series of meditative invitations 'into the woods' to remember that we are not machines, but humans. We have an absolute need for Sabbath rest in God if we are to regain equilibrium in our being and to live well. Woven around the woodland setting of the first in Wendell Berry's sequence of Sabbath poems, Slee's dialogue with its themes and her generosity with vulnerable reflections on her own Sabbatical journeyings beckon others into the trees to pause, to encounter and acknowledge fear, and to rediscover their calling. The literal and metaphorical freedoms of the woods that Slee identifies offer our physical being and our psyche space in which to play, create, imagine and dream in the tangible and symbolic realms. Although these are rich and fertile grounds for developing self-knowledge and reawakening the reality of our interconnectedness with other people and nature, they are insufficient for the nurture and rejuvenation of what is vital to our living. Something else is required.

Presenting Sabbath in varied ways, Slee portrays its opportunities for deliberate cessation of the frenetic activity and round of communication as buffering us from the interminable, energy-sapping and foolish or, at its worst, destructive chatter of the marketplace of daily life. As a theologian, poet and liturgist, the crafting and grafting of word on to word is at the heart of her vocational writing: language is the stuff of her daily bread. Yet, sharing a journalling extract, she reflects that

> If language forms the medium of my trade and I am immersed in the business of words, I need to plunge deep down beyond the surface of words into the abyss of silence. I need to recover the rhythm and the flow that will uphold my life ... after long hours inside my head.[6]

If living out her vocation is to retain its authenticity and continue to resonate with the strong and often challenging but always eloquent, passionate and empathic voice esteemed by fellow academics, students and a much wider readership, Slee recognizes the imperative for her to maintain an ongoing and intentional engagement with silence. For within its depths, outwith the realms of language and veiled in a cloud of unknowing, is the place of encounter with that mysterious knowing that is beyond self-conscious thought.

In English, silence is a somewhat ambiguous word. Whereas other tongues have different vocabulary to denote it as noun or verb, this language does not. Nounal silence is defined in terms of absence, either of speech or all sounds, the one contradicting the other. Definitions as verb are of cessation from speaking or of reduction to silence. As a feminist practical theologian, Slee has written extensively about such silencing of women and also of other groups whose stories and lived realities still have limited opportunities to find breath, form and voice.[7] Indeed, reading her statement of the need for texts to accompany women 'as an essential means of legitimating their experiences of silence and invisibility' was pivotal in identifying my own area of doctoral research, which she midwifed to completion as my supervisor and guided towards publication as a friend.[8] But in naming her need to plunge into silence's 'abyss' – seen in ancient cosmologies as the primordial ocean or formlessness from which the universe was created – Slee is clearly speaking of a different order of silence from those defined above: one that is essentially something other than absence, for within it she encounters that which sustains and heals her, and which restores direction and momentum in her return to daily life.

As this millennium began, it was suggested that practical theology engage in a 'hermeneutic of restoration' – a process of retrieval, critique and reconstruction – of Christianity's historical spiritual disciplines to identify the particularities of its authentic and meaningful practices.[9] Marie McCarthy proposed that doing so would build bridges between contemporary seekers – who have little context for understanding the roots of traditional disciplines – and the rich treasures contained within the wisdom of the past, so that today's spiritual practices will enable 'individuals and communities to function, not more effectively, but more faithfully'.[10] Nearly a decade later, Claire Wolfteich similarly emphasized that greater intercourse between practical theology and spirituality 'stands to benefit both', as all theology and spirituality is 'impoverished when separated from' the breadth of the lived encounters of faith.[11] McCarthy highlighted intentional engagement with silence as an authentically 'potent' spiritual discipline, ripe for restoration and study because of its ability to expedite transformation.[12] Her assertion is echoed by Cynthia Bourgeault, who states that the teaching of almost every traditional spirituality that holds the hope of human transformation at its heart claims that an intentional practice of silence is non-negotiable.[13] A rationale for this universal wisdom is offered by McCarthy, who implores that 'We must sit in the stillness, wait, and listen deeply. And we must be silent. The discipline of contemplative awareness is nurtured in the practice of silence.'[14] However, perhaps because practical theology's focus on practice is viewed as relating to our 'doing', as yet the discipline of silence and the 'being' associated with the more expansive awareness that it nurtures has received little of the attentive enquiry that McCarthy and Wolfteich propose.

Although Slee's extensive body of writing across many different forms emerges from the crucible of her deeply contemplative engagement with Christianity, it is *Sabbath* that contains her most sustained writing about contemplative spirituality. Here, with ideas and metaphors woven around Wendell Berry's opening stanza, in which all the poet's inner 'stirrings become quiet' and his tasks lie 'asleep like cattle', she invites readers to cessation: the 'essential *undoing* of Sabbath', whose holiness is found 'in its being a not-doing in a not-place'.[15] Berry's poem 'Sabbaths I' reads:

I go among the trees and sit still.
All my stirring becomes quiet
around me like circles on water.
My tasks lie in their places
where I left them, asleep like cattle.

Then what is afraid of me comes
and lives a while in my sight.
What it fears in me leaves me,
and the fear of me leaves it.
It sings, and I hear its song.

Then what I am afraid of comes.
I live for a while in its sight.
What I fear in it leaves it,
and the fear of it leaves me.
It sings, and I hear its song.

After days of labor,
mute in my consternations,
I hear my song at last,
and I sing it. As we sing,
the day turns, the trees move.[16]

Responding to Berry's poem, in *Sabbath* Slee writes:

> The great gift of Sabbath is to teach us that cessation, not-doing, silence, and the pause are at the heart of the rhythm of work and life. There is an essential pause at the heart of all creative work and endeavour: the silence which is integral to music, to poetry and liturgy; the wide margins around the page when we are reading or writing; all that is excised from the poem or the painting, what is left out in order for what is there to breathe ... I've come to see that the rests and pauses, the moments or hours when the mind is idling ... the walk along the beach ... are, in fact, an essential part of the work ... Sabbath is the breathing space in our labours ... in which our minds and bodies regenerate themselves and God gives gifts, treasures of darkness, to God's beloved.[17]

Ancient Daoists believed that when breathing in – the action that sustains human life and carries our speech – the egoic self becomes inflated. With the out-breath – which is, finally, our dying breath – this self-conscious identity and our sense of the body begin to diminish so that, arriving in the pause after exhalation, we stand on the shores of openness to a bigger and deeper presence. When articulation ceases and we remain in a stilled silence that deliberately refuses the inflation of egoic identity, this shift away from language and thought which reflects the open-endedness of the dying breath can be understood as an intentional disposal of self towards a different form of knowing and encounter.

Slee's invitation to cessation in *Sabbath* beckons the reader into the incremental diminishments of the out-breath and to engagement with treasures that, glinting in fading light at the edge of darkness, readily catch our eye. For the most part, the invitation to encounter that follows – and to which we will return along with the invitation to acknowledge fear – draws on the Judaic traditions of Sabbath as essentially 'social', exploring this as a relational space of conversation and intimacy, with others and with ourselves. Here, the return to equilibrium enabled by rest from doing and temporary withdrawal from others, combined with pausing on the threshold of greater openness of being – all features that draw more from Christian perceptions of Sabbath rest – elicit an increased capacity for deeper engagement in our returning to interaction with others. Relationships become 'clearer and surer, their contours and texture revealed in sharper, simpler outline' as we gather in family or friendship groups to relish the delights of resting together.[18] 'Settle back, Sabbath says, breathe deeply, ease into your chair, look into the faces of those who sit with you ... Take time to relish them ... Don't rush ... And relish human conversation.'[19]

Within Slee's discussion of the invitation to encounter, her metaphorical description of prayer as being like a bird watcher waiting for what might or might not be an extraordinary encounter over 'a long day of sitting in the rain with nothing very much happening' is particularly pertinent to this chapter's direction of travel.[20] This image is resonant with her exquisitely poised and sparse poem 'How to pray', which evokes the disciples' request to Jesus. Slee's response teaches readers the necessity of entering and leaving an empty room many times.[21]

an empty room
asks to be sat in
for a long while

at different times of the day and night
in many weathers
alone without words

perhaps hold an object in your hands
   a stone
   a cup
   a length of beads

or place something well chosen
on the floor or a window ledge
where you will look at it
for a long time

a cup
a vase
a stone
a piece of wood

without asking or telling anything
imposing your own shape on the emptiness
as lightly as possible

leave and enter
many times
without disturbing its silences

gradually over many years
a room thus entered and departed
will teach you how to furnish and dispose of
the paraphernalia of a life

With prayer stripped back to holding or gazing upon an item from nature, we are to stay with what seems the almost nothingness of this sitting, in all weathers of the day and the night, with no recourse to words. Learning to impose one's self on the space 'as lightly as possible' is the heart of the prayer practice that this poem bestows. In doing so, over time we discover what is necessary for our living while also unlearning and relinquishing what is unnecessary among all that we hold dear, as preparation for our dying. Its depiction is of contemplative awareness as movement towards the expansive openness and encounter that Daoists portray in the dying breath where, when the weight of self-conscious identity is laid aside, the perceptions of former knowing are undone as knowing of a different kind is granted opportunity to emerge.

As within Slee's poetic lesson on prayer, 'language is almost an inconvenience' in what the Chinese Christian poet Li-Young Lee sees as poetry's task.[22] Lee proposes that artists in any field inevitably become hyper-aware of their medium: dancers of the body, musicians of sound, and sculptors of wood or stone. But the medium itself is not primary to their endeavour. For Lee, poetry's subject is not its words: 'we're using language, but the real subject is silence'. If he does not move beyond a hyper-consciousness of language, he becomes ensnared in the plane of relationships between words, abandoning their greater relationship with 'mother-silence', language's ground of being. The poet's role is, rather, to deploy language in ways that 'inflect' silence, heightening its presence through the articulation of poetry, just as the hush of Sunday mornings are noticed afresh when tolling church bells cease. Where poetry succeeds in this aim, like the exhalation of the out-breath, 'It disillusions us of our own small presence in order to reveal the presence of this deeper silence – this pregnant, primal, ancient, contemporary, and imminent silence, which is God.'

While language is the medium that Slee and Lee skilfully craft, it is what they encounter in silence that is both the subject of and impetus for this work. If Christian writers are to realize the purpose of their *poiesis* – to utilize language in attempting to give fresh voice and form to the mystery of beholding and being beheld by divine love – we must venture beyond the initial diminishments that Daoists ascribe to breathing out. For, though this deposits us on the shores of silence, it can take us no further. Here, at the limits of our familiar *terra firma*, it is necessary to 'turn our back on ... one habitual mode of being' by intentionally reject-ing enticements to the inhale of self-conscious identity and its expression, and step across the threshold into the slack-tide that follows the dying breath, 'in order to face another' mode of being.[23] It is relinquishing hold on our limited knowledge at the liminality of the shoreline, voyaging into deep waters and surrendering to unknown currents flowing towards the abyss of silence, that engenders inflection of the ineffable.

The Abyss of Silence

Two theological terms help us consider the abyss of silence that lies beyond its shallows: 'cataphatic' and 'apophatic'. The former is derived from the Greek for 'to affirm' or 'to assent'. Cataphatic theology is what the fifth- to sixth-century Syrian theologian Pseudo-Dionysus described as 'the way of speech': it uses positive statements to speak of who or what God is believed to be. This contrasts with apophatic or 'negative' theology, sometimes referred to as the *via negativa*. From the Greek for 'to deny' or, more literally, 'to say away', apophatic theology denotes the Divine by negation – what God is not – emphasizing that, as God's being is beyond our comprehension, the fullness of God is ultimately unknow-able to us.

Christianity's customary ways of expressing faith and forging rela-tionship with God are through cataphatic practices, which engage the faculties of reason, emotions, memory, imagination and will. In his-toric and contemporary texts relating to the contemplative path these faculties are frequently denoted collectively as 'thoughts'. It is within this cataphatic realm that Christian practices occur and tend to remain, despite classic exhortations such as that from the anonymous fourteenth-century English author of *The Cloud of Unknowing*: 'By love may [God] be getyn and holden; bot bi thought neither'.[24] Although many of our practices reinforce the faculties that are structures of egoic selfhood, long-term engagement with those that draw us towards exploring the shores of silence can open us up to hear the call of apophatic waves lapping nearby. Journeying into apophatic 'awareness' – which, given its less dense cataphatic connotations, I will use as a more indicative word than 'prayer' – necessitates a willing surrender of self-conscious identity, perhaps best known to Christians from the apophatic movement of Christ's kenosis, portrayed by the first half of the 'Canticle of Christ's Glory' in Philippians 2.5–11. Although the theology of kenosis is appropriately interrogated by feminist theologians, the humility of this kenotic self-emptying is essential for the transfiguration of the perceptions that issue from the faculties which constitute our egoic self-consciousness:[25] it changes 'the way one figures things out',[26] shifting our epistemology away from reliance on the 'thoughts' of cataphatic knowing alone by counter-intuitively bypassing these familiar mental processes and perceptions. Instead, the apophatic engenders forms of awareness that hover at the edge of our self-conscious knowing. Apophatic awareness is therefore encountered and named as a kind of 'unknowing'. Its earliest recorded Christian usage is by Dionysius the Areopagite, referred to in Acts 17.34, whose statement, 'The most goodly knowing of God is that, the whiche is knowyn bi unknowing', is quoted by the author of *The Cloud* in support of propositions within that text.[27] Although apophatic unknowing is sometimes referred to as 'formless prayer', this can be misleading:

> once a more subtle discrimination begins to develop ... we learn that apophatic prayer is far from either formless or empty. It, too, makes use of faculties, but ones that are much more subtle than we're used to and which are normally blocked by an overreliance on our more usual mental and affective processing.[28]

Apophatic awareness is, therefore, not empty or content-free but seems to be so precisely because 'the cataphatic cannot watch the apophatic': the structures of self-consciousness cannot witness their surrender because the apophatic operates beyond the boundaries of the affective faculties that both comprise and limit our customary ways of knowing.[29] Despite the rich fruits that emerge from encounters with the apophatic, it is important to recognize that whenever apophatic awareness is advocated by theologians, across centuries of Christianity they also refute notions of a hierarchical relationship between this and the cataphatic. Neither is of greater worth. Instead, within each, faith and relationship with God are differently encountered and expressed.

In *Silence: A User's Guide*, Maggie Ross presents cataphatic know-ing as reflecting the activity of our 'self-conscious mind' and apophatic awareness as that which is engaged in by 'deep mind'.[30] On the first page of her extraordinarily rich, two-volume theological undertaking – which is far from the simple introduction belied by its title – this Anglican solitary states that if it is self-consciousness that makes us human, then it is its elision that opens the door to God.[31] Describing the capacity of self-consciousness as being significantly smaller than that of deep mind, Ross cautions that it is still able to convey the illusion that its interpreta-tions – what it believes it knows – are equal to reality.[32] Although initial reaction to Ross's assertion may be dismissive, the actuality of this illu-sion and the propensity of post-Cartesian insistence that linear thinking and interpretation alone are valid are increasingly being shown not to correspond with contemporary neuropsychological findings.[33] As these reveal that self-consciousness cannot be admitted into deep mind, Ross states that 'the purpose of the work of silence is to re-establish the flow between self-consciousness, which discriminates, dominates and distorts our lives, and the clarity and wisdom of the deep mind, which is not directly accessible, but whose activities we can influence'.[34] Ross suggests that we can open ourselves to the transfiguring insights and change that are made possible by accessing the 'vast, spacious, generous, silent' awareness that is deep mind, which 'seems to have knowledge we have never self-consciously learned', through an intention to move beyond the manipulative linear thinking of self-consciousness.[35] However, Ross cautions readers not to be misled by her phrase 'the work of silence', as the only effort required is choosing to be still and receptive, allowing the noise of self-consciousness and its perpetual grasping to fall away so that instead we can be 'grasped' by the illumination of unfiltered reality that is the epistemological abyss of deep mind. This paradoxical, kenotic move-ment, to which we will return, is the necessary requirement that enables the flow of exchange between deep mind and self-consciousness so that by combining insights from their different forms of knowing, our living can be optimal.[36]

Despite her cautioning, Ross's more than 200 repetitions of 'the work of silence' across her first volume indicates her desire to convey that sustained engagement with silence necessitates intentional discipline. Her portrayal of the commitment required challenges the oft-repeated contemporary invitations to practising silence as 'an easy cure-all' – an undemanding route towards greater personal peace and calm.[37] Initial explorations with affective or discursive practices of meditation of the kind offered in quiet services or retreat days often result in participants encountering a sense of homecoming or sanctuary in their relating with

God. Within gentle, often self-guided reflection, self-consciousness frequently lulls people into a welcome, if temporary, encounter with greater equanimity. Yet it is evident from *The Cloud* and texts by other renowned contemplatives such as Teresa of Ávila and John of the Cross that the shoreline's peace differs significantly from the tempests that assail those whose daily discipline carries them at least some way into the abyss of silence. Since before the Reformation,[38] the teachings of the church and its practices have, as with all husbandry, been employed to tame: here, the vast territories of eternal silence that so terrified the seventeenth-century theologian and mathematician Blaise Pascal.[39] However, while dipping into the sanctioned shallows of silence provides a brief refuge, engaging with silence at depth will not permit escape from the undomesticated realities that self-conscious identity prefers not to perceive. Just as current environmental concerns have led to a call for 'rewilding' – both of swathes of landscape and our relationships with other living creatures – within a broader strategy necessary to avert ecological collapse,[40] I suggest that there is a concomitant need for our engagement with silence to undergo a similar rewilding. As Ross attests, 'Silence is our natural habitat, and the work of silence is, as it were, a process of returning to the wild' that is 'essential to our survival and fulfilment as human beings'.[41] When we voyage into the abyss of silence 'we return from the exile that is our ordinary, virtual, manufactured state of mind' and, in becoming receptive to our natural habitat, we turn towards home.[42]

In the latter half of *Sabbath*, Slee addresses the 'mysterious' middle two stanzas of Berry's poem. These are the site of encounter with 'other' for that which is afraid of the poet and that of which the poet is afraid (which are not necessarily the same thing). The stanzas address first one and then the other facing their fears as they are faced by each other, and gradually what is feared departs. Slee offers an endearing picture of the animals and birds of the forest allowing themselves to be seen by the human outsider who, as he becomes silent and still, learns 'to merge with the woods and become part of the environment rather than a loud, disruptive threat' to them.[43] This reading is inevitably resonant with our own treasured encounters with timorous and enigmatic creatures in nature. However, if we allow this chapter's bearing to guide us in considering these stanzas, then Berry's depictions can be understood metaphorically: the poet representing self-conscious identity and the other unknown being representing deep mind. Both forms of knowing exist within the topography of the mind but, as within nature, the sensitive and all-perceiving awareness of deep mind is necessarily more aware of the self-conscious presence than vice versa. While it may seem counterintuitive for what Ross presents as the significantly larger capacity of deep mind to fear our self-conscious identity, the lack of symmetry in their relationship high-lighted by neuro-psychiatrist Iain McGilchrist indicates why this could be so: self-consciousness 'is ultimately dependent on, one might even say parasitic on', deep mind, 'though it seems to have no awareness of this fact'.[44] Parasites live on or in another, obtaining food, shelter and additional benefits at the expense of the host, which may be directly or indirectly harmed. McGilchrist contends that, over time, the growth of our parasitic self-consciousness has been 'relentless', significantly inhib-iting its co-operation with deep mind and restricting the exchange of different forms of knowing between them. McGilchrist and Ross both assert that communication and sharing perceptions between deep mind and self-consciousness are vital to our ability to generate 'more profound, contextualized, polyvalent interpretations' than the latter can formulate alone. Self-consciousness attempts to hide this truth from us through 'twisted ideologies and strategies' that delude us into avoiding the abyss of silence at all costs, 'even if that cost is the loss of our humanity'. Ross continues, identifying that self-consciousness fears deep mind because 'it seems to be afraid that we might realize that the would-be emperor has no clothes on'.[45] In other words, self-consciousness would prefer us to remain living solely within the limited sphere of the cacophonous noise of knowledge that it believes to be reality, embracing Maitland's 'chthonic terror' that silence will overwhelm its language and that we – that is, our self-conscious identity – will cease to exist. Unsurprisingly, it neither willingly nor straightforwardly consents to what it imagines will be its own destruction.

In metaphorically exploring Berry's 'mysterious' stanzas, it may come as no surprise that in their encounter it is deep mind, with its vast, spacious and generous awareness, that first relinquishes its fear of other. However, its risk in making its presence known is made possible by the poet's decision to embrace cessation: to 'sit still' and 'quiet' the 'stirrings' of self-consciousness. Comprehending their interdependence – the para-site cannot exist without its host – deep mind knows that our continued humanity is dependent on the irruption of its perceptions into everyday life through the flow of information exchange with self-consciousness. Despite its fears, deep mind faces self-consciousness with its challenging narrative of apophatic awareness and, in freely singing 'its song', offers self-consciousness its directly perceived forms of holistic, global and infinite awareness from the abyss of its multi-dimensional interior silence. Deep mind does so hoping that if self-consciousness will acknowledge that it is being faced with, and willingly responds to, this different know-ing, then self-consciousness' finite, linear and two-dimensional world can become more richly conceived, thus enabling self-consciousness to interact and negotiate more holistically with what it perceives as the external world.[46] Within generous, kenotic outpouring that facilitates the continuance of interdependent existence for host and parasite, deep mind's fear of being unheeded, and consequently subsumed by the agendas of self-consciousness, dissipates as stilled self-consciousness 'hear[s] its song'. In the second middle stanza, self-consciousness discovers that what it fears in deep silence – that its own identity will be overwhelmed and extinguished by the profound silence of the apophatic awareness of deep mind – is without foundation. Instead, it encounters deep mind's longing to share knowledge rather than use this for annihilation.

Within the context of this chapter it is significant that, as well as facing his own fears in the middle stanzas, the self-conscious poet is also 'being faced' by the fears and perceptions of the other who 'lives a while' close by. Similarly, our self-conscious identity is repeatedly 'being faced' by the apophatic awareness of deep mind. Terry A. Veling explains that in 'being faced' attention is shifted from our gaze's direction – the much more familiar idea of what we are 'facing' – *'to the gaze of the other,* which sees me without my knowing who is looking at me'. He continues, 'It is no longer I who faces being, but the other who faces me. I am looked upon. I am asked after ... It is almost as if the other holds me against my will, against my ravenous desire to be the center of the universe.'[47] Veling states that being faced places before us an ongoing responsibility and obligation for and towards the other who, in their facing us, call out to us to honour this duty. Although he is writing of our being faced by other humans and creatures, his words resonate with the imbalance in the uneasy relationship between self-conscious identity and deep mind. They highlight afresh the imperative for self-consciousness to intentionally turn its gaze from its rampant desires and narrow, linear agendas, which it repeatedly places centre-stage, and recognize the necessity to make space for the often less palatable but more nuanced, far-reaching and realistic narrative with which it is being faced by deep mind.

As Slee identifies in her own explication of these stanzas, things that we have feared are frequently also gifts in disguise. Once we recognize our fears for being what they are, and the fragility that these generate, 'we can discover the courage to face the fear and to await the unfolding of its gift'.[48] In the poem, these gifts are represented by the song of each individual. Yet despite the mirroring structure of engagement between the two parties across these middle stanzas, the poet's singing and hearing of his own song – Berry's discovery and offering of his 'gift' – are both delayed beyond where we anticipate. It is the other facing the self-conscious poet who, in singing first, offers up their gift in the last line of the initial middle stanza, and which the poet receives in hearing its song.

(We are never told of the other hearing the poet, maybe because this would be no unusual event.) As self-consciousness surrenders its narrative of fear in the next stanza, deep mind unexpectedly sings again at the same point – perhaps for joy or relief that self-consciousness has allowed space for its different worldview – making the most of a rare opportunity to release a further flow of insights from a score known previously only to deep mind. It is only in the final stanza, after a pointed reminder that his 'consternations' have been muted, that 'at last' the poet's singing and hearing of his song occur.

The concluding stanza adds a final and seemingly paradoxical twist: when the poet hears his own song, it is *before* he sings it. Unlike the other presence, the poet seems not to sing alone but to blend his melodic variation with the musical theme of the other. Metaphorically, the implication is that although noisy self-consciousness may live much of the time with the illusion that it is the main player, its lyricism is inspired by and carried upon the rich, multi-layered structures of deep mind that are its constant and reliable, if barely acknowledged and rarely lauded, accompaniment. As Slee proposes, in the 'utter simplicity' of their joining together in song 'the end of the poem indicates the restoration of the natural order': an active and intentional duet emerges between self-consciousness and deep mind, restoring their flow of communication.[49] This confluence of different forms of knowing enables a recovery of the balance required for harmonious, interdependent living, which the surrounding world turns to appreciate and even join in with its own dance: 'the day turns, the trees move', as poet and companion sing together. For it is not our reflexive and discriminating self-consciousness that substantiates our being as made in the image of God. Rather, this revelation is ultimately made manifest through our willingness to surrender self-conscious identity and, in venturing into the abyss of apophatic awareness where we encounter the ineffability of divine love, discover the joyous possibilities that are found in the osmotic interplay of our union with all that is.

The Paradox of Intention

If self-consciousness and deep mind are to coinhere more adequately, we are left with the question of *how* to be open to the transfiguring insights of the latter. Given that apophatic awareness appears to self-consciousness as a content-free vacuum that its nature constantly tries to colonize, the attempt seems self-defeating, for it requires the elision of self-consciousness. The nub of and solution to this paradoxical conundrum is succinctly expressed by Ross, who explains that 'we cannot self-consciously suspend self-consciousness until we find ways for self-consciousness to subvert itself'.[50] Movement into the abyss of silence cannot be made possible by the effort of self-consciousness through the ossifying application of its will. Instead, what is required is an indirect approach that cultivates the temporary suspension of self-consciousness: the paradoxical intention to leave well alone. While this may sound non-sensical, it is exemplified in small part in our self-conscious knowing that when a word refuses to come to mind, if we give up the effort to remember, it may appear a few minutes or even hours later – as if by magic – though this is not guaranteed. This 'paradox of intention' is conveyed explicitly in the subtitle of Marvin Shaw's seminal book, *Reaching the Goal by Giving Up the Attempt to Reach It*.[51] It is probably most familiar to and yet unrecognized by contemporary Christians in the Epistles, where Paul repeatedly explains how an ethic of attainment hinders believers in obtaining salvation: 'by grace you have been saved ... not your own doing' (Ephesians 2.8).[52] Understanding of the paradox of intention was common among authors of classic texts from ancient to medieval times and its role in facilitating apophatic encounter with the divine is fundamental within *The Cloud*. The author instructs that in the 'werk' of opening to apophatic awareness we must turn 'agens alle thoughtes ... coriousté of kunnyng and of kyndley witt' towards what alone 'sufficeth': a 'naked entent directe unto God'.[53]

Despite the paradoxical intention of some province of self-consciousness choosing to dispose the whole towards kenosis, its suspension is both gratuitous and imperceptible other than in retrospect, for it cannot have conscious knowledge of its own elision. As anyone who tries to still the mind's chatter will discover, the attempt to do so is ineffective and often counter-productive, just as if asked not to think about our family, their faces instantly assail us. Similarly, if self-consciousness attempts to observe deep mind – which, given its desire for control, it is likely to do once alerted to its presence – then the circuit breaker protecting these veiled, inner workings is instantly tripped. Instead, in whatever silence it permits, self-consciousness must merely wait with an intentionality that is held in the self-forgetfulness required to re-establish the flow of communication, remaining within its own bounds yet poised on 'the lip of the unknown'.[54] Here, it must surrender itself to being 'broken open' by the waves of the deep, yielding its limited knowing to an ebb tide whose return will deposit the insightful gifts that are the transfigured perceptions of deep mind, but which will only drift on to its shores unbidden.[55]

Conclusion

The centrality of establishing a regular discipline of silence in order to dispose self-consciousness to receiving the transfigured perspectives that flow from its confluence with the apophatic is widely recognized within Christianity's historic teaching of spiritual practices, and by virtually all other religious traditions. Repeated return to this paradoxical intentionality develops a patterning of surrender that, over time, becomes a kenotic disposition which ceases to be viewed as a spiritual discipline separated from and limited to designated periods within daily life. Instead, this tendency towards letting go of the grip of control that is sought reflexively by self-consciousness develops into a habitus which enables the iridescent, pearl-like insights of deep mind to infiltrate more readily the entirety of our ordinary living.

Journeying into the abyss of silence beyond our words and 'thoughts' is a pilgrimage that, with or without our willing consent, each of us must embark upon eventually. It is the voyage out from self-conscious identity that will be required when, departing this embodied, earthly existence, we 'cease to breathe' and enter into the 'perfect happiness' of 'the union which had been impossible' in our human life.[56] As a spiritual discipline that freely embraces the reality of unknowing, it becomes not only a practice that enables us to live both more faithfully and optimally but also one that bids us to encounter and be faced by our fears of the out-breaths that will eventually carry us on an unstoppable ebb-tide towards our final exhalation.

As we walk upon the shores of silence, although there is inevitable delight in discovering the treasures of transfigured perspective that drift to us on the tides of deep mind, it is in the kenotic relinquishment of self-conscious knowing into the abyss of silence that the fullness of our authentic being ultimately becomes manifest as being One with God. It is this paradoxical and yet intentional surrender into the unknowable vastness of divine love, which

    is our longest journey
    our destination   voyage
    and our final home[57]

Notes

1 Captain Lawrence Oates's last words on exiting the tent into a blizzard at -40°C and certain death during Scott's doomed *Terra Nova* expedition to the South Pole (1910–12). See Robert Falcon Scott, *Scott's Last Expedition, Volume 1: The Journals of Captain R. F. Scott*, arr., Leonard Huxley (London: Smith, Elder & Co., 1914), 592. Scott's journal entry continues, 'He went out into the blizzard and we have not seen him since.'

2 Adam Ford, *Seeking Silence in a Noisy World: The Art of Mindful Silence* (Lewes: Leaping Hare Press, 2011), 7.

3 Adam Nicholson, *Sea Room: An Island Life* (London: HarperCollins, 2004), 155.

4 Sara Maitland, *A Book of Silence* (London: Granta Books, 2008), 128–31.

5 Nicola Slee, *Sabbath: The Hidden Heartbeat of Our Lives* (London: Darton, Longman and Todd, 2019).

6 Slee, *Sabbath*, 44–5.

7 See, for example, Nicola Slee, 'Apophatic Faithing in Women's Spirituality', *British Journal of Theological Education* 1, no. 2 (2001): 23–7; *Faith and Feminism: An Introduction to Christian Feminist Theology* (London: Darton, Longman and Todd, 2003); and *Fragments for Fractured Times: What Feminist Practical Theology Brings to the Table* (London: SCM Press, 2020), 46–59.

8 Nicola Slee, *Women's Faith Development: Patterns and Processes* (Aldershot: Ashgate, 2004), 179. See Alison Woolley, *Women Choosing Silence; Relationality and Transformation in Spiritual Practice* (London: Routledge, 2019); Alison Woolley, 'Wholly Sound: A Feminist Reframing of the "Problem" of Interview Silence as a Methodology for Discovering New Knowledge', in *Researching Female Faith: Qualitative Research Methods*, eds Nicola Slee, Fran Porter and Anne Phillips (London: Routledge, 2018), 155–70; and Alison Woolley, 'Silent Gifts: An Exploration of Some Aspects of Relationality in Contemporary Christian Women's Chosen Practices of Silence', in *The Faith Lives of Women and Girls: Qualitative Research Perspectives*, eds Nicola Slee, Fran Porter and Anne Phillips (London: Routledge, 2013), 147–59.

9 Marie McCarthy, 'Spirituality in a Postmodern Era', in *The Blackwell Reader in Pastoral and Practical Theology*, eds James Woodward and Stephen Pattison (Oxford: Blackwell, 2000), 192–206 (202–4).

10 John Swinton and Harriet Mowat, *Practical Theology and Qualitative Research* (London: SCM Press, 2005), 257.

11 Claire Wolfteich, 'Animating Questions: Spirituality and Practical Theology', *International Journal of Practical Theology* 13, no. 1 (2009): 121–43 (122).

12 McCarthy, 'Spirituality', 204.

13 Cynthia Bourgeault, *Centering Prayer and Inner Awakening* (Lanham: Cowley Publications, 2004), 9.

14 McCarthy, 'Spirituality', 200.

15 Slee, *Sabbath*, 79, quoting Judith Shulevitz, *The Sabbath World: Glimpses of a Different Order of Time* (New York: Random House, 2011), 69.

16 Wendell Berry, 'Sabbaths I' (1979), in *This Day: Collected and New Sabbath Poems* (Berkeley: Counterpoint Press, 2013), 7.

17 Slee, *Sabbath*, 90–1.

18 Slee, *Sabbath*, 109.

19 Slee, *Sabbath*, 110–11.

20 Borrowed from Rowan Williams, *Being Disciples: Essentials of the Christian Life* (London: SPCK, 2016), 3–4, quoted in Slee, *Sabbath*, 108.

21 Slee, 'How to pray', *Fragments for Fractured Times*, 29. First published in Gavin D'Costa, Eleanor Nesbitt, Mark Pryce, Ruth Shelton and Nicola Slee, *Making Nothing Happen: Five Poets Explore Faith and Spirituality* (Farnham: Ashgate, 2014), 32.

22 This and subsequent quotations are from Li-Young Lee in 'An interview with Li-Young Lee' by Marie Jordan (May 2002): www.awpwriter.org/magazine_media/writers_chronicle_view/2134/an_interview_with_li-young_lee (accessed 16 January 2020).

23 Slee, *Sabbath*, 81.

24 *The Cloud of Unknowing*, ed. Patrick Gallagher (Kalamazoo: Medieval Institute Publications, 1997), 36.

25 Slee identifies 'a certain consensus in feminist liturgy' that is opposed to such 'kenotic vulnerability', which exists because of perceptions about its role in contributing to women's subjugation through the self-sacrificial expectations of patriarchy and the relinquishment of agency, leading to an impoverished self-identity. See Slee, *Fragments for Fractured Times*, 58. For the full discussion of my call for feminist theologians to nevertheless reconsider kenosis and the apophatic, see Woolley, *Women Choosing Silence*, 246–61 (esp. 254–58).

26 Maggie Ross, *Silence: A User's Guide, Volume 1: Process* (London: Darton, Longman and Todd, 2014), 98.

27 *The Cloud of Unknowing*, 96.

28 Bourgeault, *Centering Prayer*, 32.

29 Bourgeault, *Centering Prayer*, 38.

30 Ross, *Silence*, 70.

31 Ross, *Silence*, 1–2.

32 Ross, *Silence*, 95.

33 See, for instance, the extensive research presented in Iain McGilchrist, *The Master and His Emissary: The Divided Brain and the Making of the Western World* (New Haven: Yale University Press, 2009).

34 Ross, *Silence*, 23.

35 Ross, *Silence*, 1–2.

36 Ross, *Silence*, 40.

37 Sally Longley, *Conversations with Silence: Rosetta Stone of the Soul* (Eugene: Cascade Books, 2021), 5.

38 For further discussion, see Ross, *Silence*, 218–20; Diarmaid MacCulloch, *Silence: A Christian History* (London: Allen Lane, 2013), 114–60; and Thomas Keating, *Open Mind, Open Heart: The Contemplative Dimension of the Gospel* (New York: Continuum, 1995), 22–4.

39 'le silence eternal de ces espaces infinies m'effraie'. See Blaise Pascal, *Pensées*, III, ed. Francis Kaplan (Paris: Editions du Cerf, 1992), 206, quoted in Nicholas Lash, *Holiness, Speech and Silence: Reflections on the Question of God* (Aldershot: Ashgate, 2004), 77.

40 For example, see Paul Jepson and Cain Blythe, *Rewilding: The Radical New Science of Ecological Recovery* (London: Icon Books, 2020), and Marc Bekoff, *Rewilding Our Hearts: Building Pathways of Compassion and Coexistence* (Novato: New World Library, 2014).

41 Ross, *Silence*, 13 and 33.

42 Shierry Weber Nicholsen, *The Love of Nature and the End of the World: The Unspoken Dimensions of Environmental Concern* (Cambridge: MIT Press, 2002), 25.

43 Slee, *Sabbath*, 107.

44 McGilchrist, *The Master and His Emissary*, 6.

45 Ross, *Silence*, 18.

46 Ross, *Silence*, 13–14.

47 Terry A. Veling, *Practical Theology: 'On Earth as It Is in Heaven'* (Maryknoll: Orbis Books, 2005), 126–35 (127–8).

48 Slee, *Sabbath*, 131 and 139.

49 See Slee, *Sabbath*, 167; see also Ross, *Silence*, 18.

50 Ross, *Silence*, 2.

51 Marvin C. Shaw, *The Paradox of Intention: Reaching the Goal by Giving Up the Attempt to Reach It* (Atlanta: Scholars Press, 1988).

52 For a full discussion, see Shaw, *The Paradox of Intention*, 29–38.

53 *The Cloud of Unknowing*, 23, 37.

54 Ross, *Silence*, 48–9, quoting Kazim Ali, 'Doubt and Seeking', in *A God in the House: Poets Talk About Faith*, eds Ilya Kaminsky and Katherine Towler (North Adams: Tupelo Press, 2012), 32–45 (40).

55 Ross, *Silence*, 49.

56 Virginia Woolf, *The Voyage Out*, ed. Elizabeth Heine (London: Vintage, 1992), 376.

57 Nicola Slee, 'The Sea's Prayer', *Abba Amma: Improvisations on The Lord's Prayer* (Norwich: Canterbury Press, 2022), 183.

Return

*Nicola Slee**

There is an ocean I am always returning to
travelling halfway round the world
to come home to its long bay

I walk along the edges of surf
searching for greenstone and pāua shell
feel the grit under my feet

taste the tang of salt in my mouth
rinse my mind's eye clean

I want to trudge as far as the tide will sing to me
slapping bare feet on sand in time with the sea's fret and fray
walk out of my weariness and forgetfulness

stay as long as the waves come and go
til the moon rises and stars appear in the southern sky
the ocean gathering darkness, slipping me over its long white cloud.

* Originally published in *NZ Books*, June 6, 2018 (28.2), 26.

Permissions

Grateful acknowledgement is made to the following publishers for use of copyright material.

SPCK Group for material from Nicola Slee, *Praying Like a Woman* (SPCK, 2004), Nicola Slee, *The Book of Mary* (SPCK, 2007), Nicola Slee and Stephen Burns, eds, *Presiding Like a Woman* (SPCK, 2010) and Nicola Slee, *Seeking the Risen Christa* (SPCK, 2011).

Darton, Longman and Todd for material from Nicola Slee, *Sabbath: The Hidden Heartbeat of Our Lives* (Darton, Longman and Todd, 2019).

Counterpoint Press for material from Wendell Berry, *This Day: Collected and New Sabbath Poems 1979–2013* (Counterpoint Press, 2013). Copyright © 1979 by Wendell Berry. Reprinted with the permission of The Permissions Company, LLC on behalf of Counterpoint Press, counterpointpress.com.

SAGE Publications for material from Eleanor Nesbitt, 'Cathedral of Santiago di Compostella', *Theology* 118, no. 4 (2015): 283.

Index of Names and Subjects